THE PENDULUM CULTURE?

Integration of Young Muslim Immigrants in East London

Janusz Balicki

Anne Wells

Maciej Debski: Statistical Tables and Figures

Nicholas Walters: Consultation & Contributions to Sections
on UK Society - Chapters 3, 4, 6 and 7

THE PENDULUM CULTURE?

Political Science Institute
Cardinal Stefan Wyszynski University in Warsaw

Centre for Ethnic Minority Studies, School of Law
SOAS, University of London

Review: **Werner Menski**
Sham Qayyum
School of Law (SOAS), University of London.

ISBN: 978-1-4269-4581-6 (sc)
ISBN: 978-1-4269-4580-9 (e)

Trafford rev. 11/29/2010

 www.trafford.com

1663 Liberty Drive,
Bloomington, IN 47403
Phone: 888-232-4444
Fax: 812-355-4082

North America & international
toll-free: 1 888 232 4444 (USA & Canada)
phone: 250 383 6864 ♦ fax: 812 355 4082

Table of Contents

Abbreviations   9

Acknowledgements   10

Introduction   11

1. Integration   17

2. Background to Research   23
    2.1. Muslims in Great Britain   23
    2.2. London Borough of Newham   26
    2.3. Newham College   27
    2.4. Survey of Newham College Students   28
    2.5. Profile of Students   29
        2.5.1. Background   29
        2.5.2. Values   33
        2.5.3. Language   35
        2.5.4. Home life   37

3. Education - Work - Social Participation   41
    3.1. UK Society   41
    3.2. Immigrants' Culture and Traditions   49
    3.3. Newham College Students' Views   52
        3.3.1. Education   52
        3.3.2. Work   55
        3.3.3. Social Participation   61
        3.3.4. Discrimination   66
    3.4. Conclusion   68

4. Marriage - Gender Relationships   71
    4.1. UK Society   71
    4.2. Pre-marital Gender Relationships   74
        4.2.1. Immigrants' Culture and Traditions   74
        4.2.2. Newham College Students' Views   76
    4.3. Arranged Marriage   78

4.3.1. Immigrants' Culture and Traditions   78
4.3.2. Newham College Students' Views   80
4.4. Forced Marriage   83
4.4.1. Immigrants' Culture and Traditions   83
4.4.2. Newham College Students' Views   90
4.5. Conclusion   91

5. Marriage - Gender Equality   93
5.1. Polygamy   93
5.1.1. Immigrants' Culture and Traditions   93
5.1.2 Newham College Students' Views   95
5.2. Divorce   100
5.2.1. Immigrants' Culture and Traditions   100
5.2.2. Newham College Students' Views   103
5.3. Female Circumcision   104
5.3.1. Immigrants' Culture and Traditions   104
5.3.2. Newham College Students' Views   109
5.4. Conclusion   109

6. Dress   111
6.1. UK Society   111
6.2. Immigrants' Culture and Traditions   122
6.3. Newham College Students' Views   129
6.4. Conclusion   136

7. Identity: Religion – Culture and Nation   139
7.1. UK Society   139
7.2. Immigrants' Culture and Traditions   145
7.3. Newham College Students' Views   149
7.3.1. Identity and Belonging   149
7.3.2. Religion   153
7.4. Conclusion   163

8. Real Life Stories   167
8.1. Sana   167
8.2. Abdul   171
8.3. Isma   173
8.4. Sultana   180
8.5. Maya   185
8.6. Fuzia   189

8.7. Moonisah   190

8.8. Usman   193

8.9. Imran   195

8.10. Jabz   196

8.11. Waheeda   197

8.12. Manna   198

8.13. Rabiah   200

8.14. Conclusion   202

Bibliography   211

Tables and figures   219

Appendix   223

   1.   Questionnaire   223

   2.   Questions for short Interviews   234

   3.   Support Groups   235

Abbreviations

AIMPLB = All India Muslim Personal Law Board
BME = Black and Minority Ethnic
FGM = Female Genital Mutilation
FMU = Forced Marriage Unit
GDP = Gross Domestic Product
NCW = National Commission for Women
Ofsted = Office for Standards in Education
UNCRC = United Nations Convention on the Rights of the Child
UNESCO = United Nations Educational, Scientific and Cultural Organisation
WHO = World Health Organisation

Arabic Terms

Al-Fatifa = 'The Opening' the first chapter of the Qur'an.
burka = an enveloping outer garment worn by women
hadith = collection of traditions or records of the Prophets deeds, sayings and tacit approval.
hijab = often refers to the head covering that Muslim women wear.
Izzat or *izzet* = 'honour', particularly in relation to the status of the family.
khul = a particular type of divorce, often called a 'women's divorce'
juma = Friday prayer
mahram = an unmarriageable member of the kin with whom sexual intercourse would be regarded as incestuous.
mahr / dower = amount of money or property settled or paid by the husband to his wife as an incident of marriage. Without mahr marriage is not valid.
niqab = face veil, a piece of cloth which covers the face.
purdah = curtain or screen. The practice of preventing men from seeing women, including veiling or segregation of women.
qadi = judge ruling in accordance with the shari'a, a recognised marriage official
Qu'ran = Koran
shalwar kamiz = a trouser suit worn by Muslim women
talaq = triple divorce
wali = guardian or representative of a woman in her marriage, usually the father

Statistical Symbols

Ch2 = chi-squared test of independence
Df = Degrees of Freedom
P = P-value
Vc = Cramer's V

Acknowledgements

We are deeply indebted to all those who made possible the questionnaires and interviews which constituted our core research. Our particular gratitude is owed to the students who so generously gave up their free time to answering the lengthy questionnaire and during the interviews shared their opinions with us. We are also grateful to the staff of Newham College for their invaluable support.

We are especially grateful to:

- Brian Cooper, Facility Director, Newham College of Further Education, East Ham Campus who in allowing us unlimited access to the college, made the whole research possible.

- Sabi Rashid who initially put us in touch with many of the students and teachers whose support was invaluable to us in our research. We are especially grateful for his help in securing interviews.

- All of the site staff and teachers who made us most welcome and co-operated so generously.

- Maire O'Donnell RSHM for her careful and painstaking proof reading, her patience and encouragement.

- Professor Werner Menski (SOAS) for reviewing our publication and his extremely helpful suggestions for editing the text.

- Sham Qayyum (SOAS) for his invaluable expertise and support, his reading and clarification of the text from a Muslim perspective.

- Dr Maciej Debski for producing the Tables and Figures for this publication and in particular for his advice and help with the methodology and statistics.

- Professor Nicholas Walters from Surrey University for his time, suggestions and writings on the UK Society point of view.

- Special thanks to the Sisters of the Sacred Heart of Mary and Father Denis Hall, Forest Gate. Their generous hospitality has made this publication possible.

Introduction

The main purpose of this publication is to help people from different cultures to understand each other better. In the UK there are many immigrants from different ethnic and religious backgrounds. It is obvious that this creates a lot of dilemmas and tensions, especially for the younger generation. Many authors express the opinion that the most challenging experiences are for those with a Muslim background.

We want to help our readers to be able to understand where young Muslims are coming from - their backgrounds, beliefs and cultures. We hope that the book will be useful for anyone who just wants to understand the relationship between people from different cultures, especially for those who are dealing with the young in their professional work and want to help them to integrate: teachers, social workers, youth workers, the government, any one in public services.

This book is also addressed to the Muslim young people themselves and their parents, who often cannot understand why the UK society has a problem with their customs, religion or way of life. Our aim is to help Muslim immigrants especially to understand the society into which they have come.

Many people do not have any problems with the fact that Britain is becoming more and more multicultural. They welcome the richness that other cultures bring to our society. Some people, however, are afraid. They worry about the fact that so many immigrants are coming to the UK, which is after all only a small island with limited space. They are especially anxious about Muslims who in their opinion do not want to integrate. This impression was initially given by the first generation of Muslim immigrants who had no intention of spending a whole lifetime in the UK. They considered their time here as temporary before they returned, hopefully richer, to their home country. However, they realised eventually that returning was a 'myth'. They would never go back to their own country to live. Trying to keep their religion and identity in what they considered an alien land, they endeavoured to preserve their home culture and traditions as faithfully as possible. Their children born in the UK grew up to hear their parents' native country called 'home' while at the same time in a natural way they were becoming part of British society. We are all aware that youth is a time for seeking and establishing one's identity. For the second generation of Muslim immigrants, that is no less true. However it leaves them with a dilemma: what is their identity? Is it tied up with their parents' home nation or the UK, their ethnic group, their culture, their religion, or is it a combination of many aspects?

Esposito (2010) considers that Muslim integration into society in America is easier than into Europe. While immigrant American Muslims, arrived with education and skills, most Muslims who came to Europe arrived as labourers and blue-collar workers with limited education, skills, and social mobility. Consequently:

> Many Muslims in Britain, are trapped in social ghettos, plagued by poverty (…). Gallup polling of life evaluations provided by Muslims living in Europe reveals their problems. Seventy-two percent in the United Kingdom consider themselves 'struggling,' while only seven percent of Muslims in the U.K. say they are 'thriving' (2010:25).

Authors, like Melanie Philips see a great danger for the UK created by the flow of immigrants from Muslim countries. The urban landscape of London and many cities in the UK has changed dramatically over the last ten years or so. Philips regards Islamic religious dress seen frequently on our streets as a welcome contribution to the variety of the British nation, but worries: Is it really a religious requirement commanding respect, or a political statement of antagonism towards the British state? She says:

> The effect is to create a niggling sense of insecurity and unease, as the open nature of London's society is vitiated by such public acts of deliberate concealment, with faces and expressions - not to mention the rest of the body - hidden from sight. In the wake of the London bombings in July 2005, such concealment appears to be a security issue too (2006:33-34).

Continuing, she says that walking through some areas listening to the various South Asian languages one might feel that one has stepped into a village in the Punjab that has somehow been transported into an English city. She states also that what becomes even clearer in northern UK cities than it is in London is that these Muslim enclaves are just that: areas of separate development which are not integrated with the rest of the town or city.

For anyone moving to another country integration is not easy. Because Muslims appear to hold different values, beliefs and traditions to the majority of British society they are often accused of not wishing to integrate. It is important to try to understand the difficulties they experience in integrating.

In attempting to understand their difficulties we considered the attitudes of young Muslim immigrant students at college. There is no doubt that the younger generation of Muslims who go on to higher education have the good will to integrate with the host society, but they often find themselves creating their own culture between two cultures.

We have called the young immigrants' culture – 'The Pendulum Culture'. They appear to be in a difficult place, between two different ways of life. At home they are faithful to their family culture, often preserved by their parents, and when away from home, whether with their friends or in college, they live what appears to be an adapted Western culture. The young people sometimes seem to swing almost effortlessly between the two cultures but at other times it is obviously a challenge. Some authors call this 'skilled cultural navigation.'

Culture is a vast area covering the whole of our lives but for the purpose of this research we are only considering areas where obvious differences can be observed and where it is possible to ascertain to what extent the students are living between different cultures. We clearly observed that the students could create their own 'culture' in the same terms as Bhikhu Parekh (2006) describes in his book *Rethinking Multiculturalism*:

> The term 'Our' culture refers not to one in which we were born, for we might emigrate or be given up for adoption and raised in another culture, but one in terms of which we understand and organise our individual and collective lives. Our culture is one we live, which has shaped us and with which we identify (2006:155).

Our publication is based on research which took place in Newham College in London in 2006-2009. In our survey we analysed 217 questionnaires which we supplemented with 100 short interviews given to different students, all of whom were Muslim. We completed our field study with 13 in-depth interviews of Muslims. The student profile of

Newham College is highly multicultural. The majority of the students were children of immigrants (second generation) or immigrants themselves and were Muslims from Asia (Bangladesh, Pakistan and India) or from African countries. In addition we used literature which was relevant to the issues and analysed in our research.

Our main question is: do the young Muslim students from Newham College swing as a pendulum between cultures, creating a new 'culture'? If so, where are they in that swing? What does their 'culture' look like?

We asked the students, among other questions: what they think about education and women having a profession, bearing in mind that traditional Muslim culture sees women as mainly working at home; their opinion regarding participation in social and political activity; how they see gender relationships, marriage - arranged and forced, polygamy, gender equality, divorce, dress regulation, identity and religion.

The book has eight chapters. The first one is about integration. It shows the problem of integrating immigrants from different countries. It explains basic terms and refers to different models of integration and the integration policy in the UK.

The second chapter has a methodological character. The authors chose one specific college of further education, in the London Borough of Newham, where there is a high ethnic minority population. It is important to remember that all the young people in this study had opted to go to a college of further education. The study does not look at the attitudes of young people who left school with few qualifications and are unemployed, or young people who on leaving school immediately joined the work-force, or young women who married straight after school. Nor does the study include those who went on to the 6th form in their own school or into a 6th form college.

It explains details about our research in Newham College and gives some fundamental information about the students who took part in our study – their countries of origin, religion, languages and family life.

The third to seventh chapters are based on the results of our survey and cover the following topics: education – work – social participation; marriage – gender relationship; marriage – gender equality; dress and identity related to religion, culture and nation. We begin each chapter by looking at the UK society's position on the relevant topic. This is followed by information on the students' cultures and traditions. We describe the Newham College students' views, giving the questions asked and the results of our survey on each topic. We sum up each chapter with our conclusions.

In chapter eight we relate thirteen real life stories as presented by Muslim students. The students were interviewed separately and asked to tell the authors about their life and attitude to the topics covered in our research. Each interview took approximately thirty minutes. We try to answer the question: does our research show that Muslim students create a different 'culture' to British society and their parents' country of origin?

The authors were conscious that they were dealing with a different culture to their own and touching very sensitive religious topics. They are aware that at times they may have unintentionally generalised an opinion which was held only by a particular group of Muslims or in fact is more cultural than Islamic.

CHAPTER ONE

Integration

These days there is a great deal of debate and confusion about what is meant by 'integration'. The UK host society sometimes looks aghast at immigrants and observes that they have a different culture and lifestyle. They dress distinctively, eat different food and worship in a different way and the host society feels their own British culture to be under threat. They accuse the immigrants of leading parallel lives while being fearful that the immigrants will dilute or totally change what the UK host society considers to be essentially British culture and values. Meanwhile many of the immigrants are bemused and intimidated. They do not know what the host society actually expects of them. They like living in the UK but they don't approve of everything that happens in UK society any more than the locals do. They don't know what it means to be integrated and they are afraid of losing their own values, culture and religion and therefore their own identity. Ed Husain in his book *The Islamist* wrote in 2007:

> Since my return (to the UK) I have observed British Muslims being browbeaten by certain sections of the media and government, demanding 'integration' and an end to 'parallel lives'. The implied accusation, of course, is that Muslims are guilty of terrorism and that an undefined 'integration' will put a stop to it (2007:283-4).

He goes on to say:

> Many of my Muslim friends rightly ask what we are supposed to integrate into. 'Big brother' life style? Ladette culture? Binge drinking? Gambling? (2007:284).

Husain talks about the despair he felt when walking home with his wife, after a night out. They saw 'rowdy, drunken teenagers vomiting on the streets.' He says:

> Anti-social behaviour in our cities, high rates of abortion, alcohol abuse and drug addiction are abhorrent to all right-thinking people,

not just Muslims. The neglect of the elderly, shunting them off to 'care homes' does not sit comfortably with most Muslims. When the centre of social life in modern Britain is the local pub, where do Muslims and others fit in? Can an orange juice ever be enough? (2007:284).

He continues to explain that many Muslims have managed to develop a rich, vibrant subculture in Britain. Amidst the myriad of lifestyle choices they are able to integrate the best aspects of their home nation's traditions, ethnic diversity, British upbringing and Islamic roots. According to Husain the majority of Muslims are hard working and quietly go about their lives without attempting to turn religion into politics. They work right at the centre of national life, helping to maintain our schools, transport system and the National Health Service (2007:284).

The confusion is largely brought about by a lack of clarity or definition of what is meant by integration. Three terms frequently used are acculturation, integration and assimilation.

The word '*acculturation*' is generally understood to mean that immigrants keep their own culture and values while adopting also the culture and values of the recipient country. In other words they are part of two cultures. This raises several questions:

- o Is it possible to live out of two cultures at the same time?
- o Will one culture dominate or will the person oscillate between the two cultures?
- o What happens when the two cultures are so different that they clash?
- o Is acculturation necessary before integration can take place?
- o Does religious affiliation have any effect on integration?

The word 'Integration' means different things to different people. Some people speaking of integration actually mean 'Assimilation' whereby the immigrants are expected to give up their own culture totally and take on the values and culture of the recipient country so that there is no longer any difference between people. In this view assimilation is considered to be one-sided and:

(…) would come down to conformity to mainstream, dominant cultural patterns. The assimilation process would occur in phases.

(...) Whatever the precise course of the process would be, at its end no significant differences between the newcomers and their offspring and the established society would persist, neither in their social situation nor in their cultural orientation (Entzinger, Biezeveld 2003:7).

Others view integration also as assimilation but expect all cultures to merge, amalgamate, to be watered down until the recipient country becomes one large melting pot, like the USA. After many generations even names merge and skin becomes coffee coloured. The result, of course, would be a new culture. This was the accepted view of integration and it was not until the 1960s that people began to challenge this viewpoint. The question arose from the fact that although the UK had experienced several generations of immigration it was perfectly obvious that the cultural differences remained within both the immigrant society and the host society.

Grzymała-Kozłowska represents 'integration' as an interaction between the immigrants and the host society whereby different groups or individuals have lasting associations with a host society, taking part with due respect in various aspects of its life, while maintaining their cultural identities (2008:35-36).

The European Commission report *Benchmarking in Immigrant Integration*, (2003) written by Han Entzinger and Renske Biezeveld, considers that there are four dimensions to integration 1) socio–economic 2) cultural 3) legal and political 4) the attitude of recipient societies towards migrants.

Immigrants have reached the first dimension, 'socio-economic' when the host country treats the immigrants like the local people. They are allowed to work and their living conditions are similar to those of other local people in their area. Regarding the second dimension, 'cultural' the immigrants keep their own system of values and religion as long as it doesn't contradict the host nation's system of values. The benchmarking report agrees with the sociologist Marc Granovetter (1973) when he states that cultural integration has various dimensions. The first he identifies as the 'incidence' dimension which he claims has two characteristics: 'frequency' and 'intensity' which do not necessarily have any link. Frequency refers to the actual number of connections/ relationships a person or group has with their surroundings and with others, while intensity refers to the feelings of familiarity the person has with their surroundings and with other people. Obviously a person's sense of belonging to other family members will probably be stronger than their sense of belonging to the people they work with even though they see more of their work colleagues.

Granovetter calls the second dimension 'identification.' Naturally the more a person identifies with another, the closer they feel. That doesn't mean they necessarily have frequent or meaningful contact with each other. It was obvious from the responses of the young people the authors interviewed, that many strongly identified with their parents' country, calling it 'their home country,' even though they had been born in the UK and had almost no contact with that country.

Of course frequent encounters with others can lead to quite a strong identification. However, unless a person identifies in some way with a group, that person is highly unlikely to cultivate a strong bond with that group.

The third dimension of integration is legal and political. The immigrants are granted citizenship, allowed to participate in local government and they have the right to vote in national elections.

The fourth dimension depends largely on a positive attitude of the recipient society towards the migrants, although clearly the migrant's attitude can have a profound effect on the host society's willingness to welcome the migrant.

Obviously the act of integration is not solely dependent on the immigrant's attitude but also relies heavily on the recipient State's attitude as well as that of its individual inhabitants. A person can claim to be fully integrated only if they personally fulfil the above four dimensions. According to the Report *Benchmarking in Immigrant Integration:*

> The more a society is integrated, the more closely and the more intensely its constituent parts (groups or individuals) relate to one another. In recent years, the term *social cohesion* has become widely used as an equivalent for integration as a characteristic of a society. Integration can also be perceived from the perspective of groups and individuals. All groups and individuals display a certain degree of integration within a given society, and we can measure to what extent this is the case.

Integration

According to Hellyer:

> The EU has attempted, quite strongly, to ensure that any deepening of ties between member states does not impinge upon individual member states' fundamental national identities, otherwise the European project would fail. However, at the.... member state level – often such efforts are not made, whether with regard to religion or to other signatures of identities (2009:107).

In furthering understanding in the area of freedom of religious belief it is important to know what is meant by certain symbols in certain communities and thereby to avoid unintentional errors. Hellyer cited Tariq Ramadan who noted that while integration might take place on the basis of shared values, it included a respect for diversity which entailed the understanding of which forms of diversity were acceptable and which forms were not:

> They (non-Muslim citizens of Europe) need to accept that Europe's population has changed, that it no longer has a single history and that the future calls for mutual understanding and respect. They need to face up to their ignorance and reject the clichés and prejudices that surround Islam. They must start discussing the principles, values and forms that will enable us to live together (Hellyer 2009:112).

Ramadan (2002:207) sees integration as a challenge. Addressing his co-religionists in Europe, he appealed to them not 'only to live in Europe but to feel part of it.'

Ramadan (2004:55) disagrees with Muslims being treated as a minority group in Europe. He says: 'Europe is their home and they should feel at home, not only say so.' If the host society and the Muslims think that way they will be better able to co-create European society along with the local population.

In the past nations were relatively clear about how they saw their identity. In the not too distant past if a person claimed to be British that person was white, Christian, born in the British Isles. However it hasn't been so clear cut since the time of the British Colonies. If a Muslim calls himself British, he is in essence asking the British as a nation, the question: What does it mean to be British? (Hellyer 2009:107). We need to redefine our understanding of what it means to be British. We will explore this whole area in Chapter Seven.

CHAPTER TWO

Background to Research

In this chapter we will look briefly at the history of Islam in the UK before considering more closely our survey and the area in which our research took place including the characteristics of the students involved.

2.1. Muslims in Great Britain

The prophet Mohammed died in 632 AD. During the first thirty years after his death Islam spread to the four corners of the world. History records different starting points for the UK's relationship with Islam. However as Egypt and Palestine were trading with Britain during the seventh century it is quite probable that the Celts came into contact with Muslims (Rosser-Owen 1998). Some scholars suggest that the first Muslim settlers arrived as early as 775 AD. Hellyer wrote that a coin of that period had been discovered in the UK with the Islamic Declaration of Faith on it. He added that we can find records indicating the presence of Muslims in London during the twelfth century. Relations with Muslims are recorded as cordial throughout the centuries. With apparently many Spanish Muslims 'wandering' around Britain, intermarriages occurred between non-Muslim Britons and Muslims even during the Crusades (Hellyer 2009:145). There is an archive apparently showing that King John I of England proposed marriage to the Muslim daughter of the Sharif of Morocco.

England was not the only European country with links to Islam. From 632 until 1258 Islam was a major world influence. According to Abbas, by the height of the Middle Ages nearly every area of learning and art in Europe, was influenced by Islam. This all changed with the advent of the Renaissance. As Abbas states:

> The West not only turned against its own medieval past but also sought to forget the long relation it had had with the Islamic world, one which was built on intellectual respect despite religious opposition. A defining event for the changing relation between

Islam and the Western world was the series of Crusades declared by the Pope and supported by various European kings. The purpose although political, was outwardly to recapture the 'holy land' and especially Jerusalem for Christianity. (…) English participation in the Crusades was minimal and Richard I was the only king of England to participate personally. Edward I participated when he was heir to the throne (Abbas 2005:6).

According to Abbas during the Crusades the Islamic world was also going through a period of division caused by feuds and the corrupt and luxurious lifestyles of the rulers. He explained that it was important to note that at the end of the 15th century, an event took place in the Islamic world which in essence froze the interpretation of the Koran:

> The *Ulama* (religious scholars) reduced the concept of *Ilm* from 'all knowledge' to 'religious knowledge,' reduced *Ilma* from meaning the 'consensus of the community' to that of the *Ulama* itself. The interpretation of the Qur'an was frozen in history. It lost its dynamism; this transformed society from an open to a closed one (Abbas 2005:7).

India had been conquered by the Muslims in 1526. The Moghul Empire lasted for over three hundred years. It eventually ended in 1857 with the rise of British power in India. In the 19th century much of the Ottoman Empire was under foreign rule, apart from a few regions in the Middle East – Persia, Afghanistan, Yemen and certain parts of Arabia. The Ottoman Empire broke up after the First World War and while some countries gained independence, for example Iraq and Jordan became a new entity, others became French colonies – Palestine, Syria, Lebanon.

By the first half of the twentieth century, much of South Asia was part of the British colonies and many of the area's citizens were Muslim. With the formation of the British Commonwealth and the colonies' move to independence, a significant number of Pakistani, Indian and Bangladeshi Muslims chose to emigrate to the UK. To cater for this sizeable Muslim community the first large Mosque was opened in Regents Park in 1944. England gave Pakistan and India independence in August 1947. The whole area was at the time in turmoil and Pakistan was divided into two areas East and West.

The number of Muslim immigrants grew considerably in the 1960s and 1970s. By 2003 there were an estimated 1.8 million Muslims in the UK, living mainly in London, Birmingham, Manchester, Bradford and Glasgow. About half the population were born in the UK and although the others came from many nations, the majority came from South Asia.

Table 2.1 Numbers of Britons of Pakistani and Bangladeshi descent, and percentage born in Britain (1951-2001)

Year	Number	% born in UK
1951	5,000	-
1961	24,000	1.2
1971	170,000	23.5
1981	360,000	37.5
1991	640,000	47.0
2001	1,030,000	46.0

Source: S. Gilliat-Ray, *Muslims in Britain. An Introduction*, Cambridge University Press, Cambridge 2010:47.

According to the UK Labour Force Survey there were 2,422,000 Muslims in the UK in 2008 and 42,657,000 Christians. The following table gives a break-down of the number of Muslims according to age group.

Table 2.2 Muslims in Britain by age (2008)

Age	Number
0-9	538,000
10-19	405,000
20-29	502,000
30-39	440,000
40-49	257,000
50-59	156,000
60-69	68,000
70+	56,000

Source: Labour Force Survey, UK Government Office of National Statistics, January 2009, as quoted in S. Gilliat-Ray, *Muslims in Britain. An Introduction*, Cambridge University Press, Cambridge 2010:121.

The majority of Muslims prefer to be recognised as a faith community than to be seen as an ethnic group. This fact poses fundamental questions to British Society where ethnicity, nationality, class and fashion are usually seen as the major determining factors of identity. If a group primarily defines itself in terms of religious identity it creates a major break with the established social culture (Hellyer 2009:153).

Many of the Muslim community's requests have been met by the UK authorities. Mosques have been built, there is provision for prayer in the work place, facility for slaughtering animals and preparing *halal* (ritually acceptable) food, provision of *halal* food in schools, hospitals and prisons. There are some Muslim schools and also same sex schools in areas with a large Muslim population. Women and girls are free to wear the *hijab* in school and many schools with a large Muslim population have adapted their school uniforms to conform to the Islamic strict dress code for girls. There are also Muslim sections in cemeteries. They have their own media producing 'Q-news' a Muslim magazine that began in the early 1980s and also a magazine called 'Muslim News.'

In the UK there are many Muslims who are involved in politics including approximately 150 Muslim councillors and a number of mayors. Since 1997 five Muslims have been made life peers and have been appointed to the House of Lords. The five life peers were mostly originally from the Indian sub-continent - Lord Ahmed is Kashmiri, Baroness Uddin is Bangladeshi, Lord Bhatia is Tanzanian, Lord Patel is Indian and Baroness Falkner is Pakistani (Hellyer 2009:153). In the 2010 National Election eight Muslim MPs were elected, including the first woman.

2.2. London Borough of Newham

According to *Focus on Newham 2006,* the London Borough of Newham's statistical magazine published yearly, Newham has the largest proportion of non-white ethnic groups in the country with almost two-thirds (61%) of Newham's population coming from a non-White ethnic group. Newham has the second highest percentage of Asians in England and Wales and it also has the second highest percentage of black Africans in England and Wales. Newham has communities from almost every corner of the world.

The 2001 Government census revealed that there were 243,891 people in Newham. By 2005 that number had risen to 246,200 people. In 2001 the top ten countries of non UK born citizens represented in Newham were: India - 12,701; Bangladesh - 11,724; Pakistan - 9,856; South & Eastern Africa[1] - 6,023; Central & Western Africa[2] - 5,441; Nigeria - 5,423; Caribbean & West Indies[3] - 4,131; Sri Lanka - 3,591; the Far East - 3,399 and Somalia - 3,163 (UK Census 2001). In 2007 Newham published its ethnic statistics for 2005 showing that there were 84,200 White people, 30,282 Indians, 23,635 Pakistanis and 23,635 Bangladeshis in Newham (Newham 2007).

The examiners from Ofsted inspected Newham College in June 2009 and described the Newham Borough in their final report:

Newham is an area of extreme and multiple deprivations and is rated the sixth most deprived English local authority district. Unemployment is double the national average and 41% of adults are workless; nearly twice the London average. Newham has the youngest population of any borough in London. Child poverty, including risk to health, is the second worst in England (...).

Employment in Newham is largely within micro and small and medium-sized businesses with a very large concentration of minority ethnic owned businesses. The largest single employers are in the public sector. Newham is experiencing significant economic and infrastructure development, amounting to some £19bn of investment, including work for the 2012 Olympics and Paralympics and the Stratford City and Canning Town developments (Newham 2009:4).

2.3. Newham College

Newham College of Further Education was the result of a merger between East Ham and West Ham technical colleges in 1985 with the aim 'to better serve the needs of the people of Newham'. There are two main campuses: East Ham Campus, High Street South, London and Stratford Campus, Welfare Road, London and several local centres. Our survey was carried out on both of the main sites.

---

[1] Not including Kenya, Somalia, South Africa, Zimbabwe.
[2] Not including DR Congo, Nigeria, Sierra Leone.
[3] Not including Jamaica.

The college has excellent facilities which alongside the fact that many students live close by contributes to building a strong community atmosphere. According to its on-line prospectus the college has a rich cultural diversity due to the fact that many of the students are members of ethnic minority groups.

According to the Ofsted report in June 2009, 70% of the students are from ethnic minorities and 59% of the students are women. Newham College is one of:

> the largest further education colleges both nationally and in the Greater London area, with over 20,000 full- and part-time students. Many of the students are local, and over 80% are aged over 19.
>
> The college has a vision of 'a learning revolution spurring local economic and social regeneration, and full participation by local people.' The college's Mission is 'to expand and improve lifelong learning' and it aims to achieve this by making an open access provision, relevant to the diverse range of needs in its local communities, and regardless of prior attainment (Newham 2009).

Many of the students go on to further education, apprenticeships or employment. Over 272 students progressed to university in 2009.

2.4. Survey of Newham College Students

In our survey all the students were aged between 17 and 24 years in 2006-07. As expected, the student profile was significantly multicultural. The majority of the students were children of immigrants (second generation) or immigrants themselves. A vast number were Muslims from the Indian subcontinent (Bangladesh, Pakistan and India) or from African countries and the majority of the respondents were Muslim.

We gave out approximately 250 questionnaires in the autumn of 2006. A few were returned blank as the students' ability in English was too poor to even attempt answers. Others were left incomplete; a few were spoilt. In all 217 returned questionnaires were analysed. As to be expected some of the questions were left unanswered so the percentages shown in the Tables/ Figures in the following chapters are based on the valid results. The authors returned to the college in 2007-08 and supplemented the questionnaires with 100 short interviews given to different students, all of whom were Muslim. After each interview the interviewee was asked if they would be happy to have their photograph included in the results of our research. The majority agreed while a few were uncomfortable with the idea and declined the offer. We included some of these photographs in our book but the photos are not linked to any particular statement. In 2009 we completed our research with 13 in-depth interviews with Muslim volunteers. Their stories are included in this book as complete articles in themselves.

2.5. Profile of Students

2.5.1. Background

The profile of students is based on the students who answered the questionnaires. Significantly more young women, 114 answered the questionnaire, with just 89 men doing so (Table 2.3). However 14 students who answered the questionnaire did not state their sex.

Table 2.3 Sex of students

	Number	Percentage
male	89	43.8
female	114	56.2
Total	203	100.0

Interestingly at first the authors attempted to complete the questionnaires in the cafeteria when the students were freer and had time between lessons. Nevertheless that proved quite difficult from the start, as a couple of the male students felt very uncomfortable with the procedure and attempted to prevent others from taking part by harassing them. After that experience the authors sought permission to carry out the questionnaires in a more conducive environment: empty classrooms and during tutorials, and were very grateful to staff members who went out of their way to accommodate them.

Almost two-fifths (39.8%) of the students initially questioned were born in the UK and therefore are second generation immigrants. As we can see from Table 2.4 the next largest group was born in India 10.2%, with Bangladesh 5.8%, Somalia 5.8%, Nigeria 3.4% and Pakistan 2.9%. We also questioned many individuals or small groups of students who were born overseas (see Table 2.4). Just over half the group (50.1%) who completed the questionnaire were born in Europe. Almost a third (28.8%) were born in Asia, 20.1% were born in Africa and 3% were born in South America.

Table 2.4 Distribution of students according to country

Europe	N	%		Africa	N	%
UK *	82	39.8		Somalia	12	5.8
Lithuania	5	2.4		Nigeria	7	3.4
Portugal	4	1.9		Ghana	4	1.9
Kosovo	3	1.5		Zanzibar	3	1.5
Russia	2	1.0		Congo	2	1.0
Poland	2	1.0		Zimbabwe	2	1.0
Slovakia	1	.5		Uganda	2	1.0
Spain	1	.5		Angola	1	.5
Latvia	1	.5		Burundi	1	.5
France	1	.5		Cameroon	1	.5
Italy	1	.5		Egypt	1	.5
Asia				Dem. Rep. Congo	1	.5
India	21	10.2		Equador	1	.5
Bangladesh	12	5.8		Guinea Bissau	1	.5
Pakistan	6	2.9		Morocco	1	.5
Sri Lanka	4	1.9		Sierra Leone	1	.5
United Arab Emirates	3	1.5		Americas		
Afghanistan	2	1.0		Columbia	2	1.0
Jordan	2	1.0		St. Kitts Nevis	1	.5
Saudi Arabia	2	1.0				
Thailand	2	1.0		Sum total	206	100.0
Burma	1	.5				
Hong Kong	1	.5				
Philippines	1	.5		* UK second generation immigrants		
Syria	1	.5				
Ukraine	1	.5				

In Table 2.5 we see that 194 of the students were willing to declare which passport they held. Of course it is possible that some of the young people may not have had a passport. Although only 39.8% (Table 2.4) of the students were born in the UK, 55.1% (Table 2.5) hold British passports.

30

Table 2.5 Distribution of students according to passports

Passport	Student		Passport	Student	
	N	%		N	%
British	107	55.1	Afghani	1	.5
Indian	18	9.3	Bashish	1	.5
Somali	8	4.1	Burundian	1	.5
Bangladeshi	6	3.1	Cameroonian	1	.5
Portuguese	6	3.1	Dutch	1	.5
Pakistani	5	2.6	Equadorian	1	.5
Lithuanian	4	2.1	Finish	1	.5
Nigerian	4	2.1	Kosovan	1	.5
Congolese	2	1.0	Latvian	1	.5
Filipino	2	1.0	Sierra Leone	1	.5
French	2	1.0	Slovak	1	.5
Ghanaian	2	1.0	Sri Lankan	1	.5
Polish	2	1.0	Swiss	1	.5
Russian	2	1.0	Tanzanian	1	.5
Sudanese	2	1.0	Thai	1	.5
Burmese	1	.5	Ugandan	1	.5
Columbian	1	.5	Zanzibar	1	.5
Italian	1	.5	Zimbabwean	1	.5
Moroccan	1	.5			
			Total	194	100

The authors were particularly interested to compare the integration and views of young Muslims with other faith groups. It quickly became obvious that the two largest faith groups in Newham College were Christian and Muslim with a handful of other faiths or sects plus some non believers (Table 2.6). Consequently it was decided for the purpose of our survey that we would consider the replies only of the students who were either Muslim or Christian and ignore the responses of the other 22 students.

In the 2001 census Islam was the largest of the non-Christian religions with 2.78% of the whole UK population proclaiming to be Muslims. According to the census over two-thirds of the Muslims lived in the 44 urban districts the populations of which were over 5% Muslim. The highest proportion was in the two London boroughs of Tower Hamlets with 36% and Newham with 24%. They were closely followed by two areas in the north of England - the Blackburn area 19% and Bradford 16% (GIS Project 2009). The Muslim community in the

UK comes from a wide range of countries including Somalia and Afghanistan but the majority have origins in Pakistan, Bangladesh and India.

Table 2.6 Students according to declared religion

Students' Religion		N	%
Islam		129	62.3
Christian	Roman Catholic	22	10.6
	Church of England	16	7.7
	Christian	9	4.4
	Methodist / Baptist	4	1.9
	Pentecostal	3	1.4
	Greek / Russian Orthodox	2	1.0
Other Faiths	Hindu	4	1.9
	Sikh	4	1.9
	Buddhist	3	1.4
Others	Adventist	1	.5
	Mormon	1	.5
	Jehovah's Witness	1	.5
	Celestial Church of Christ	1	.5
Atheist	(non-believer)	7	3.4
Total		207	100.0

The ratio of Muslims to Christians in the questionnaire group was as follows: Muslim males 69.2%, Christian males 30.8%, Muslim females 70.1%, Christian females 29.9%. The high percentage of Muslims questioned does not indicate the percentage in the college.

Figure 2.1 Ratio of Muslims to Christians in questionnaire group (%)

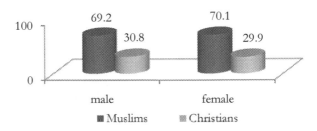

Concentrating on solely the Muslim and Christian students we saw that half of the students were born in Europe (50.8%) although it has to be said, almost all of those were children of immigrants. Almost the same number originated from Asia (24.6%) as Africa (22.9%) and a few came from South America (1.7%).

Table 2.7 Distribution of Muslim and Christian students according to continent

	N	%
Europe	91	50.8
Asia	44	24.6
Africa	41	22.9
Central America	3	1.7
Sum of Total	179	100

Table 2.8 shows the distribution of students according to continent of birth and their religion. As we can see a slightly higher percentage of Christians (54.4%) were born in Europe than Muslims (49.2%). A much higher percentage of Muslims (32%) came from Asia than Christians (8.8%) whereas a lower percentage of Muslims (18.9%) came from Africa than Christians (31.6%). All three respondents from South America were Christian, perhaps to be expected, as there are few Muslims in that part of the world.

Table 2.8 Apportionment of students - religion & continent

Religion		Continent				Total
		Europe	Asia	Africa	Central America	
Christian	N	31	5	18	3	57
	%	54.4	8.8	31.6	5.3	100.0
Muslim	N	60	39	23	0	122
	%	49.2	32.0	18.9	0	100.0
Total	N	91	44	41	3	179
	%	50.8	24.6	22.9	1.7	100.0

(Chi2=17.878; df=3;p<0,001; Vc=0.316)

2.5.2. Values

Many people worry that immigrants' values are different from UK society's values. They believe that there are clear differences, for example between perceived Asian values and Western values. However, it cannot be declared that all Asians hold exactly the same values or that all Westerners hold identical values. Bearing this in mind, it is generally thought that there are distinct differences between the values of the east and west. One perceived Asian value is community whereas Westerners are seen to put more value on the individual. Asians appreciate order and harmony whereas Westerners put a greater emphasis on personal freedom. Other values considered to be 'Asian' are respect for leaders, family loyalty, saving and thriftiness and hard work (BBC World). We would add respect for parents and the supreme value of 'honour.'

Forster in 1983 stressed that Africans' concept of family is totally different to our Westerners' concept. Here in the west people are very aware of their nuclear family but often live in isolation from their family members. Africans, however, have a very broad concept of family, with extended family members often living together.

Naturally there are differences between cultural values but interestingly, even with the UK's ethnic mix, according to a UK Citizenship Survey[4] conducted in 2007-08 the most commonly chosen UK values were: Respect for the Law (57%); Tolerance and Politeness towards others (56%); Equality of Opportunity (38%); Freedom of Speech (36%) and that everyone should speak English.

The Newham College Students were asked what their parents' attitudes were in relation to the values of their country of origin. In the question: What do you think about your parents' attitudes to the values of their country of origin? - 62.2% of Christians and 63.2% of Muslims agreed that their parents 'always keep those values'. 'They sometimes keep those values' was chosen by 31.1% of Christians and 32.6% of Muslims, while 6.7% of Christians and 4.2% of Muslims chose the answer - 'They sometimes ignore those values'.

---

[4] UK Citizenship Survey: Identity and Values Topic Report – national representative sample of 10,000 adults + additional sample of 5,000 adults from ethnic minority groups.

Table 2.9 Students' reflections on parents' attitudes to values of their country of origin

Religion		They always keep those values	They sometimes keep those values	They sometimes ignore those values	Total
Christian	N	28	14	3	45
	%	62.2	31.1	6.7	100
Muslim	N	60	31	4	95
	%	63.2	32.6	4.2	100
Total	N	88	45	7	140
	%	62.9	32.1	5.0	100

(Chi2=0.395;df=2;p=0.821;Vc=0.053)

2.5.3. Language

The authors were interested to discover whether the students normally spoke in English at home or whether they used the language of their country of origin. Obviously that can be an indication of how integrated their family situation is. The assumption was that they are more integrated if they speak English at home, because presumably this means that their parents are fluent or at least feel at home speaking English.

In Table 2.10 we look at the student responses to the question: What language do you normally speak at home? The majority of the young people answered this question. We discovered that the young people speak a total of 41 different languages at home as their first language. Only 21.1% speak English as the norm at home.

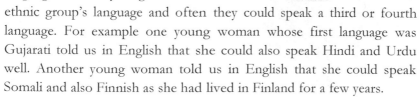

We also discovered that the majority of the young people were fluent in at least two languages – usually English and their ethnic group's language and often they could speak a third or fourth language. For example one young woman whose first language was Gujarati told us in English that she could also speak Hindi and Urdu well. Another young woman told us in English that she could speak Somali and also Finnish as she had lived in Finland for a few years.

Table 2.10 Distribution of students according to first language

European	N	%			N	%
English	44	21.1		Tamil	2	1.0
Portuguese	6	2.9		Sinhalese	2	1.0
French	4	1.9		Hindi	1	.5
Spanish	4	1.9		Thai	1	.5
Albanian	3	1.4		Pakistani	1	.5
Lithuanian	3	1.4		Marathi (India)	1	.5
Russian	3	1.4		Chinese	1	.5
Polish	2	1.0		Turkish	1	.5
Ukrainian	1	.5		Baji (China)	1	.5
Slovak	1	.5		Dhan (India)	1	.5
Dutch	1	.5		Myanmar (Burma)	1	.5
Latvian	1	.5		African	N	%
Greek	1	.5		Somali	12	5.7
Creole	1	.5		Arabic	8	3.8
Asian				Swahili	3	1.4
Bengali	29	13.9		Yoruba	2	1.0
Gujarati	20	9.6		Bravanese (Somalia)	2	1.0
Urdu	20	9.6		Lingala (Congo)	2	1.0
Panjabi	10	4.8		Twi (Ghana)	2	1.0
Malayalam	4	1.9		Akan (Ghana)	1	.5
Tanalog	3	1.4		Shona (Zimbabwe)	1	.5
Pashto	2	1.0		Sum total	209	100

In Table 2.11 the young people tell us how good they are at spoken and written English. As expected we see by these results that they consider their spoken English to be better than their written English. Indeed those we actually interviewed were well able to express themselves in English. Only one young person thought they would fail if tested on Spoken English and only five considered their spoken English poor.

When we asked the question: How good are you at written English? we saw that 31.8% of the students thought they were excellent, and 25.6% considered themselves very good. Only 6.8% admitted they thought their written English was poor.

Table 2.11 Ability to speak English and to write English

Spoken English	N	%	Written English	N	%
Excellent	70	39.5	Excellent	56	31.8
Very good	42	23.7	Very good	45	25.6
Good	59	33.3	Good	63	35.8
Poor	5	2.8	Poor	12	6.8
Fail	1	.6	Fail		
Total	177	100	Total	176	100

The authors thought that it would be helpful to see how many of the students watched English TV channels. The percentage of those born in the UK who always watched English TV was slightly higher (81.1%) than those born abroad (75.5%).

Figure 2.2 Students who watch English channels on television (%)

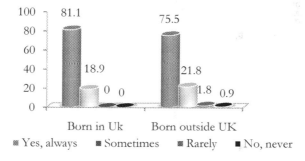

Only two people born abroad rarely watched English TV and one person born abroad claimed that they never watched English TV. However it is doubtful whether they watch other stations out of their own preferences or whether their parents, with perhaps limited English, prefer foreign language stations. While in 2010 we were visiting an Albanian family (who had arrived in the UK in 1999), an Albanian station was on the TV and even though her ten year old son couldn't speak Albanian, the mother stated that they always watched TV from their home country.

2.5.4. Home Life

Regarding home life the authors wanted to see if the young people stuck rigidly to their families' customs/traditions or whether their attitudes were moderated by their contact with English customs. The students were asked if they could evaluate their families' attitudes to following their home country's customs and traditions. Table 2.12 shows the students' responses to the question: Does your family follow the customs and traditions (including: eating habits, holidays, clothing, music, art, etc.) of your or your parents' country/countries of origin? It is hardly surprising that most students (94.9%) follow those customs to a certain extent. 'Yes, very much.' was the enthusiastic response of 42.6%, Very few never observed their customs (2.8%) and even fewer felt strongly that their parents didn't agree with following traditions (2.3%).

Table 2.12 Family attitudes towards following the customs/traditions of their parents' home country

Religion		Yes, very much	Yes, to some extent	Some-times	No, never	Strongly against	Total
Christian	N	24	11	19	1	2	57
	%	42.1	19.3	33.3	1.8	3.5	100
Muslim	N	51	39	23	4	2	119
	%	42.9	32.8	19.3	3.4	1.7	100
Total	N	75	50	42	5	4	176
	%	42.6	28.4	23.9	2.8	2.3	100

(Chi2=6.553;df=4;p=0.161;Vc=0.193)

When asking the students more specifically about attitudes towards eating national food, over half (58.6%) said that they always ate their national food; 39.7% said that they sometimes did so and only 1.7% said that they rarely ate their national food (Table 2.13). However, it was clear that Muslims (63.3%) were far more likely always to eat their national food than Christians (48.1%) probably largely due to the Muslim's ritual preparation of food, the fact that only some food is permitted *(halal)* and needs to be prepared in a particular way. On the other hand more Christians (51.9%) sometimes ate their national food and only 34.2% of Muslims sometimes did so.

Table 2.13 Family attitudes towards eating national food

Religion		Always	Sometimes	Rarely	Total
Christian	N	26	28	0	54
	%	48.1	51.9	0	100
Muslim	N	76	41	3	120
	%	63.3	34.2	2.5	100
Total	N	102	69	3	174
	%	58.6	39.7	1.7	100

(Chi2=5.752;df=2;p=0.056;Vc=0.182)

When asked about their family attitudes towards traditional weddings/ birthday celebrations, just over half (52.4%) agreed that they always had traditional celebrations; 37.2% said 'sometimes' and 10.4% said 'rarely.' (Table 2.14). Almost the same percentage of Christians (48.1%) and Muslims (54.4%) said that they always observed traditional family celebrations, with a fraction more of the Christians stating that they rarely did so.

Table 2.14 Family attitudes towards traditional weddings/ birthday celebrations

Religion		Always	Sometimes	Rarely	Total
Christians	N	25	19	8	52
	%	48.1	36.5	15.4	100
Muslims	N	61	42	9	112
	%	54.5	37.5	8.0	100
Total	N	86	61	17	164
	%	52.4	37.2	10.4	100

(Chi2=2.135;df=2;p=0.344;Vc=0.114)

Generally speaking we found that the Muslims tried to keep their family customs and values. In the next four chapters we will consider more controversial topics regarding the customs and traditions that the immigrant families brought from their original countries. We will look at several areas and consider how the students differ regarding their religion and in particular the Muslim male and female responses.

CHAPTER THREE

Education – Work – Social Participation

In this chapter we want to answer the question: How much do the young Muslims swing between two cultures in the area of Socio-Economic Integration into UK Society, by comparing Muslim students with Christian students. After looking at the UK society's attitudes to education, work and social participation we will reflect on the Newham College Muslim and Christian students' background and then the students' attitudes to those topics.

3.1. UK Society

After the Second World War special schemes were promoted by the UK government to encourage migrant labour to come to the UK to fill vacancies that had been generated by post war reconstruction and regeneration. There was a labour deficit. Waves of migrant workers from Commonwealth countries arrived in the UK in the 1950s. Socially, first generation migrants were not always welcomed and there were many instances of widespread discrimination and racism. The 1960s were characterised by antipathy towards the newly arriving Asians, especially in the West Midlands (Grillo 2010:51). This led to incidents of civil unrest and 'race riots'. The sheer number of migrant workers and their families was seen as a threat and right-wing politicians capitalised on this. The result was the attempt to control immigration and integration.

Many hapless attempts have been made to control immigrant flows. From the late 1970s the situation became more problematic with the growth of migration from countries other than Commonwealth countries. Systems of control led to confusion between refugee and asylum seeker migration and economic migration. By the 1980s, the only way open for many economic migrants to achieve residence was through the asylum system and this was perceived as abuse. The beginning of the 1990s was a time of political upheaval in Eastern Europe with the collapse of Communism which meant that many people in Eastern Europe joined the thousands of people seeking safety from conflict by moving to Western Europe. At the end of the 1990s war broke out in South Eastern Europe after Yugoslavia collapsed, and even more people sought refuge in Western Europe (Balicki, Wells 2006:19). The numbers of immigrants grew alarmingly in the early 2000s with people also seeking refuge from conflict in other parts of the world. In a period of high economic activity and wealth generation it is easier to absorb migrant groups and their families. However, a downturn in economic activity and resultant rises in unemployment, particularly in the current economic crisis and credit crunch, puts settled migrant communities at greater risk of marginalisation. The UK tightened its immigration regulations in 2009 and introduced a selective points-based immigration policy and probationary citizenship.

The Prime Minster in 2009, Gordon Brown, declared that migrants to the UK have made over the years a tremendous contribution both economically and socially to Great Britain. He believed that if Britain were to continue to be a significant player in the global economy it needed the specialist skills of migrants. He expressed his belief that immigrants knew that rights in a community also brought responsibilities. British values were not an option to take or leave. They were a condition to becoming part of our UK community. He stressed the value of diversity:

> British society has gained immeasurable benefit from its diversity, from being continually refreshed by new talent and new perspectives, from the confidence that comes from defining ourselves positively by our values, rather than negatively by any hostility to others. And we must continually remind ourselves also that net inward migration from both within and outside the EU is not rising but it is falling, with the annual figures showing that overall net immigration is down 44% on last year, and with independent migration experts like Oxford Economics predicting further sustained falls. And we must also point out the fact that over the past decades, people who have come from abroad to our country have boosted employment and growth; have filled key skills gaps in both our public and private sectors (Brown, 2009).

The British socio-economic policy reflects that of the European Union's Lisbon Agenda of 2000; although at times a somewhat reluctant member state of the European Union, Britain sees its future in being economically successful in an increasingly competitive global market. The new wealth generation will be dependent on high skilled employment driven by the new Knowledge Society which will in turn be supported by a highly qualified labour force in a cohesive society, enjoying wealth and full employment. Such well-sounding policy seems a long way from the reality of life in Newham. Over-confidence in such policy principles has now been tempered by the global economic recession, but this vision remains.

The history of many economic migrants is one of being encouraged to fill the jobs that no one else has wanted to do. Migrant patterns of residence driven by poor income tend to result in large concentrations of migrants in inner city areas such as Newham and this presents second generation migrant students with particular challenges. Their parents have low paid jobs and many do not speak English. Some place little value on education particularly for girls, expecting them to follow in their cultural tradition of marrying young. The lads are expected to succeed but find themselves in areas with few jobs or opportunities.

What is of vital importance to second generation migrant students is that the main mechanism for realising this policy aim remains education, and an education that increasingly achieves higher levels of qualification. The unskilled manual jobs that were a key driver for migration in the past have all but disappeared. According to the 2001 UK census, Bangladeshis represent one of the poorest minority ethnic groups in Britain with Pakistanis a close second. The majority of both communities originated from rural backgrounds. These two groups have the highest percentages of those who have 'never worked' or 'long term unemployed'. They also have the highest percentage of people who look after the home whereas the UK average is 4.7%, Bangladeshis are 13.1% and Pakistanis are 12.2%. They also perhaps unsurprisingly have the highest percentage of people with no educational qualification (Peach 2005:29). Bangladeshi and Pakistani women had the lowest economic participation rates of any ethnic minority group in Britain. Their percentages were half those of Indian women (Peach 2005:28). Seventy percent of Muslim women aged 25 and over were economically inactive, compared with 41% overall in the 2001 census (Bowlby, Lloyd-Evan, 2009:39). The percentage of 16% of Muslims who have 'never worked' or 'long term unemployed' compared to the national average of 3% appears to reflect traditional Muslim values of *purdah* (female segregation) and *izzat* (family honour). Naturally these traditional values create serious economic consequences. In essence it means that the family has only one income per household whereas Hindu and Sikh families usually have two incomes, as both husband and wife work. Bangladeshi and Pakistani women tend to marry earlier and have larger families than Hindus and Sikhs so consequently their incomes are low and their homes often over-crowded (Peach 2005:30). A worrying trend is mentioned by Peach:

> within the urban areas in which they have settled, Pakistanis and (particularly) Bangladeshis have shown high rates of segregation. On a scale from 0 (no segregation) to 100 (complete segregation) Pakistanis segregated from whites averaged 54 while Bangladeshis average 65 (2005:28).

The South Asian communities are not the only groups who are deprived. Dirie in her book *Desert Children* quotes Kwateng-Kluvitse, the director of Forward, speaking about female circumcision, who said that a lack of proper integration in the UK has not helped the Africans:

> Look at how Africans live here. They have poor housing and are crowded together. Many of them cannot read or write, especially the women, and they have little English. Even the immigrants who are educated have problems assimilating. Their degrees or professional qualifications are not recognised here in the UK. And because of their refugee status they are not allowed to work for a long time. This is very hard to take. In a situation like that there is little incentive to adopt the customs and values of the host country. On the contrary – you hold fast to the traditions you brought with you from home. These people have been uprooted and are completely isolated (2005:105-106).

She goes on to explain that the situation is even worse now for the men. They were the bread-winners in their home country while here they can't work. They see their lives collapsing around them. In general the men feel a need to reinstate that they are the head of their family and consequently some become aggressive, mistreat their wives and often insist on keeping up traditions from their home countries (2005:106).

The question of education is particularly tense in the UK as Hellyer explains:

> When the Muslim community was small and predominantly composed of immigrants from other countries, education for the younger generation was not a particular pressing concern; however, as it became clear that the 'myth of return' for many of the immigrant population was, for the most part a myth, the subject of 'Islamic education' subsequently became an issue for both the Muslims and the mainstream (2009:155).

In 1997 the first Muslim schools supported by the state were opened in the UK. According to the Department for Education and Skills in 2007 there were 126 full-time Muslim schools in England; of those 8 were state funded. These are regulated in the same way as other faith schools. England's education watchdog, Ofsted, checks that they meet set standards. They have to follow the national curriculum (BBC 2007).

In 2007 there were 115 Muslim independent schools. Like all private schools these schools are subject to inspections by Ofsted and they are free to follow their own curriculum. However most Muslim schools follow the national curriculum and all schools enter pupils for GCSE exams.

It is important to remember that the Muslim community also supports many of its own places of study (Madrassas) which educate their young people in the recitation of the Koran after school, often for a couple of hours every day. According to Ataullah Parkar of the Association of Muslim Schools, the vast majority of independent Muslim schools teach citizenship to fulfil Ofsted. He states that they are increasingly looking at how to maintain faith, but be an active, contributing member of society, too (BBC 2007).

Universities have a new emerging role. Further Education Colleges are a key way to access both vocational and university higher education. The UK has been fairly active in the role of Muslim higher education. There is a formal exchange agreement between the University of Birmingham, al-Azhar University in Cairo, Egypt and the University of Kuwait. There are also two colleges in the UK where students can pursue Qur'anic studies, law and ethics alongside subjects found in mainstream Universities. In 2007 the Prime Minister recommended that an institution be established to educate future Muslim religious authorities. Many students also opt to go abroad for classical Islamic education in Egypt, Syria and Yemen (Hellyer 2009:157).

English language is difficult even for those who were born in the UK and come from English speaking homes, so it may be wrong to see English language as a single skill to be mastered. The global use of English in the media and in the world of work means that many migrants arrive with some degree, however small, of fluency. Varied forms of English are used in different contexts and there is different provision to develop fluency for these contexts. English is now part of the citizenship testing system, but there is still a popular insular belief that the world speaks English.

It is clear that Britain has become a multicultural new nation and while its teachers might still be predominantly white, its pupils are often black and brown and have a rich and varied cultural history. They are also fluent in a number of languages, with many young people speaking English as their second language and speaking their parents' native language at home, as we saw in the previous chapter. The UK Home Office decided in 2006 to introduce mandatory tests for anyone wishing to settle in Britain to help them to qualify for British nationality:

> It will help maximise their contribution to the economy by increasing their job prospects, assist their integration into local communities and generate a greater understanding of the rights and responsibilities that come with living in Britain. Immigration Minister Liam Byrne said it is essential that migrants wishing to live in the UK permanently recognise that there are responsibilities that go with this. Having a good grasp of English is essential in order for them to play a full role in society and properly integrate into our communities (Home Office Press Release 2006).

Of importance is that most migrants will have at least a second language which gives them a potential advantage in a global labour market.

The burgeoning concentration on anti-discrimination and human rights has focussed a new awareness. The Equality and Human Rights Commission was established in 2006. The new legislation and the

Commission may have resulted initially in an over concentration on legalities, but there is an increasing popular awareness about racism and ethnicity now set in a wider context of equal opportunities and anti-discrimination.

There are of course exceptions and contradictions. The importance of role models should not be underestimated. Many second generation migrants achieve many things and at the highest level. The EU Single Market, and the impact of globalisation itself, promote economic and social mobility. Yet for the British there is a migrant issue. There are fears about numbers and limited social resources, as there is a fear of perceived different cultures and an ignorance of different values. The future threat to migrant communities is one of isolation, poverty, long term unemployment and of living in sub-standard housing in ghettos. This is the potential downward spiral that British socio-economic policy is aimed to reverse.

While some Muslim groups such as Pakistanis (69%) own almost as many homes as white households (70%), they have a much higher rate of owner-occupied homes compared to Bangladeshis (34%). There is a strong correspondence between the employment status of Muslims and the type and quality of their housing. However the condition of many Muslim owned houses is of poor quality and often inadequate, with shared bathrooms and no central heating. Abbas stated in 2005 that a significant number of houses occupied by Muslim groups were overcrowded, with 43% Pakistani and Bangladeshi compared with white households which were only 2%. Overcrowding is a major problem for most Muslim families and it threatens their extended family. The main reason is that their families are considerably larger than the average UK family and there are no four bedroom council houses; of course there are also economic factors that come into play (Abbas 2005:36-38).

Another important factor is that most Muslim Bangladeshi family housing is usually in the run-down areas of inner cities. Many Muslim families prefer to live in areas where there is a mosque close by and they often choose an area near to their own family and community group, even if they can afford a more prosperous area (Abbas 2005:36-38).

In Newham over the last twenty years or more there has been a rapid ethnic change in the population. Like some other areas Newham is now experiencing some inter-ethnic tensions. These tensions are hardly surprising as there is competition for housing, worry about pressures on schools and generally mixed feelings.

According to Mumford and Power (2003) in their case study of one hundred families in the boroughs of Hackney and Newham:

> Families saw the dangers of segregation and were three times more worried about racial harassment than the London average. But 68% of families think that an ethnic mixture is a positive thing, almost all children play together across racial boundaries and 86% of interviewees asked had friends of other races. A total of 57% think that people of different backgrounds live well or were 'okay' together (2003:89).

The research showed that not everyone held the same view. It revealed that white families were more likely to have negative feelings regarding living in a racially mixed area than black and minority ethnic families. The report continued:

> There are several possible reasons for this. Minority families were conscious of having arrived more recently, having overcome initial racial hostility, having broken through into previously inaccessible areas. (...) Some white families in contrast, feel squeezed by the population shifts, particularly on the housing front because of difficulties in gaining a transfer to better housing, wanting but failing to be rehoused near family members because newcomers get priority. (...) They were also worried about schools when they saw white children rapidly becoming a minority. Their fears about growing segregation and a feeling of displacement were real and clearly articulated (Mumford, Power 2003:89).

Regarding social participation and in particular political involvement the UK has a concern in general about the political alienation and disaffection of young people. While there is evidence of a rise in single issue political engagement, for example, in environmental and climate change issues, there is a decline in interest in involvement in traditional party politics at all levels. A survey by MORI into Black and Minority Ethnic voting, conducted for the Electoral Commission, after the 2005 general election found:

> There were significant differences in claimed turnout between the different ethnic groups in the survey, over and above the differences

in levels of registration. Three-quarters (76%) of all Bangladeshis, 70% of Pakistanis and 67% of Indians said that they voted, while the figures fell to 61% for Caribbeans and 54% for Africans. Much lower still, though, were turnout rates among 'other' ethnic minorities (46%) and among those of mixed race (just 40%); in the latter case, however, this may partly reflect that the mixed race group has a much younger age profile than do the other ethnic groups, and turnout was very much lower among the young than among the middle-aged and old across the board.

Overall among BMEs [Black and Minority Ethnic], claimed turnout was lower among 18-24 year olds (48%) and 25-34 year olds (48%) than among 35-54 year olds (63%) and those aged 55 and over (79%). While voting was also lower among the young in the population as a whole, in that case there was a marked difference between 18-24 year olds and 25-34 year olds.

There was no difference in claimed turnout between those born in the UK (58%) and those born elsewhere (59%), nor much by gender (men 57%, women 60%) and surprisingly no systematic difference by class. While it was very much lower than average among third-generation residents (46%) this simply reflects that that group consists disproportionately of the young (Electoral Commission 2005:30-31).

Hellyer (2009) commented in his book 'Muslims of Europe' that although there have been moderately progressive moves to help the Muslim community in the UK. it is difficult to generalise about such a diverse community.

3.2. Immigrants' Culture and Traditions

There is a considerable gap between Europe and developing countries regarding education and specifically the education of girls. As we read in the Arab Human Development Report 2005, the Arab world is currently experiencing an extraordinary rise in the education of women, ahead of other regions although it has not yet succeeded in eliminating illiteracy among Arab women. The index of illiteracy in Arab countries is higher than the world average, and even higher than the average for developing countries. Arab countries have entered the twenty-first century with 60 million illiterate adults, 40% of the adult population. The majority of the illiterate adults are poor women from villages.

International figures show, that in the Arab countries, girls (who actually attend school) are more successful than boys. However, it does not give them the same opportunities as boys (Arab Human Development Report 2005:80)[5].

According to UNESCO, Pakistan ranks second in the world regarding growth in illiteracy. Pakistan has 6.5 million children who are not in school and 80% of those have never been to school at all. The country spends a little over 2% of its GDP on education. Nigeria has first place with 8 million children not in school and India ranks third with 4.5 million. One of the main causes is poverty, with many girls needed at home to help with chores and younger siblings. Approximately, 65.6% of the population of Pakistan lives on less than $2 per day. The average duration of schooling for boys in Pakistan is 3.8 years and 1.3 years for girls (Syed 2006). The situation may also be a consequence of tradition. In some families, parents remove their daughters from the schooling system, in order to marry them young (Heritier 2007:609).

The Arab Charter of Human Rights (Cairo, 15 September 1994) Article:34 speaks of the commitment of Arab states to combat illiteracy:

> The eradication of illiteracy is a binding obligation and every citizen has a right to education. Primary education, at the very least, shall be compulsory and free and both secondary and university education shall be made easily accessible to all (1994:80).

Irrespective of religion, in many African countries the education of children is neglected. Schools clearly reflect the problems many African countries have regarding inefficient or dysfunctional authorities. Tradition plays a major role which is compounded by political problems, social and armed conflicts. The obligation to go to school does not mean that parents are forced to send their children to school. Free education doesn't mean parents feel obliged to send their children. At present in Africa the younger generation is more literate. However there are still some children under 14 years old who have never attended school. Some children in that age group drop out of school early and

---

[5] Discrimination against women in the Arab countries continues to limit their access to knowledge despite the mass of statistical and other evidence indicating that Arab girls are the better learners, especially on the first rungs of the educational ladder (7-8 years).

the higher the level of education the less are girls likely to attend (Michalowska 2008:379-380).

Souad, a woman brought up in Jordan wrote in her book *Spalona żywcem (Burned Alive)*:

> I was born in a tiny village. I was told that it lies somewhere in the territory of Jordan (…) but because I never went to school, I don't know the history of my country. (...) I have never moved away from my village by more than a few kilometers from the last house, but I knew that further away, there are cities. However, I didn't see them. I also didn't know whether the Earth is round or flat, I had no idea at all about the world! (...) Instead, I had to pray at least twice a day, recite prayers as my mother and sisters did, but I learned about the existence of the Koran many years later, in Europe. My only brother, the king in our house, attended school, but we girls, didn't. In my country having a girl is a curse. Wife should first give birth to a son, at least one, and if she keeps having only daughters, everyone sneers at her. There is no need for more than two or three girls for the household chores, the cattle and field work. If more daughters are born, they need to be got rid of. That's how I lived for almost seventeen years, knowing nothing except that if I was brought into this world as a girl, I am worse than an animal (Souad 2008:8).

That many communities in the world do not see a need to educate girls is confirmed by Ayaan Hirsi Ali in her autobiography *Infidel*, as a temporary immigrant in Kenya:

> When I went back to school, things were different. Girls I used to know had left; when I asked about it, people shrugged and said they had probably gone to be married. This had happened before, from time to time; even in primary school, one girl left because she was betrothed. Somehow, though, I had never really noticed it before.
>
> Now I saw that Latifa, one of the Arab girls from the coast, had suddenly disappeared from our classroom. According to Halwa, one Saturday afternoon Latifa's father told her that she was never going back to school; the time had come for her to prepare to become a woman (2007:77).

Immigrants living in Europe may also underestimate the need to send their daughters to school. Some immigrants believe that the education of girls is unnecessary because their daughter will marry and her husband has an obligation to maintain his wife, while she looks after the home.

After analysing the situation in the UK and countries of origin we come to our research in Newham College. In order to understand better how the young see themselves becoming involved in the area of socio-economic integration we asked them a number of questions. We will reflect on the responses the students gave us regarding the following topics:

- ➢ Education - whether they hope to study at university.
- ➢ Work - the students' opinions on whether they think it is appropriate for a young woman to be allowed to have a job outside the home; whether a young wife should stay at home, live with and look after her parents-in-law; their parents' expectations regarding their children's future and the students' aspirations regarding their situation when they are 30 years old.
- ➢ Social Participation - the students' involvement in social activities – taking part in sports or dance clubs, being a member of a library, voting in elections.
- ➢ Discrimination – we wanted to know if discrimination had ever been a problem for the students or their families and we invited them to explore their own attitude to other ethnic groups. We also asked the students about their friendship groups and whether their friends were from the same ethnic group or not.

3.3. Newham College Students' Views

3.3.1. Education

One of the first questions we asked the students was: Do you hope to study at university and get a degree? (Table 3.1). The responses were as follows: 79.6% of Christians and 89.4% of Muslims agreed while 20.4% of Christians and 10.6% of Muslims chose the option 'No'.

We can see that while the majority of the students who answered this question were motivated to go on to University, Muslim students were 10% more likely to want to study at university and get a degree. Of course it is important to remember that all the young people questioned were already at a college of further education and therefore had an interest in education.

Table 3.1 Aspirations of students to go to university

Religion		Yes	No	Total
Christian	N	39	10	49
	%	79.6	20.4	100
Muslim	N	101	12	113
	%	89.4	10.6	100
Total	N	140	22	162
	%	86.4	13.6	100

(Chi2=2.019;df=1;p=0.080;Vc=0.135)

Looking just at the Muslims' responses to the question: Do you hope to study at university and get a degree? (Figure 3.1) we can see that there is very little difference between the Muslim men and women when it comes to aspirations to further study.

Figure 3.1 Attitude of Muslim students to future education (%)

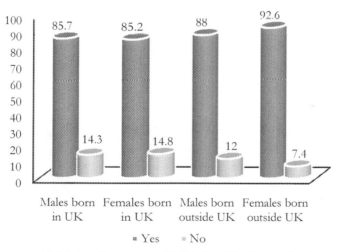

The percentage is high in all groups. 85.7% for Muslim males born in the UK and 88% for Muslim males born outside the UK. Regarding the Muslim females there is a greater difference with 85.2% for Muslim females born in the UK and considerably higher number of those born outside of the UK 92.6%. Possibly due to the cultural differences in their home countries where boys are more likely to be educated to a higher level than girls, it is possible that many young women come to the UK specifically to study although we did no research on their reasons for coming to the UK.

Fewer than a half of the students answered the question: Do you think you will fulfill the desire to go to University? - 83.3% of Christians and 72.7% of Muslims chose the answer 'Yes, because, I am hard working & clever'. The answer 'Yes, because, my parents want me to go to university' was chosen by 16.7% of Christians and 27.3% of Muslims. The group that did answer appeared to have an overwhelmingly desire to go on to further study at university (Table 3.2).

Table 3.2 Students' expectations with reference to further study

| Religion | | Yes, because... | | Total |
		I am hard working & clever	My parents want me to go to university	
Christian	N	25	5	30
	%	83.3	16.7	100
Muslim	N	40	15	55
	%	72.7	27.3	100
Total	N	65	20	85
	%	76.5	23.5	100

(Chi2=0.696;df=1;p=0,204;Vc=0.119)

During the research one of the teachers confidently argued that a large proportion of female students will not work or complete their education, but will get married as soon as possible. He may be correct, for very few actually answered this question, but we cannot be sure as they gave no opinion.

However the 100 short interviews with the students suggested, to the contrary, their high self-determination to learn a profession (maybe even graduate from higher education). When asked about marriage plans, nearly 100% of the girls answered that they didn't know or didn't expect to get married soon.

The experience of girls in literature shows that being encouraged to go to school doesn't prevent arranged or forced marriages. Shah in her book *The Imam's Daughter* writes about the fact that she was surprised her parents let her go to college. However she began her studies and was making excellent progress. She hoped eventually to go to university:

> Somehow I had convinced myself that there were no secret wedding plans afoot. I had started to believe there was a way out via my studies. (...) If I studied hard and did well, maybe my parents would let me go to university. (...) For the past few months I had lived in false hope and with a false sense of security. Now I knew different. I knew that my abduction was planned and ready for the very next day. I would be bundled on to a flight in the evening, after college finished, over night to Pakistan (2009:165-166).

Only twenty-five students actually answered the question: Do you think you will fulfill the desire to go to University (No. because...)? The results were as follows: three Christians and eight Muslims chose the answer 'No, because I have difficulty with English'. The authors went into one class of approximately twenty-four students who had just arrived at the college to find that no one spoke the same language. There were twenty-four different languages including Albanian, Dutch, Somali, Urdu and Hindi and the majority of those students only had a few words of English. Unsurprisingly these students were unable to even attempt the questionnaire. Naturally many young people are keen to start earning some money, yet only three Christians and six of the Muslims chose the answer 'My parents want me to start work as soon as I leave college'.

It is possible that the students did not want to acknowledge that they suspected they would never qualify for university and didn't wish to admit it. Whatever the reason only five of the Muslims disclosed that their parents would want them to marry as soon as they left college and only nine of the group thought their parents would expect them to start work immediately.

3.3.2. Work

The question: Should a young woman be allowed to have a job outside the home? (Table 3.3) refers also to a traditional custom found amongst many Muslims, where it is considered unusual for a young woman to work outside the home. However we see that there is not a big difference between Christian and Muslim students: 87.5% of Christians said 'Yes, definitely' and 74.6% of Muslims. The answer 'May be' was chosen by 8.9% of Christians and 19.7% of Muslims. 'Definitely not' was chosen by 3.6% of Christians and 5.7% of Muslims.

Table 3.3 Students' attitudes towards young women being permitted to work outside the home

Religion		Yes. definitely	May be	Definitely not	Total
Christian	N	49	5	2	56
	%	87.5	8.9	3.6	100
Muslim	N	91	24	7	122
	%	74.6	19.7	5.7	100
Total	N	140	29	9	178
	%	78.7	16.3	5.1	100

(Chi2=3.889;df=2;p=0,143;Vc=0.148)

In Figure 3.2 we see that there is practically no difference between the Muslim male and female students' attitudes towards the females having a job outside the home. However, there is one exception; Muslim males born outside the UK who are less likely to agree to women working outside the home.

Figure 3.2 Comparison of Muslim male and female students' attitudes towards young women being permitted to work outside the home (%)

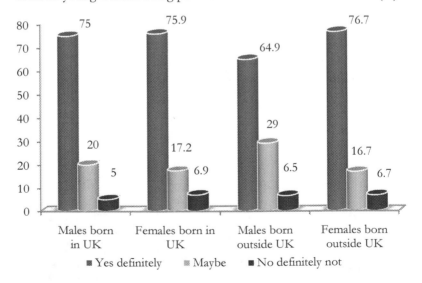

It would appear that very few young immigrants consider that custom to be relevant in today's UK society. Certainly some of the young

.people when interviewed felt that if they lived 'back home' for example in Bangladesh their lives would be more traditional and they would be more likely to follow the customs of their elders.

In the interviews we asked each of the male students how he felt about his future wife working: An Indian Muslim was adamant. He wanted his wife to work. As he said: *Want her to work, we have a family business if she can get involved great.* A Bangladeshi stated: *Would like wife to work but not as hard as me.* A Somali Muslim declared that he was *happy for wife to work, help family budget... expenditure. Wife will choose (her own) work.* While a Tanzanian Muslim told the authors: *If the woman chooses to work it is for herself. In Islam the husband must provide.*

An Afghani felt the choice was hers: *If she wants to work she can. If she doesn't want to work she can.* And another lad who described himself as a British Afghani told us the same: *If she wants to work, she can. It is up to her.* However a Pakistani felt quite strongly: *(My) wife will have to stay at home. I will support her.* A Turkish Muslim was also strong in his opinion: *I believe my wife should not work but stay at home and look after the children. In Muslim tradition the man works and the woman stays at home.*

A Nigerian Muslim agreed with him: *Women should not work. The man should be the bread winner.* Another Nigerian was a little more accommodating: *(I would) prefer wife not to work for someone else but would like her to have a good education and a career of her own, in case anything happened (to me).*

Some of the Muslim women were asked if they expected to have a job/ career outside the home after they married. An eighteen year old Bangladeshi told the authors: *I would like to work. But I would put my children first and think about work later on.* A 19 year old Pakistani told the interviewers: *Would like to work in beauty after college. Will not work after marriage.* A British (Turkish) Cypriot Muslim aged 18 told us: *(I) will be working and then going home to do my house cleaning.*

The question: Do you think a young wife should stay at home, live with and look after her parents-in-law? (Table 3.4) refers to the tradition in Muslim countries of the young wife moving into her husband's home and looking after the home and her in-laws. As expected, more Muslims than Christians felt this was acceptable. 5.5% of Christians answered 'Yes, definitely' and 12.7% of Muslims, 'May be'

– 25.5% of Christians and 42.4% of Muslims, 'definitely not' - 69.1% of Christians and 44.9% of Muslims.

Table 3.4 Attitudes of students towards a young wife staying at home to care for her parents-in-law

Religion		Yes, definitely	May be	Definitely not	Total
Christian	N	3	14	38	55
	%	5.5	25.5	69.1	100
Muslim	N	15	50	53	118
	%	12.7	42.4	44.9	100
Total	N	18	64	91	173
	%	10.4	37.0	52.6	100

(Chi2=8.970;df=2;p=0.011;Vc=0.228)

However Muslim males born in the UK were less sure whether it was acceptable for a young wife to stay at home, live with and look after her parents-in-law with only 10% saying 'yes' and 60% saying 'maybe' compared to Muslim males born outside the UK who appeared to feel it was more acceptable, with 25.8% saying 'yes' and 41.9% saying 'maybe.'

Figure 3.3 Points of view regarding whether a young wife should stay at home, live with and look after her parents-in-law (%)

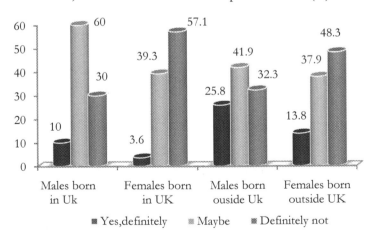

Muslim females born in the UK were far more certain of their thoughts on the matter with 57.1% saying 'definitely not' and of those born outside the UK 48.3% saying 'definitely not.' Only 3.6% of Muslim

females born in the UK agreed that a young wife should stay at home, live with and look after her parents-in-law (Figure 3.3).

In the question: What would you like to be doing when you are 30 years old? (Table 3.5) - 80.9% of Christians and 74.8% of Muslims chose the answer 'Married with children, working as a...' 12.8% of Christians and 19.6% of Muslims chose the answer 'Married, working as a....' 6.4% of Christians and 5.6% of Muslims chose the answer 'Single, working as a...' Very few young people actually completed the sentence with the work they would like to be doing.

Table 3.5 Students' hopes for future lifestyle

Religion		Married with children, working as a..	Married. working as a..	Single. working as a...	Total
Christian	N	38	6	3	47
	%	80.9	12.8	6.4	100
Muslim	N	80	21	6	107
	%	74.8	19.6	5.6	100
Total	N	118	27	9	154
	%	76.6	17.5	5.8	100

(Chi2=1.068;df=2;p=0.586;Vc−0.083)

In the question: What do you think your parents would like you to be doing when you are 30 years old? (Table 3.6) - three quarters of the group (76.2% of Christians and 74.7% of Muslims) who had answered this question chose the answer 'Married with children, working as a....' 16.7% of Christians and 17.2% of Muslims chose the answer 'Married, working as a...' Only a very small percentage (7.1% of Christians and 2.0% of Muslims) chose the answer 'Single, working as a....'. Again very few young people actually completed the sentence '...working as a......' with the work they thought their parents would like them to be involved in.

Table 3.6 Parents' aspirations for their children aged thirty

Religion		Married with children working as	Married. Working as a	Single. working as a	Other	Total
Christian	N	32	7	3	0	42
	%	76.2	16.7	7.1	0	100
Muslim	N	74	17	2	6	99
	%	74.7	17.2	2.0	6.1	100
Total	N	106	24	5	6	141
	%	75.2	17.0	3.5	4.3	100

(Chi2=4.740;df=3;p=0.192;Vc=0.183)

The authors were interested in whether the students planned to stay in Newham or the London area (Table 3.7). In the question: Where would you like to be living when you are 30 years old? 31.9% of Christians and 32.4% of Muslims chose the answer 'Where I am now'. 17.0% of Christians and 26.7% of Muslims chose the answer 'Somewhere else in the UK'. 8.5% of Christians and 3.8% of Muslims chose the answer 'Somewhere in Europe outside the UK'. 17.0% of Christians and 16.2% of Muslims chose the answer 'Somewhere else in the world'. 25.5% of Christians and 21.0% of Muslims chose the answer 'I do not know.'

Unfortunately the question was close to the end of the Questionnaire and only 152 students actually answered the question. However we can see that almost a quarter of the group had no future plans to move abroad and only a very small percentage felt that they would like to live somewhere else in the UK.

Table 3.7 Students' hopes for future residence

Religion		Where I am now	Another place in the UK	Another place in Europe outside UK	Another place in world	I do not know	Total
Christian	N	15	8	4	8	12	47
	%	31.9	17.0	8.5	17.0	25.5	100
Muslim	N	34	28	4	17	22	105
	%	32.4	26.7	3.8	16.2	21.0	100
Total	N	49	36	8	25	34	152
	%	32.2	23.7	5.3	16.4	22.4	100

(Chi2=2.959;df=4;p=0.565;Vc=0.140)

3.3.3. Social Participation

In figure 3.4 we look at the students' responses to the question: How many really close friends do you have among people of your own ethnic group? We can see that the majority of students, 62.5% of Muslims and 47.3% of Christians, feel that they have six or more close friends in their ethnic group. Perhaps the fact that more Muslims (15% more than Christians) feel that they have six or more ethnically related friends is due largely to the close knit family bonds within the Islamic faith plus their close-knit cultural backgrounds.

Figure 3.4 Comparison of Muslim & Christian number of close friends within own ethnic group (%)

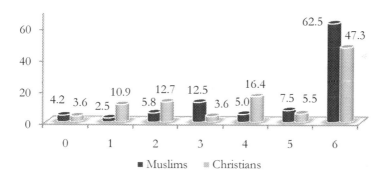

Figure 3.5 Comparison of Muslim & Christian number of close friends within other ethnic groups (%)

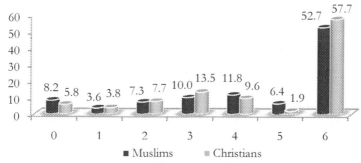

In Figure 3.5 when we compare Muslim & Christian number of friends within other ethnic groups the results are closer. Over half of both groups consider that they have six or more friends from other ethnic groups. The Christians (57.7%) have slightly more than the Muslims (52.7%). More Muslims think that they have no close friends in other ethnic groups (8.2%) while among Christians the percentage is 5.8%.

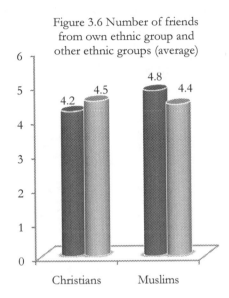

Figure 3.6 Number of friends from own ethnic group and other ethnic groups (average)

■ other people of your ethnic group

▨ members of other ethnic groups

In Figure 3.6 we look at the average result and can see that there appears to be very little difference between the two groups. Christians have slightly more close friends in other ethnic groups while Muslims have slightly more close friends in their own ethnic groups.

It is heartening to read that two thirds of the Christians questioned and almost the same number of Muslims had no problems with another ethnic group living next door to them. However it is a matter of concern that forty-three of the young people are uncertain of their feelings on the matter and it is very worrying that fifteen of the young people would be unhappy with another ethnic group living next door (Table 3.8).

Table 3.8 Position taken on having another ethnic group living next door

Religion		Yes, definitely	May be	Definitely not	Total
Christian	N	34	10	6	50
	%	68.0	20.0	12.0	100
Muslim	N	71	33	9	113
	%	62.8	29.2	8.0	100
Total	N	105	43	15	163
	%	64.4	26.4	9.2	100

(Chi2=1.870;df=2;p=0,393;Vc=0.107)

In order to understand better the students' willingness to become involved in local society they were asked if they already belonged or would consider belonging to either a sports/dance or drama club.

In Table 3.9 we can see that a higher percentage of Christians (65.4%) than Muslims (44.6%) either belonged already or would choose to belong to either a sports, dance or drama group. There is a particularly marked difference when you look at the percentage in each group who would not consider belonging, only 5.8% of Christians while 20.5% of Muslims when asked, said 'no,' they would not consider joining one of those group.

Table 3.9 Christian/Muslim aspiration to belong to a sports/dance or drama club

Religion		Yes	Maybe	No	Total
Christian	N	34	15	3	52
	%	65.4	28.8	5.8	100
Muslim	N	50	39	23	112
	%	44.6	34.8	20.5	100
Total	N	84	54	26	164
	%	51.2	32.9	15.9	100

(Chi2=8.252;df=2;p=0.016;Vc=0.224)

The authors were particularly interested in whether there was any difference in the number of Muslim males and females who would consider joining such groups. The results show that almost 20% more males (56%) were likely to belong to such groups than females (35.7%) and females (26.8%) were less likely to join such a group compared with males (16%). However the Muslim females (37.5%) were also more undecided and would possibly consider joining one of the clubs whereas the males seemed to have already made up their minds with only 28% still undecided (Table 3:10).

Table 3.10 Muslim male/ female aspiration to belong to a sports/dance
or drama club

Muslims		Yes	Maybe	No	Total
male	N	28	14	8	50
	%	56.0	28.0	16.0	100
female	N	20	21	15	56
	%	35.7	37.5	26.8	100
Total	N	48	35	23	106
	%	45.3	33.0	21.7	100

(Chi2=4.539;df=2;p=0.103;Vc−0.200)

The young people were asked if they belonged to or would like to belong to a library. Again we see that Christians were more likely to belong than Muslims with 60.9% of Christians and only 49.5% of Muslims. Roughly the same percentage in each group would consider belonging, Christians 32.6% and Muslims 36.2%. Again more Muslims stated that they would not join a library, 14.3% compared to Christians 6.5% (Table 3.11).

Table 3.11 Christian/Muslim wish to belong to a library

Religion		Yes	Maybe	No	Total
Christian	N	28	15	3	46
	%	60.9	32.6	6.5	100
Muslim	N	52	38	15	105
	%	49.5	36.2	14.3	100
Total	N	80	53	18	151
	%	53.0	35.1	11.9	100

(Chi2=2.512;df=2;p=0.285;Vc=0.129)

When it came to comparing male and female Muslims' opinions regarding belonging to a library, only 99 students gave their views. Just over half the female group (55.8%) said that they would consider belonging to a library and less than half the males (46.8%) agreed. Very few students, just 14 in total declared that they wouldn't consider belonging to a library (Table 3.12). This result is maybe a little surprising, when one takes into account the fact that they are all studying at a college of further education and perhaps could be expected to have some interest in learning and reading. Perhaps the college provides everything for them, or does this indicate a lack of ambition to reach higher?

Table 3.12 Muslim male/female wish to belong to a library

Muslims		Yes	Maybe	No	Total
male	N	22	20	5	47
	%	46.8	42.6	10.6	100
female	N	29	14	9	52
	%	55.8	26.9	17.3	100
Total	N	51	34	14	99
	%	51.5	34.3	14.1	100

(Chi2=2.917;df=2;p=0.233;Vc=0.172)

There is little difference between the percentage of Muslims (67%) and Christians (65.3%) who would give to charity (Table 3.13). Both Christians and Muslims are encouraged by their faith to do so, but the authors wondered if they saw their giving as part of their responsibility to the society they lived in and whether it made any difference if they were male or female. If you take into account the number of 'maybes' it is heartening to see that so many young people are willing to give either voluntary help or to give to charity and it is clear that there is little difference between males and females in their willingness to donate, although it is perhaps surprising to find that 7 of the Muslims declared that they wouldn't give to charity.

Table 3.13 Christian/Muslim desire to give voluntary help or charity

Religion		yes	maybe	no	Total
Christian	N	32	17	0	49
	%	65.3	34.7	0	100
Muslim	N	77	31	7	115
	%	67.0	27.0	6.1	100
Total	N	109	48	7	164
	%	66.5	29.3	4.3	100

(Chi2=3.699;df=2;p=0.157;Vc=0.150)

In Table 3.14 we see that slightly more Muslim females (69%) than males (64.7%) were willing to give to charity. That number is evened out by the 'maybes' as we see that 27.5% of males and 25.9% of females would consider giving to charity.

Table 3.14 Muslim male/female desire to give voluntary help or charity

Muslims		Yes	Maybe	No	Total
male	N	33	14	4	51
	%	64.7	27.5	7.8	100
female	N	40	15	3	58
	%	69.	25.9	5.2	100
Total	N	73	29	7	109
	%	67.0	26.6	6.4	100

(Chi2=0.401;df=2;p=0, 188;Vc=0.061)

Although more of the group answered the question: Do you think it is important to vote in elections? the students' general lack of enthusiasm to vote mirrors the trend of young people all over the UK to be disillusioned about politics and therefore indifferent. Considerably less than  half the group stated that they would vote. As we can see approximately 10% more Muslims would vote: 47.1% of Muslims and 38.6% of Christians. However, 10% more Christians than Muslims would consider voting. Almost the same percentage of Muslims and Christians would not even consider voting.

Table 3.15 Muslim & Christian willingness to vote in elections

Religion		Yes	Maybe	No	Total
Christian	N	17	19	8	44
	%	38.6	43.2	18.2	100
Muslim	N	48	34	20	102
	%	47.1	33.3	19.6	100
Total	N	65	53	28	146
	%	44.5	36.3	19.2	100

(Chi2=1.344;df=2;p=0.511;Vc=0.096)

3.3.4. Discrimination

In the question: Have you ever suffered from discrimination/ or been treated badly because of your ethnic group? - 28.0% of Christians and 22.3% of Muslims chose the answer 'Yes, definitely.' 'May be' was chosen by 18.0% of Christians and 26.8% of Muslim while 54.0% of Christians and 50.9% of Muslims chose the answer 'Definitely not'.

Table 3.16 Students discriminated against or badly treated because of
ethnicity

Religion		Yes, definitely	May be	Definitely not	Total
Christian	N	14	9	27	50
	%	28.0	18.0	54.0	100
Muslim	N	25	30	57	112
	%	22.3	26.8	50.9	100
Total	N	39	39	84	162
	%	24.1	24.1	51.9	100

(Chi2=1.636;df=2;p=0.441;Vc=0.100)

Interestingly when asked in the interviews very few students had anything to say about discrimination. Only three Muslim students made any comment at all. A 19 year old Indian stated that she had *experienced discrimination in Britain outside London, especially in the employment sector*. An Afghani said that she hadn't noticed any discrimination: *No discrimination here. Everyone very friendly*. One student from the Congo thought that there was *discrimination in media*.

In the question: Have your parents suffered from discrimination or been treated badly because of their ethnic group? - 28.0% of Christians and 23.2% of Muslims chose the answer 'Yes, definitely' while 46.0% of Christians and 36.6% of Muslims chose the answer 'May be'. Definitely not' was chosen by 26.0% of Christians and 40.2% of Muslims.

Table 3.17 Parents discriminated against or badly treated because of
ethnicity

Religion		Yes, definitely	May be	Definitely not	Total
Christian	N	14	23	13	50
	%	28.0	46.0	26.0	100
Muslim	N	26	41	45	112
	%	23.2	36.6	40.2	100
Total	N	40	64	58	162
	%	24.7	39.5	35.8	100

(Chi2=3.034;df=2;p=0.219;Vc=0.137)

It was apparent that the students found this question harder to answer, as they did regarding any question about their parents. Of course it is a well known fact that many teenagers are more in tune with the attitudes and feelings of their peers than of their parents.

3.4. Conclusion

The task of this chapter was to find out if the young Muslims in Newham College swing as a pendulum between two cultures, creating a new culture regarding education, work and social participation.

Regarding education we see that Muslim students were ten percent more likely to want to go on to study at university than the Christian students in Newham College. As mentioned earlier, we were dealing with people who were already at a college of further education and therefore had an interest in education. A very important finding was that there was very little difference between Muslim men and women when it came to aspirations to further study and an insignificant difference between Muslim males born in the UK and Muslim males born outside the UK. Regarding Muslim females, a considerably higher percentage of those born outside of the UK were keener to pursue an University degree than Muslim females born in the UK, perhaps due to the fact that many of the young people came from countries where education for girls was a low priority. Of course it is questionable whether the young women will achieve their ambitions for further education due to the pressure of their culture to conform, marry and start a family at an early age. Less than half of the group gave their opinion on whether they would fulfil that desire. However the hundred short interviews with Muslim students suggested that these students had a high self-determination to learn a profession, maybe even graduate from higher education.

Considering the area of work – we wanted to know if the tradition of a young woman staying at home after marriage rather than going out to work was still acceptable to young students in the UK. The majority of young people were in favour of women being allowed to work outside the home. However, there was almost thirteen percent more support from Christians than from Muslim students (respectively 87.5% and 74.6%). But if we take into account that in both cases the percentage was high and that the answer 'Definitely not' was chosen by less than four percent of Christians and less than six percent of Muslims we can say that it would appear that very few young immigrants consider that custom to be relevant in today's UK society. Similarly in our hundred short interviews only a few students were against women working outside the home.

We found a greater difference between Muslim and Christian students regarding the tradition in Muslim countries of the young wife moving into her husband's home and looking after the home and her in-laws. As expected more Muslims than Christians felt that this was acceptable. Almost seventy percent of Christians and forty-five percent of Muslims were totally against this custom. It is good to observe some independence of women in this area with fifty-seven percent of Muslim females born in the UK and forty-eight percent of those born outside the UK absolutely against this custom. We can see that regardless of the tradition of the countries of origin, the students appreciate the fact that there is a greater need for women to work. It might be worth adding that a desire to work does not necessarily mean that work is possible. Ramadan commented:

> In addition to cultural norms discouraging women from working, the unequal participation of both genders in the structure of employment may also be affected by factors such as sex discrimination or lack of appropriate facilities for mothers with children (2004:55).

When it came to social participation we asked the students about their levels of involvement with their own ethnic group and others regarding – friendships, belonging to a drama group, sports club, library and if they were willing to vote. We asked also if they or their parents had experienced any form of discrimination.

On the subject of friends there was very little difference between Christians and Muslims. It appears that Christians have slightly more friends in other ethnic groups while Muslims have slightly more friends in their own ethnic groups. Two thirds of the Christians and almost the same number of Muslims would accept another ethnic group living next door to them.

Just over twenty percent more Christians than Muslims either belonged already or would choose to belong to either a sports, dance or drama group. While more than twenty percent of Muslims would not consider joining one of those groups, there was a significant difference in the proportion of Muslim males to females, with almost twenty percent more males (56%) likely to belong to such groups than females (35.7%). Again we see that Christians are ten percent more likely to belong to a library than Muslims. There is little difference between the percentage of Muslims and Christians who would give to charity. It is interesting to note there is also little difference between Muslims and Christians in their desire to participate in voting.

Because integration is a two-way process and equally depends on the attitude of the receiving society or country it is important to be aware that approximately half of the Muslims and Christians chose the answer 'definitely not' regarding their experience of discrimination based on ethnicity. We have to remember that these students are living in a very multicultural setting so it is rather sad to realise that almost half of them have experienced some kind of discrimination. Regarding their parents the situation is even worse.

Thus to answer the question: Do the young Muslims swing between two cultures – Country of Origin and British regarding social/ economic integration? we found that they were very determined to finish their college studies and to go even on to further education. The female Muslim students' attitudes towards having a job outside the home indicated a desire to be, as many Western women are, contributing to the wider society. Also many of the Muslim males appear very willing to allow their wives to go out to work. In the whole area of social/ economic integration we did not find a significant difference between Muslim and Christian students.

CHAPTER FOUR

Marriage – Gender Relationships

In this chapter we want to consider marriage and gender relationships. We try to answer the question: Do the young people swing between the culture of their parents and British society in their attitude towards marriage? We will look closely at the following aspects of marriage: male/female pre-marriage relationships, arranged marriage and forced marriage. We will consider other aspects regarding marriage in chapter five – polygamy, divorce and female circumcision.

4.1. UK Society

Until the end of the 1950s English society was fairly traditional. However, the 1960s brought a period of rapid cultural change. This can be described as the inexorable growth of individualism and the decline in the authority of social structures. The authority of these structures had long been taken for granted and was deeply embedded in the British psyche, but with popular acceptance of individualism this was, and is still, questioned more and more.

The institution of marriage is of central concern as changes in attitudes towards marriage reflect these cultural changes:

> Since the 1960s there has been a steep decline in marriage and fertility rates, an increase in the mean age at marriage, and a substantial increase in divorce rates. In the United Kingdom alone, the number of first marriages in a year fell by nearly two fifths between 1961 and 1993 (Office of National Statistics 1996).

More than a third of all marriages in 1993 were remarriages. However in 2008 this changed. There were 147,130 marriage ceremonies where both partners were being married for the first time, an increase from 146,220 in 2007. Remarriages fell from 89,150 in 2007 to 85,860 during 2008. It is important to note that whereas in the 1970s and 1980s it was common for divorced couples to go on to remarry and this trend continued into the 1990s, couples tend to marry later now and with the expense of weddings plus the social acceptability of cohabiting, second marriages have fallen from favour (Wallop 2010).

However, although divorces in the UK peaked at 153,176 in 2003, since then the number of divorces in the UK has steadily dropped. In 2008 there were 121,779 (Rogers 2010).

This statistical portrait of changes in rates of marriage and divorce suggests that the nature of marriage itself has also changed greatly. The concept which emerges from the range of writings on this subject is that of a move from marriage as an institution to marriage as a relationship. In 2010 Dave Percival, Coordinator of National Marriage Week, stated:

> Living together and marriage are increasingly seen as the same by the public, yet the outcomes are radically different. Two thirds of all the first marriages in 2008 can be expected to last a lifetime. Less than 10 per cent of cohabiting relationships last even to their tenth anniversary (cited in Cassidy 2010).

What does marriage mean for modern men and women who have alternatives to wedlock, and for whom institutional motives for matrimony are less pressing?

Far fewer people look to religion to provide meaning for the married state, but meaning is derived in other ways. Giddens (1991) identifies the problem of identity for the individual in modern times, and the importance of personal relationships in creating a stable sense of self. For Giddens, modern marriage differs quite dramatically from 'typical marriage institutions in pre-modern Europe'. He describes the 'pure relationship': a relationship not anchored in external conditions of social-economic life but focused on intimacy, and kept going for as long as it delivers the emotional satisfaction to be derived from close contact with another. While this emphasis on pure relationship is perhaps over-stated, it is true that, for modern marriage, commitment and the quality of the marriage outweigh the importance of institutional anchors (Reynolds, Mansfield 1999:10-13).

In the UK 'engagement' has ceased to be a legal contract. Legally no one can be forced to marry against their wishes, but both parties have to be over 16 years old (with parents' consent if under 18 years). Those who are legally married cannot marry again, as bigamy and polygamy are illegal (Vertovec 2002:31). However since 2008 there has been an exception in England and Wales. If such a marriage has already taken place legally in another country, it is possible for a man to claim welfare benefits for more than one wife (Slack 2008).The question of whether it is accepted in the UK officially is a different matter, complicated by Private International Law.

In the UK a marriage recognised by UK law can be a civil ceremony that usually takes place in a Registry Office, or in a place registered for civil marriages, or in a church. In the case of a church ceremony the marriage is both a civil and religious ceremony, if the church is a 'registered building.'

The above are some examples of specific cultural difficulties related to marriage and personal relationships posed by migration. Much UK discourse about migration has been questioned as it tends to be based on the concept of a single migrant arriving in the UK with a fixed culture that has to be integrated with a fixed British culture. The reality is much more multifaceted and fluid. Many migrants are only in the UK for a certain period. There are many instances where migrants are in the UK intermittently. However, for those who settle, it is of course to be expected that they will maintain very real contact with the country of origin and with the values and culture of their origin. This presents some real tensions for the UK.

More remains to be done in understanding the cultural relationship between host cultures and cultures of origin. One specific difficulty that has come to light in later years is forced marriage among some immigrant communities. Forced marriage is totally unacceptable in the UK. The incidence of forced marriages has recently received more attention. The Forced Marriage Unit has been established to address the issue and provides practical support for those subjected to forced marriage. We address this subject later in this chapter.

On the topic of marriage we looked only at areas where we felt that there could be a discrepancy between UK society's proclaimed perspective to be Christian but taking an increasingly secular view-point, and Islamic viewpoints.

In Islam, there are two basic areas of family law, which are opposed to the UK's current perception of gender equality: divorce and polygamy. We will look at these two areas in the next chapter and also at female circumcision as many immigrant societies consider female circumcision to be a prerequisite for marriage.

4.2. Pre-marital Gender Relationships

4.2.1. Immigrants' Culture and Traditions

The majority of religions do not allow their members to have sexual pre-marital relationships. But in some religions including Islam any type of relationship between a man and woman, who are unmarried and not closely related is *haram* (prohibited) and can be punished. In classical Islam girls and boys are separated from puberty for purposes such as education and sports activities. Teenagers are expected to go out in same sex groups or with older family members. It is not acceptable, for a young woman and man to go out together on a date. If on the rare occasion, their families have declared a relationship acceptable the young couple are expected to marry each other in the not too distant future. Naturally young people mix in higher education where there is no segregation of sexes but not outside of the educational space. While a young Muslim is studying or working he/she needs to be aware of acting modestly and chastely. Muslim men and women have a duty under Shariah law to wear modest, loose-fitting clothing that does not attract the other sex. Both are instructed to lower their gaze in the company of the other sex (Ghiza 2005).

Marriage under Islamic law is normally preceded by an engagement, which, in turn, is preceded by gathering information about each other's families. After a candidate is selected, the representatives (guardians) of both parties agree on the terms and conditions of the marriage contract. (Sometimes the couple make these arrangements themselves). According to Zyzik's description this could be done in the following way: The son's father approaches the daughter's father and declares his good will, proposing his son to the man's daughter, a woman of untarnished and unspoiled background, on behalf of his son. The names of the bride-to-be and of the groom-to-be are mentioned.

Then the wali (woman's guardian in marriage) responds: 'Your wish will be granted if you accept my terms and conditions'. The sentence is repeated three times before the groom's guardian asks to be shown the terms and conditions. The woman's *wali* presents his requirements, mainly concerning the payment of *mahr* (*dower*) which corresponds to the value of the basic *mahr* (marriage gift paid by the groom to the bride as a demonstration of his commitment to her). After the requirements are heard, the groom's representative responds: 'I accept'. The statement is followed by a joint recitation of the first Surah of the Koran: *Al-Fatifa* (The Opening), which constitutes an informal agreement between the couple and their commitment to one another as husband and wife. Often on the same day or shortly afterwards, an official marriage contract is signed (Zyzik 2003:60).

Zyzik writing about her experiences in Kuwait emphasizes that in order to understand the customs of the Muslim engagement ceremony in that community, one must take into account two factors that determine Muslim society: a) segregation of the sexes; b) marriage as the union of two families rather than two individuals (Zyzik 2003:47). The engagement is publicly announced. Often the ceremony is the sole opportunity for the future husband and wife to meet, and it is required to be carried out in the presence of witnesses. Once the proposal is accepted, other candidates can no longer approach the woman's family, unless the first candidate is rejected or he marries the chosen girl, but then divorces her (Witkowski 2009:85-86).

In accordance with Islamic principles, neither men nor women are allowed to look at a person of the opposite sex, unless, with regard to the degree of consanguinity, they are relatives (*mahram*) and therefore cannot marry one another. In a few Muslim countries like Kuwait it is permissable for an engaged couple to meet and get to know each other beforehand, as physical attraction may affect their feelings and marital stability. The meeting is permitted even before the official engagement ceremony, on condition that they truly intend to start a family (Zyzik 2003:62).

Depending on the Islamic law school, lawyers' opinions vary regarding the compensation to be granted should the engagement be broken off. In particular, different opinions apply regarding the return of gifts. Claims may also be made to cover the engagement costs (Witkowski 2009:86).

The institution of engagement needs to be viewed in the context of the local culture, which in terms of the extended family structure, renders it difficult for the European to imagine the degree to which the family is more interested in an individual's life, than would be the case in our society. This fact also explains the concept of arranged marriages described further on in this chapter.

4.2.2. Newham College Students' Views

The students in Newham College were asked their views on pre-marital gender relationships. In Figure 4.1 we see the comparison between male and female Muslims born in the UK and those born abroad in relation to the idea of cohabiting. Very few Muslims supported the idea of cohabitation. Of Muslims born in the UK 28.6% of males agreed but only half that number of females 14.4% agreed. Muslims born outside the UK felt more strongly that it was not acceptable: 51.6% of males said 'definitely not' and a significantly higher percentage of females (76.6%) agreed with them.

Figure 4.1 Comparison between male and female Muslims born in UK and born abroad in relation to the idea of co-habiting (%)

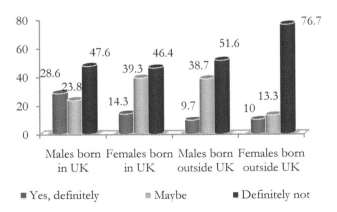

■ Yes, definitely   ▓ Maybe   ■ Definitely not

The difference between Christian and Muslim students is more obvious, with 43.9% Christian students saying 'Yes, definitely' compared with 13.2% Muslim students in response to the question: Do you think it is okay for a man and woman to live together without marrying? However exactly the same percentage of Christians and Muslims chose the answer 'May be'. We see again a significant difference in the answer 'definitely not': 26.3% Christians and 57% Muslims (Table 4.1).

Table 4.1 Attitude of students towards co-habiting

Religion		Yes. Definitely	May be	Definitely not	Total
Christian	N	25	17	15	57
	%	43.9	29.8	26.3	100
Muslim	N	16	36	69	121
	%	13.2	29.8	57.0	100
Total	N	41	53	84	178
	%	23.0	29.8	47.2	100

(Chi2=23.532;df=2;p<0.001;Vc=0.364)

The following question was put to the students: Do you think a young woman should marry the first young man she goes out with? Table 4.2 is referring to a tradition or custom in many countries, connected partially to the arranged marriage but mostly to the strong principle that a woman should be a virgin at the time of her marriage. Rather than put temptation in front of the young people they are not permitted to go out with someone of the opposite sex unless accompanied by others. If they do go out unaccompanied they are expected to marry that person even if they haven't had a sexual relationship. Fewer than 9% of Christians and 15% of Muslims thought a young woman should marry the first man she went out with. The answer 'May be' was chosen by 26.8% of Christians and 44.2% of Muslims. 'Definitely not' was chosen by 64.3% of Christians and 40.8% of Muslims.

Table 4.2 Students' attitude towards woman marrying first boyfriend

Religion		Yes, definitely	May be	Definitely not	Total
Christian	N	5	15	36	56
	%	8.9	26.8	64.3	100
Muslim	N	18	53	49	120
	%	15.0	44.2	40.8	100
Total	N	23	68	85	176
	%	13.1	38.6	48.3	100

(Chi2=38.441;df=2;p=0.015;Vc=0.219)

4.3. Arranged Marriage

4.3.1. Immigrants' Culture and Traditions

According to Zyzik (2003), the concept of an arranged marriage is based on the assumption that close family members may help a person to make the right choice, hence avoiding disappointments and failures in the future. A special role in this process is played by the groom's mother who, according to the author, has a very high position within the family hierarchy, based on Muhammad's words: 'may Allah's peace and blessings be upon him: Your Heaven lies under the feet of your mother.' From the man's perspective, due to a segregation of the sexes in Muslim countries, he does not have too many free opportunities in finding a candidate to be his wife. Therefore, the closest women within his family (mother or sisters) are able to help in this process. It is quite logical, for the reason that only women have the opportunity to contact and observe the potential fiancée (Zyzik 2003:54).

Zyzik cites the opinion of Soraya Altorki that even though Muslim girls talk openly with their parents about choosing a candidate to be their husband, they rarely mention the word 'love', because 'love' suggests secret premarital relationships, which would certainly have a negative impact on the honour of the girl and her relatives (Altorki 1986:137). Moreover, she cites further example of that sort of explanation in Muslim society, for according to Abdur-Rahman Abdul-Kha-liqa true and deep love may only develop in a legal relationship (Abdul-Khalid 1997:33-35). It is important to mention that Marlena Zyzik is married and to remember that she lives in Kuwait and therefore her experiences are based on a more open society than exists in some other countries.

Ayaan Hirsi Ali describes how marriage formalities seem in practice, at least in Kenya:

A *qadi* is a recognised marriage official and weeks after the *nikah*, my father took the marriage certificate drawn up by the *qadi* and officially registered my wedding with the Kenyan marriage bureau. I knew this because one day in June he brought me home an official Kenyan Government document written in English and Arabic, with a special box to indicate 'whether Virgin or Not' and the 'amount of Dowry' [*dower*]. The boxes were all filled in for me – the answers were 'Virgin' and 'ten books of the Quran' – and the documents also indicated that I had been represented at my wedding in February by my father. My father told me I must sign the Kenyan document.

    I hesitated, but I was already married to Osman Moussa in the eyes of Islam and every Muslim I knew. What difference could it possibly make if I signed, I thought? So right under my father's signature in Arabic, I signed it A. H. Magan (2007:177-178).

Arranged marriages are not only part of Islam, but also culturally ingrained. They are encountered among Catholics who have arrived from Asia or Africa or some parts of South East Europe, at least in the first generation. It is possible to give examples of happy relationships which have lasted for several decades. Nevertheless, it is not uncommon to have difficulty in drawing a line between arranged marriages, accepted by European governments, and forced marriages. The question is: When do we deal with the first scenario, and when with the second? Do parents' preferences, especially in a culture which assumes absolute obedience of a child to the father, not amount to coercion?

    Nowadays the situation of women has changed and, in many cases, a woman is no longer dependant on her husband. Many women graduate from higher education and work professionally. Therefore, the attitude towards women is changing. Countries such as Tunisia and Somalia have recognised these changes and have adapted their law to the new situation. In other countries, such as Egypt, the pressure to revise and recognize the new role of woman in marriage is on the increase.

    The South Asian communities in the UK practise a wide range of arranged marriages. It is still common for parents to choose a marriage partner for their daughter or son from the Indian subcontinent. Pakistani Muslim families in the UK often still marry first cousins, although in recent years that has caused considerable concern in the

NHS due to the high predominance of birth defects among their offspring (Reid 2008:181-184). These marriages are accepted unless there is evidence of significant coercion (evidence of kidnapping or deceit. For example the young person understands he/she is going on holiday and is unaware of the marriage intention), in which case it is recognised as a forced marriage (Vertovec 2002:31). Parekh said:

> The practice of arranged marriages (...) covers a wide spectrum ranging from the almost automatic parental endorsement of spouses freely chosen by their offspring to parental imposition of them (...). Most cultures who support arranged marriages are able to give a reasonable defence of it. They argue that marriages are likely to be happier and last longer if parents consent to them and feel morally and emotionally committed to their success (2006:274).

4.3.2. Newham College Students' Views

Maya is seventeen and her parents are Indian. They had an arranged marriage and Maya and her siblings are also expecting their marriages to be arranged. In her interview Maya told the authors what she understands by arranged marriage: *In our town the definition of 'arranged' means my dad will look for a girl or maybe my brother himself will look for a girl and will tell my dad about it. My dad will look into it, like their family background, how the person is herself. Then they will probably arrange a meeting from there and if they are still not sure arrange another meeting and if they want to go for it say 'yes.' If they want to say 'no' they look for someone else but nothing like forced. Nothing like that comes into it. It mainly comes down to the person who is going to get married.*

Using a questionnaire we asked the students: Do you think arranged marriages should be allowed in the UK? Regarding this whole area of arranged marriages the students' answers show significant differences. Even though arranged marriages are practised in both Muslim and Christian communities: 'Yes, definitely' was chosen by 10.5% of Christians and 37.1% of Muslims when giving their views on arranged marriage (Table 4.3). Although the answer 'May be' does not show a big difference, respectively 40.4% and 44% of most young people are quite definite in their views, so this score is a possible indication that the young people are not so certain what they agree with, regarding arranged marriages. There is a noteworthy difference in choosing the answer 'definitely not' with a significantly large number of Christians 49.1%, but only 19% of Muslims agreeing.

Table 4.3 Students opinions with reference to the allowance of arranged marriages in UK

Religion		Yes, definitely	May be	Definitely not	Total
Christian	N	6	23	28	57
	%	10.5	40.4	49.1	100
Muslim	N	43	51	22	116
	%	37.1	44.0	19.0	100
Total	N	49	74	50	173
	%	28.3	42.8	28.9	100

(Chi2=21.650;df=2;p<0.001;Vc=0.354)

Looking purely at the Muslim responses we can see that only 35% of Muslim males born in the UK think that arranged marriage should be allowed, whereas 42.9% of Muslims males born outside the UK think in this way. With Muslim females it was the other way round. More young Muslim women born in the UK think arranged marriage is desirable than those born outside the UK (31%). We wonder if the freedom to choose looks more attractive at a distance.

Figure 4.2 Comparison between male and female Muslims born in UK and born abroad, in relation to arranged marriage (%)

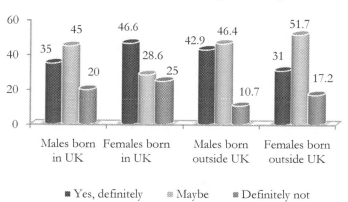

With the exception of Muslim females born in the UK, with only 28.6% being unsure of the benefits of arranged marriage, the other groups are uncertain how they feel; Muslim males born in the UK 45%, Muslim

males born outside UK 46.4% and Muslim females born outside the UK 51.7% (Figure 4.2). In spite of the fact a fairly low percentage thought arranged marriage should be allowed in the UK, in our one hundred short interviews almost 100% of the young people who were asked the question whether their marriage would be arranged stated emphatically that it would be. We got the impression that they were surprised at the question because for the majority of them arranged marriage was totally normal.

One nineteen year old born in London and describing herself as British Pakistani when asked if she would have an arranged marriage replied: *I'm not thinking of marriage yet but will choose my own husband. I don't believe my parents have a choice in the matter as they are divorced and I don't live with either of them.* She went on to say that she would not care about his background *as long as he takes care of me.* If she takes a Muslim husband she will allow him to take another wife if the circumstances are appropriate, *if it is for the same reasons as the Prophet.*

The following question: If you accept arranged marriages do you think the UK Government should stop the bride/bridegroom being brought to the UK from abroad? Table 4.4 refers to the relatively common practice of finding spouses for immigrants' children in the country of origin and bringing them to the UK.

There are at least two main reasons for that practice. The first one is to find a husband or wife from relatives. Sometimes it is connected with under age marriage or even forced marriage, with some young people promised in marriage while still infants. Another reason is to have a spouse from the same culture. That scenario of bringing a spouse from abroad usually has a negative influence on the process of integration of the whole family. The cycle of integration begins anew.

Only a few of the students thought it was unacceptable to bring a spouse from abroad. Almost 22% of Christians (21.7%) and 14.0% of Muslims said 'Yes, definitely' unacceptable. However 52.2% of Christians and 43.9% of Muslims showed that they were uncertain of whether or not the Government should interfere. The remaining 26.1%

of Christians and 42.1% of Muslims said 'Definitely not,' indicating that they thought it was acceptable to bring a spouse from abroad.

Table 4.4 Students' opinions on the government stopping brides/ bridegrooms being imported from abroad

Religion		Yes, definitely	May be	Definitely not	Total
Christian	N	10	24	12	46
	%	21.7	52.2	26.1	100
Muslim	N	16	50	48	114
	%	14.0	43.9	42.1	100
Total	N	26	74	60	160
	%	16.3	46.3	37.5	100

(Chi2=3.930;df=2;p=0.140;Vc=0.157)

In answering the question: Do you know anyone who went abroad as a single person and came back with a husband/wife, born in another country? - 51.1% of Christians and 43.8% of Muslims chose the answer 'Yes'. 35.6% of Christians and 40.2% of Muslims chose the answer 'No'. 13.3% of Christians and 16.1% of Muslims chose the answer 'Not sure'. We did not ask if the people they knew were from their own ethnic or religious group.

Table 4.5 Knowledge of husband/wife being chosen from overseas

Religion		Yes	No	Not sure	Total
Christian	N	23	16	6	45
	%	51.1	35.6	13.3	100
Muslim	N	49	45	18	112
	%	43.8	40.2	16.1	100
Total	N	72	61	24	157
	%	45.9	38.9	15.3	100

(Chi2=0.713;df=2;p=0.700;Vc=0.067)

4.4. Forced Marriages

4.4.1. Immigrants' Culture and Traditions

Firstly it is important to be clear that a forced marriage is not the same as an arranged marriage. In arranged marriages, although the parents or families of both spouses have considerable say in actually arranging the marriage, the choice to accept remains with each spouse. In a forced marriage one or both people are forced into a marriage that the families want but at least one of the young people does not consent to. Forced marriages, according to the 2009 Council of Europe Report, even if they are not treated as 'deplorable' actions against women, fall under the category of visible or invisible forms of violence, psychological pressure, moral blackmail or physical violence from their parents, which prevent future spouses from choosing their life partners (Council of Europe 2009:9). Coercion is often involved which might also be financial or sexual and is nearly always emotional.

Often the person is a minor (under eighteen years old). However there is no 'typical' victim of forced marriage. It can happen to both men and women, although most cases involve young women and girls aged between 13 and 30. Some may have a disability, some may have young children and some may be spouses from overseas. The people responsible for forcing the individual are usually the parents or family members. In some cases people may be taken abroad without knowing that they are to be married. When they arrive in the country their passports may be taken by their family to try and stop them from returning home. Often the family makes the young person feel that they are bringing shame on their family by their lifestyle or choices and are told that the only way they can bring honour to their family is by marrying their parents' choice of husband or bride.

How do parents justify forcing their children to marry? Firstly they rarely consider that they are doing anything wrong. Parents often believe that they are protecting their children, fostering stronger family links by forcing young people to marry relations (often those marriages have been arranged when the spouses were only young children, little more than babies and the young people do not realise that they have a right to choose their spouse). The parents are often attempting to preserve perceived cultural or religious traditions and perceived honour.

Hannah Shah in her book *The Imam's Daughter* describes how important 'honour' was to her Pakistani community when she grew up in the north of England, where all her neighbours were Pakistani:

> The culture in our street was very much centred around how you could gain honour, how you could maintain honour and how you could avoid bringing shame on yourself or your family. The women were obsessed with honour and shame. It was by listening to their

gossip that we learned what was appropriate and what was not, and how an individual's family's honour and shame were computed (2009:23).

In the UK, the Home Office and Foreign Office jointly administer an organisation called the Forced Marriage Unit (FMU). It is important to remember that forced marriage is a violation of children's rights under the UN Convention on the Rights of the Child (UNCRC) as well as a form of violence against women and an abuse of human rights (Stobart 2009:11). The FMU received 1,600 reports in 2008 and intervened in 420 actual cases. By early July 2009 the FMU had received 770 calls, up 16% on 2008 (Casciani 2009).

Most forced marriages are assumed to involve women, which is not quite true, because men, too, are involved. However 85% of reported cases involve women. It is estimated that the total number of forced marriages in the UK could have been 10,000 in 2009. The majority of cases consisted of teenage girls, the daughters of immigrants from Pakistan, Bangladesh and India. The report gives several reasons for which women are being married off abroad: namely, to associate them with the roots of their community, to keep promises to their clan or to obtain visas for a family member or a friend to stay in the UK (Jones 2009).

According to the Forced Marriage Unit the following key motives for forced marriage have also been identified: attempts to protect family honour; control the behaviour and sexuality of women; control unwanted behaviour or behaviour in a perceived 'westernised manner' and prevent relationships with members of other ethnic, cultural or religious groups. In 2009 Stobart wrote:

> The majority of cases of forced marriage reported to date in the UK involve South Asian families. This is partly a reflection of the fact that there is a large, established South Asian population in the UK. However, it is clear that forced marriage is not solely a South Asian problem and there have been cases involving families from East Asia, the Middle East, Europe and Africa. Some forced marriages take place in the UK with no overseas element, while others involve a partner coming from overseas or a British national being sent abroad (2009:10).

There is a certain link between forced marriages and so-called 'honour killings', in cases when the girl objects and her parents treat this opposition as violation of the family honour. According to the report of the European Monitoring Centre on Racism and Xenophobia, the problem of forced marriages varies depending on the country of origin.

It is important to note that there is a very high rate of suicide within the British Asian community. Women aged 16 to 24 from Pakistani, Indian and Bangladeshi backgrounds are three times more likely to kill themselves than the national average for women of their age (The Independent 2008). The Centre for Social Cohesion published a report in 2008, cited in The Independent newspaper, which uncovered the fact that many Asian women felt unable to defy their families and therefore:

> suffer violence, abuse, depression, anxiety and other psychological problems that can lead to self-harm, schizophrenia and suicide (The Independent 2008).

The majority find themselves in an impossible position. Their family situation is abusive and they are trapped in a forced marriage but to escape means that they have to cut off all ties with their family. For an Asian woman brought up to believe that the family is everything this is an intolerable choice to have to make. Consequently many who seek help retract their statements and return to their family, going through with a forced marriage rather than live alone or in hiding, disowned by their family.

Speaking of her own experience of being estranged from her family, Sanghera, described how close she had been to her sisters Robina, Lucy and Ginda. She wrote:

> Our oldest sister, Ginda would line us up, three in a row and wash our hair. We were as close as sardines in a tin in those days and now look at us: all three dead to one another. And Ginda – who all but brought me up – as distant as a stranger to me and my children. I made a choice and that's the price I paid (Sanghera 2009:226).

A former policeman recounted how he had seen 395 cases of forced marriage in the city of Bradford last year:

> 'I had a case of a 14-year-old girl at school,' he recalled. 'The teacher tells me that the girl claims to have been married. So I went along to

the school with a Muslim colleague. We saw the girl. We asked her a few questions and we were not sure.' Then the girl said: 'If you don't believe me I have the video at home' (The Independent 2008).

In 2007 a total of 250 girls aged between 13 and 16 were taken off the Bradford school rolls because they failed to return from trips abroad. Possibly many were victims of forced marriages (The Independent 2008).

McVeigh (2009) wrote in the Observer that police estimate that at least 12 young women are killed in the UK, in the name of honour each year but other young women are dying – forced suicides and murders made to look like suicide are widely believed to take place undetected. It seems guaranteed that there are many more suffering from honour-based abuse who are hidden away in concealed communities.

Many do not realise that all the main faith groups strongly condemn forced marriages and often the traditions they think they are preserving may have changed. One needs to be aware, at least in theory, that this type of marriage is not related to Islam as a religion, because the Koran according to Muslims stresses the necessity of free will while taking a vow. Therefore, forced marriage is based on cultural traditions.

It is worth noting that such practices were condemned in 1981 by the Universal Islamic Declaration of Human Rights. Article XIX (i) reads:

> The Right to Found a Family and Related Matters, states that no person may be married against his or her will, or lose or suffer diminution of legal personality on account of marriage.

The Council of Europe condemned forced marriages under Resolution 1468 (2005): *Forced marriages and child marriages*, which proposed the use of specific measures to be taken by Council of Europe members, in order to eliminate these practices in Europe.

Jones believes that, given the reported cases of forced marriages which may, in the event of disagreement with the family, be linked with honour killings, the British Government should put British law above the interests of some groups. The Report has new recommendations and helpful resources for police, teachers and doctors, to recognize the warning signs of forced marriages. This material was released before the summer holiday in 2009, which is a period when hundreds of children are sent abroad in order to marry, although some of them return to Britain (Jones 2009).

One girl, whose parents from Birmingham wanted to marry her off in that way (Shazia Qayum), explains the false concept functioning in some Asian societies:

> To refuse marriage to a candidate chosen by parents is probably the worst thing one could do in one's life. You risk losing the relationship with your family, forever (Jones 2009)!

In her case, her parents chose a cousin to be her husband for the first time when she was seventeen years old. Her refusal, however, caused her parents to take her out of school. The next attempt was two years later when her parents forcefully deceived her into visiting the family in Pakistan. When she arrived at the parents' village, it became obvious that she was going to get married. Everything was already prepared and for the first time she also saw the man to whom she was about to be married (Jones 2009).

In 2009 Hannah Shah wrote in her book *The Imam's Daughter* about her friend Skip:

> Skip's greatest worry was that her father was going to force her into an arranged marriage. (…) This wasn't about religion – it was all about culture and tradition. And of course it was about 'honour' (2009:97).

Skip's fear was well founded. When Skip, aged seventeen, went on holiday with her parents to Pakistan her fear became reality. She was taken to visit some distant relatives and presented to her husband to be - a Pakistani man she had never met before. She was locked into a dark room with no food or water until she agreed to go through with the marriage. After the marriage she managed to phone Hannah in England and seek help and she eventually escaped. Hannah Shah wrote:

> I wasn't exactly surprised. How many other girls did we know who this had happened to? Dozens, for sure. And in the back of my mind I feared that the same fate might be awaiting me.
>
> Skip's wasn't an isolated case. What made it so unusual was that she managed to escape. All too often the trap of a forced marriage became a prison for life (2009:97-99).

In the UK there are several 'hotlines', which young people call, looking for help to avoid getting married against their will. The Forced Marriage Unit co-operates with the Ministry of Foreign Affairs. Among others, there was a case, in which they rescued a woman who called for help from a toilet at Heathrow Airport in London. In cases of forced marriage, the police of the immigrant country of origin might help. However, it is not always possible, for instance in rural areas of Pakistan or Bangladesh (Jones 2009).

Currently, courts have an instrument to combat forced marriages in the country or abroad: *The Forced Marriage Act 2007* (which came into force in November 2008). Under this law, one can lose parental responsibility for a minor. However, in practice it is quite complicated.

Nevertheless, in 2009 the law was used to release Humayra Abedin, a medical student, who had been deceitfully brought to Dhaka, the capital of Bangladesh, and then abducted in order to force her to marry against her will (Jones 2009).

In June 2009, in the UK a guideline for various institutions was prepared by the FMU, created for identification and registration of cases of forced marriages. The guidance discusses and explains the existence of this phenomenon, and then gives practical advice on how to help the victims of such marriages. Moreover, it gives helpful guidelines for health care organisations, schools, the police, social services dealing with children and adults, and finally, for local authorities and home administrators.

In 2007 Jasvinder Sanghera brought the question of forced marriage into the public domain and was instrumental in helping the Forced Marriage Bill to go through Parliament. She co-founded Karma Nirvana, a community-based project in Derby that supports South Asian women, after her sister Robina killed herself to escape the misery of her forced marriage. Sanghera has published two books. The first entitled *Shame* recounts the true story of how she escaped from a forced marriage and the second book *Daughters of Shame* tells the story of many of the survivors of forced marriage who with the help of Karma Nirvana have rebuilt their lives. The project Karma Nirvana received 4,000 calls to its helpline during its first year and is now taking 300 calls a month from people under threat of honour-based violence, often linked to forced marriage. Sanghera believes that about 3% of women manage to escape forced marriage in the UK and when they leave they have to live with fear and rejection not only by their families but also by their communities and sometimes their friends (Bawden 2009).

Sanghera went on to explain why she thought that such a large proportion of the Asian community never seem to assimilate into British culture. She thought that it was connected with arranged marriages or forced marriages, with people from abroad. A man comes from abroad, marries, has a baby. However, as soon as he has secured a right to stay in the UK the couple split up. He goes for a divorce and he brings over another bride from India, Pakistan or Bangladesh. This means that the community continues to go backwards rather than move forwards (2009:109-110).

4.4.2. Newham College Students' Views

The authors didn't ask the students the direct question whether they were afraid of being forced to marry. They were asked only if they expected an arranged marriage. Although, as we saw, almost all of them expected to have an arranged marriage, when asked if there was an element of choice no one appeared to expect to be forced. However the authors, aware of the sensitivities of this subject, knew it was highly unlikely that they would admit that they were afraid they could be forced.

The young people, however, were asked if they knew anyone who had been forced to marry. Their answers show quite a high level of awareness. The answer 'Yes' was chosen by 25.5% of Christians and 30.9% of Muslims. The answer 'No' was given by 70.2% of Christians and 55.5% of Muslims while 4.3% of Christians and 13.6% of Muslims chose the answer 'Not sure' (Table 4.6).

Table 4.6 Students' awareness of others in forced marriages

Religion		Yes	No	Not sure	Total
Christian	N	12	33	2	47
	%	25.5	70.2	4.3	100
Muslim	N	34	61	15	110
	%	30.9	55.5	13.6	100
Total	N	46	94	17	157
	%	29.3	59.9	10.8	100

(Chi2=4.199;df=2;p=0.123;Vc=0.164)

In response to the question: Do you know where you could go for help if your friend was being forced to marry someone against her/his will? (Table 4.7) the following are quite worrying statistics - only 26.7% of Christians and 25.2% of Muslims chose the answer 'Yes'. While 53.3% of Christians and 44.1% of Muslims chose the answer 'No'. The answer 'Not sure' was chosen by 20.0% of Christians and 30.6% of Muslims.

Table 4.7 Students' awareness of help available to those in danger of forced marriage

Religion		Yes	No	Not sure	Total
Christian	N	12	24	9	45
	%	26.7	53.3	20.0	100
Muslim	N	28	49	34	111
	%	25.2	44.1	30.6	100
Total	N	40	73	43	156
	%	25.6	46.8	27.6	100

(Chi2=1.916;df=2;p=0.384;Vc=0.111)

4.5. Conclusion

The task of this chapter was to discover if there is a difference between British society and Muslim students' attitudes towards pre-marital gender relationships, arranged marriage and forced marriage.

    The students in Newham College were asked first their views on pre-marital gender relationships. As is commonly known, the incidence of cohabitation in Western Europe is very high. According to UK National Statistics the percentage of men aged 30-34 who were cohabiting in 2007 was approximately 40% and women almost 43%. Very few Muslims supported the idea of cohabitation. Muslims born outside the UK felt more strongly than Muslims born in the UK, with over half of Muslim males and over three quarters of Muslim females agreeing that cohabitation was not acceptable. The difference between Christian and Muslim students is more obvious with less than fourteen percent of Muslim students thinking it acceptable for a man and woman to live together without marrying compared to almost forty-four percent of

Christians. Similarly the answer to the next question showed that only fifteen percent of Muslims thought a young woman should marry the first man she went out with. Almost sixty-five percent of Christians thought it was not necessary while just over forty percent of Muslims agreed with them.

The students were asked if they thought that arranged marriages should be allowed in the UK. Our one hundred short interviews showed that almost all Muslim students were expecting an arranged marriage. However, nineteen percent of Muslims when answering the questionnaire said that arranged marriages should not be allowed in the UK. The Christians felt far more strongly, with more than forty-nine percent against arranged marriages. Many immigrant parents choose their child's spouse from their home country. Nearly sixteen percent more Muslims (42.1%) than Christians (26.1%) supported the UK Government allowing spouses to be brought from abroad. More than fifty percent of the Christians questioned whether the practice should be allowed and almost forty-four percent of Muslims were undecided. Over half of the Christians and almost forty-four percent of the Muslims were aware of spouses being brought from abroad. However, we need to remember that the students were not asked if their knowledge was limited to their own religious or ethnic group.

There was quite a reasonable level of awareness of the prevalence of forced marriages, with almost a quarter of the Christians having knowledge of someone who had been forced to marry and roughly a third of Muslims being aware. When it came to information about where to seek help the Muslim (44.1%) students seemed more au fait than the Christian (53.3%) students, but this still indicates that the students need to be better informed in this area. Hopefully the UK Government: *Forced Marriage (Civil Protection) Act 2007* which came into force in November 2008 plus the new British guidelines: *Multi-agency practice guidelines: Handling cases of Forced Marriage* which were published in July 2009 will give a higher profile to the problem and clearer guidance to any young person finding themselves in that situation.

CHAPTER FIVE

Marriage – Gender Equality

In this chapter we attempt to answer the question: Is the young Muslims' attitude towards gender equality in marriage, including polygamy, divorce and female circumcision so very different from British society's viewpoint (as seen in the last chapter).

5.1. Polygamy

5.1.1. Immigrants' Culture and Traditions

There are two main forms of polygamy – polygyny (one man having multiple wives) and polyandry (one woman having several husbands). When we refer to polygamy in this book we are referring only to polygyny. Polygamy is thought of as an Islamic practice but in actual fact it was an accepted custom in much of the ancient world. It was practised in ancient Egypt and in ancient Persia as well as practised by Jews and can be found in the Old Testament. Some European Jews still practised polygamy in the Middle Ages.

Many Hindus in India practised polygamy legally until 1955 when it was abolished by the Hindu Marriage Act and also in China until 1951 when it was made illegal. According to Jamila Hussain (2004) polygamy is still practised in many societies today. It is recognised under civil law in many countries which are not thought of as Islamic. For example it is legal in some countries in Africa including Tanzania, where one quarter of women live in a polygamous marriage. It is also legal in Zambia. A 2003 Demographic and Health Survey found that 16% of women in Zambia are in polygamous marriages (OECD 2009). In Zambia polygamy is allowed however:

> the first wife is required to consent to polygamy at the time of marrying; in practice, men rarely consider their wives' opinions before taking a second (or subsequent) wife. The prevalence of the practice varies according to region and level of education: it is more common in rural areas, although the figures have recently risen in

urban areas, and the incidence is very low among women who have received higher education (OECD 2009).

In Zimbabwe polygamy is accepted by the traditional religions and about one in ten women live in polygamous unions (OECD 2009). Hussain explains how this Islamic law came about in her book *Islam- Its Laws and society*:

> The Quranic rules on polygamy were originally a limitation on the then current Arab practice which allowed men to marry as many women as they chose, and a provision for women who were left without male support at a time when there was no social security and every woman was expected to be dependent on a man (2004:86).

In Islamic law polygamy is a licence available only to men. A man is allowed (but it is not recommended) to have up to four wives at a time and it is a rare occurrence even in Islamic countries. If a man wants a second, third or fourth wife he must fulfil certain conditions: be able financially to support each wife; be able to treat every wife equally; have a good reason for needing another wife, for example if the first wife is too old or ill to perform her marriage duties or is unable to bear children; he must inform his first wife/wives (in this respect polygamy is not the same as bigamy. In bigamy each wife is usually unaware of the other wives).

It is important to remember that just because a country is recognised as Islamic this doesn't mean that polygamy is prevalent. For example polygamy is legal in Pakistan, but there are strict formal pre-conditions and the practice is generally considered as unacceptable. It is estimated that approximately 5% of the men have polygamous marriages. However reports state that men who choose to have more than one wife rarely obtain consent and the required letter of permission from their first wives. Polygamy is also legal in Bangladesh. However the prevalence has decreased, particularly in the cities, since the 1960s. Many of the population consider it to be an outdated tradition and now only 10% of men are in polygamous relationships (OECD 2009).

For non-Muslims and also many Muslim women the whole question of polygyny is a matter of great concern. The thought that your husband is free to take a second or even third or fourth wife doesn't sit comfortably with most women. Hence the possibility or prospect often fills the wife with alarm. For some it is a no-go area; for others they have a sense of being trapped. They consider it allowed under Shariah law and therefore almost inevitable. Historically it was quite common and even in the first part of the twentieth century it was fairly common in Arab Gulf States (Roald 2001:201-202).

In 1995 Badawi, who lived in the UK, wrote that while Islam did not outlaw polygyny, it did restrict it. He went on to remark that it was not encouraged and certainly not required. It was quite simply just permitted. He indicated that polygyny was initially suggested as a solution to the growing problem of that time - an imbalance between the number of males and females, due to a war (Roald 2001:203).

Many westerners cannot understand the ruling in Islam that allows a man to have more than one wife but a woman to have only one husband. They see it as another example of Islam being discriminatory towards women and not treating them as true equals. Badawi (Roald 2001) explains the ruling as follows:

> In the case of polygyny, the lineal identities of children are not confused. They all have the same father and each of them knows his or her mother. In the case of polyandry, however, only the mother is known for sure...in addition... polyandry raises problems relating to inheritance law (2001:203).

5.1.2. Newham College Students' Views

Sana, a 20 year old Pakistani explained her understanding of the meaning of polygamy to us: *Muslims can have more than one wife - people so often misunderstand that phrase. It's not really a cultural thing. It is more religious. If you are going to have more than one wife you have to treat her equally. All the wives must have the same facilities. If you look at it it's not really easy. It's very, very difficult. I mean if you are going to give one, I don't know ....£10,000...you have to give the other three the same, can that be done? I wouldn't want my husband to have another wife.*

Responses to the question: Do you think UK law should allow immigrants to have more than one wife? - showed a significant difference between the two religions (Table 5.1). 'Yes. Definitely' was selected by 8.9% of Christians and 16.4% of Muslims and 'May be' by 25.0% of Christians and 41.0% of Muslims with 'Definitely not' by

66.1% of Christians and 42.6% of Muslims. However the interviews revealed less of a difference. Many of the young Muslim men were not in favour of more than one wife and even those who found the idea appealing didn't think it likely, as it would be too difficult to treat the wives equally. The Muslim women however found the idea far from appealing and although accepting that it was allowed within Islamic law, were adamant that they would not readily agree to their husband taking a second wife.

Table 5.1 Comparison between Muslim and Christian attitudes towards UK law allowing polygamy

Religion		Yes, definitely	May be	Definitely not	Total
Christian	N	5	14	37	56
	%	8.9	25.0	66.1	100
Muslim	N	20	50	52	122
	%	16.4	41.0	42.6	100
Total	N	25	64	89	178
	%	14.0	36.0	50.0	100

(Chi2=8.471;df=2;p=0.014;Vc=0.218)

In Figure 5.1 it is noticeable that about a quarter of the Muslim males questioned were in favour of polygamy – 23.8 of those born in the UK and 25.8 of those born outside the UK, while considerably fewer females agreed – only 13.8% of those born in the UK and even fewer, only 6.9% of those born outside the UK. The results can be better understood if we listen to the young people's views.

The majority of the Muslim young women when asked: Would you be happy if your husband wanted a second wife? were very adamant when they answered. We list eighteen of their replies:

o *No, I wouldn't agree*, said a 21 year old Indian who came to the UK with her husband in 2006. He is 30 years old.

o *Don't agree. Not good to take another one. Not good to live with another woman*, declared an 18 year old Bangladeshi born in the UK.

o *Would not like my husband to take a second wife*, said an 18 year old born in Norway of Somali parents.

o *My husband cannot take another wife. Absolutely not*, a 17 year old Afghani told us. She had lived for 14 years in Holland before coming to the UK.

Figure 5.1   Muslim attitudes towards polygamy (%)

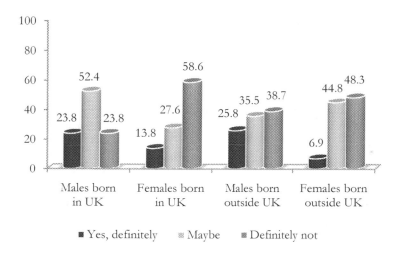

o *Certainly not. If he takes another wife I would leave him*, said a 17 year old born in Pakistan.

o *No, because a girl wants her husband for herself - would never want husband shared with another woman*, a British Asian 19 year old born in England told the authors.

o *I don't agree that my husband have more than one wife*, said an 18 year old Pakistani who came to the UK in 2004.

o *Would kill husband if he took a second wife*, declared a Congolese Muslim.

o *If my husband wants to take another wife. I will definitely leave him. How can I share my husband?* said an 18 year old Pakistani who came to the UK in 2006.

o *Want my husband all to myself*, an 18 year old Pakistani born in London told us: *I am a very greedy person. If he decides to take another wife I will not live with him any more. I wouldn't give him permission to marry again.*

o *I'd divorce him*, an 18 year old Bangladeshi told us.

Five other young women gave reasons for not wanting their husband to have another wife:

o *Wouldn't allow husband to marry another woman as it causes arguments, unless he has good reason, i.e., first wife is infertile. My father took second wife for this reason. So I have 2 mums and I treat them both with love and respect*, stated a 19 year old, born in London whose parents were Pakistani.

o *Wouldn't agree for my husband to have a second wife... (hesitation) .. Might cause problems*, said another 19 year old Pakistani.

o *He must have a good reason to take another wife but I still would not agree*, said a 19 year old born in India who came to the UK in 2006.

o *I don't like the fact husband can take a second wife. Husband must have a good reason and have permission of first wife*, said an 18 year old who had come to the UK from Afghanistan in 2005.

Some of the young women went as far as saying that the concept of having more than one wife was wrong. For example: *When you get married it is you and your husband. Why should he marry someone else? It is not right*, a 17 year old Bangladeshi stated. And others: *Up to him but what can I say? I can't stop him. No, I didn't say I'd agree but it is part of our religion*, an 18 year old born in Somalia who came to UK as a child declared.

Another young woman aged 17 born in Bangladesh spoke. While telling us that she was not thinking of marriage yet she stated, *I will not allow my husband to take other wives*, and added, *will choose my own husband from community*. Only one young woman, also born in Bangladesh appeared to agree: *Would not mind (if my husband took a second wife) as long (as we were) treated equally, no favourite.*

The majority of the young men likewise seemed to think that one wife was enough. Like the young women they were quite adamant. We list below fifteen of the answers given to the question: Would you like more than one wife?-

o *Wouldn't agree to more than one wife*, said an 18 year old Turkish Muslim.

- *One more than enough*, said an 18 year old Indian born in the UK.

- *No point in marrying a second wife*, a 23 year old Nigerian declared.

- *Have to take responsibility for more than one wife. Will choose one wife*, a 19 year old Afghani told us. He came to the UK in 2006.

- Another Afghani aged 17 said: *I will have only one wife*. He came to the UK in 2005.

- *Only one wife. One is good. One is enough*, said a 17 year old Pakistani who came to the UK in 2006.

- *Just one wife – one is enough*, a 19 year old born in Bangladesh who emigrated to UK as a child, told the authors.

- *Definitely wouldn't agree to another wife*, said a 19 year old born in Bangladesh.

- An 19 year old who arrived in England from Bangladesh when he was 11 years old stated: *Not thinking of marriage. Would prefer to choose own wife, but will be willing to enter an arranged marriage. Would only marry once or there will be bickering.*

- *It would be my choice as well as my mother's. It has to be. Most probably not an English woman because family is not really that open minded. Probably Asian. Would like 3 or 4 children. If my wife allowed me to have more [wives] I would love to but one is enough … one is enough … too much headache*, said a 19 year old Afghani who wants to wait at least 6 years before he marries.

- *Haven't thought about marriage yet. Don't mind whether my parents arrange a marriage for me or if I'm allowed to choose my own wife. Will only have one wife as I prefer monogamy*, said a 19 year old Pakistani who had come to the UK when he was 11 years old.

Of the hundred interviewed one man, a Bangladeshi born in London, mentioned that he didn't think he could legally marry more than one wife, here in the UK. *Don't think wife or country will allow me to have more than one wife. Have to treat wives equally.*

Only two young men considered that they might have more than one wife: *Maybe I will have more than one wife, depending if I need one. If your sexual drive is high you can or if I see someone you can help, say a woman has lost her husband. I don't know what is in front of me but if I feel can handle it, be equal to my other wife and to her. All depends on condition,* asserted a 17 year old who was born in England to Bangladeshi parents.

o Another Bangladeshi, who was also born in the UK said: *Like more than one wife but one would be enough.*

o Only one actually said he wanted more than one wife: *Want two wives... Have to treat them equally,* the 18 year old Somali announced. He came to the UK in 2006.

5.2. Divorce

5.2.1. Immigrants' Culture and Traditions

Under *Shariah* (Islamic law) when it comes to divorce a man has far more scope than a woman. He is free to divorce his wife when he feels like it while his wife can only initiate divorce on limited grounds and generally has to do so through the courts. A man can divorce his wife by pronouncing a set formula three times. He does not have to go through the court; his wife cannot contest the divorce and he has very limited obligations towards her while she waits three months. These three months are to ensure that she is not pregnant with his child before all ties are finally broken (Tucker 2008:86).

Hussain wrote that according to the Koran divorce is allowed and there are many different kinds of divorce in Islamic Law. However for many years divorce was the prerogative of the husband and a Muslim wife was virtually unable to obtain a divorce in Islam. If the husband wanted a divorce all he had to do:

> was to pronounce a talaq at the appropriate time and under the proper conditions. The word talaq means literally to snap off or to separate, and thus to sever the bond of the marriage relationship (Ur Rahman 1984:309). This can be done at will and without any prior formalities. Providing that he observes the conditions laid down in the Koran (Hussain 2004:101).

In recent years many Islamic States including Algeria, Iraq, Iran, Indonesia and Tunisia all chose to either ban or restrict this form of divorce. Pakistan sought in its Muslim Family Law Ordinance to eliminate it in 1961, instituting the formal requirement that arbitration was required for every divorce. However in practice men are still free to walk out of a marriage when they wish to do so because traditional *shari'a* law prevails over the modern statute.

In the 1990s a number of women's groups in India tried to address the issue of triple divorce by drawing up several model marriage contracts which were aimed at discouraging the husband from pronouncing a 'triple divorce.' One specification suggested that a husband who chooses to divorce in this way must pay his wife double the *dower*. In April 2000, the National Commission for Women (NCW) issued a report on the minority Muslim community and called for a ban on 'triple divorce.' However the ban was not backed by the Islamic jurist-theologians, the *ulama* (Tucker 2008:124-126).

India had set up an umbrella organisation: 'The All India Muslim Personal Law Board' (AIMPLB) in 1972 to represent its forty plus different Muslim groups in the country. In July 2004 AIMPLB took up the question of 'triple divorce'. There had been a growing campaign in India calling for the end of 'triple divorce.' Tucker explained that it was generally felt that 'triple divorce' -

> being a male prerogative, sowed insecurity and creating hardship for Muslim women who could find themselves divorced and cast immediately out of their homes in an extra-judicial process against which they had no recourse (Tucker 2008:128).

However, AIMPLB also did not succeed in banning 'triple divorce' and in Indian law, too, Muslim husbands can simply terminate the marriage by pronouncing the triple *talaq*. They may now have to pay maintenance to the ex-wife for a long time, but the right to divorce itself remains intact. In India it is still the law that -

> a husband may divorce his wife by repudiating the marriage without giving any reason. Pronouncement of such words which signify his intention to disown the wife is sufficient (Gupta 2009).

The big issue in India now is that Muslim women are divorcing their husbands under another law, and the men are running for cover – because they now have to pay maintenance to the ex-wife till she remarries or dies.

There is a proposed plan to allow in Egypt a 'Women's divorce' a *khul* (the Khul is a particular type of divorce. There are disagreements between its exact interpretations but a common interpretation is that it is initiated by the wife, who foregoes her mahr, with the husband pronouncing talaq) to enable a woman to escape an abusive or dysfunctional marriage with more success. However it is a lengthy process which has to go through the courts and can result in the woman facing social disgrace and it can cause long term problems such as difficulty in collecting child support

Overall, then, Islamic law on divorce is discriminatory and varies according to which doctrine is predominant in a particular region or state. Men and woman have very different options and women in particular are less free to choose divorce. With the exception of Tunisia[6], when it comes to divorce it is easier for the man and it is very difficult for the woman to prevent a divorce she wishes to avoid.

Tucker states that divorce law is still influenced by a highly gendered vision of the power and place of male and female in marriage. It is seen as the birthright of a male to be able to divorce his wife without interference and this has proved difficult to supersede. When states have pronounced reforms that restrict *talaq* and expand women's access to divorce, the courts and the judges have often dragged their heels (2008:132).

The call for *Talaq* or 'triple divorce' to be accepted by British Law remains highly contested (Vertovec 2002:31).

Today most Muslim countries have legislation allowing divorce initiated by the wife. However a wife must obtain a divorce through the court in almost all circumstances whereas men are often allowed an extra-judicial divorce. This difference between the rights of men and women offends most western societies (Hussain 2004:106). There appears to be a discrepancy between the judicial treatment of men and women in some countries as we can see in the book: *Women's Rights in the Middle East and North*

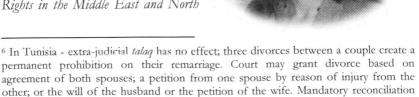

---

[6] In Tunisia - extra-judicial *talaq* has no effect; three divorces between a couple create a permanent prohibition on their remarriage. Court may grant divorce based on agreement of both spouses; a petition from one spouse by reason of injury from the other; or the will of the husband or the petition of the wife. Mandatory reconciliation efforts by family judge precede any award of divorce.
www.law.emory.edu/ifl/legal/Tunisia2.htm.

Africa – Citizenship and Justice (Nazir 2005):

> With the exception of Morocco and Tunisia, the existing family laws of MENA countries relegate women to an inferior position within marriage and within the family. Family laws in these countries declare that the husband is the head of the family, require the wife to obey her husband, and give the husband power over his wife's right to work and travel, among other rights. The reports in this study cite specific articles that enshrine a condition of legal inequality for women. The reports further explain how courts have interpreted these laws to deny legal protection to women whose husbands have forbidden them to accept certain jobs. The reports also detail how, in many countries, the law allows a husband to divorce his wife at any time without stated reason and without going to court but requires a wife to meet specific conditions in order to initiate a divorce in a court of law (2005).

However, most countries now insist on at least some formalities, even if it is only the registration of the divorce and certainly such formalities are required in the UK.

5.2.2. Newham College Students' Views

The answers to the question: Do you think a woman should be allowed to divorce her husband? showed hardly any difference between the two groups – 'Yes, definitely' was chosen by 58.9% of Christians and 53.7% of Muslims while 'May be' was picked by 23.2% of Christians and 27.3% of Muslims. 'Definitely not' was chosen by 17.9% of Christians and 19.0% of Muslims (Table 5.2).

Table 5.2 Position of students on divorce instigated by wife

Religion		Yes, definitely	May be	Definitely not	Total
Christian	N	33	13	10	56
	%	58.9	23.2	17.9	100
Muslim	N	65	33	23	121
	%	53.7	27.3	19.0	100
Total	N	98	46	33	177
	%	55.4	26.0	18.6	100

(Chi2=0.457;df=2;p=0.796;Vc=0.051)

However Muslim answers to the question: Do you think a woman should be allowed to divorce her husband? took a different stance. While 47.6% of Muslim males born in the UK agree that their wives could instigate a divorce, only 40% of Muslim males born abroad would agree to their wife doing so. It is significant that 75% of Muslim females born in the UK (thus 25% more) think that they have a right to instigate divorce while 50% of their counterparts born abroad think so. Muslim males born in the UK are only 7.6% more likely than males born abroad, to agree to their wives instigating a divorce. This considerable discrepancy in opinion between males and females is likely to cause problems within the Muslim community in the UK.

Figure 5.2 Position of Muslim students on divorce instigated by wife (%)

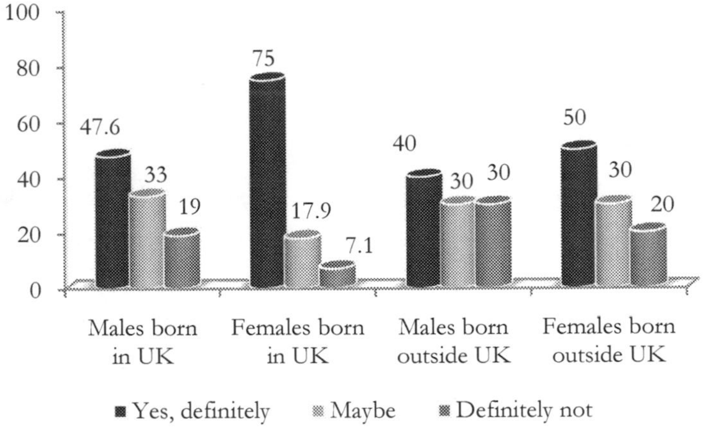

5.3. Female Circumcision

5.3.1. Immigrants' Culture and Traditions

Female circumcision is officially known as female genital mutilation. The precise origin of female circumcision is unknown. It is often thought of as a Muslim ritual but in fact it is thought to predate Islam. Although it is a common practice in many Muslim countries, in others it is not practised at all. It has certainly existed for centuries. Evidence that women had been circumcised has been found in mummified bodies of ancient Egypt. Even in 19th century England, France and the USA circumcision was practised supposedly to cure epilepsy and insanity.

The Koran makes no mention of female circumcision and the *hadith*s only briefly and rather ambiguously refer to it:

> A woman used to perform circumcision in Medina. The Prophet said to her: Do not cut severely, as that is better for a woman and more desirable for a husband.

Most Muslim schools of thought believe that female circumcision is recommended but not compulsory, apart from the Shafi school of Islam whose followers believe that it is mandatory (Goodwin 2008:175).

According to the World Health Organisation approximately 100-140 million women in the world have been subject to this practice. It is performed in many regions of Africa - in particular in Sudan, Somalia, Ethiopia, Kenya and Chad. It is also a tradition in the Muslim communities of Malaysia and Indonesia and in a number of countries in the Middle East, including Egypt, the UEA and parts of rural Saudi Arabia. Many women among the Coptic Christians in Egypt and the animist tribes also undergo this operation as well as Muslims (Goodwin 2008:175).

There are four major types of female genital mutilation (FGM)

1) Clitoridectomy: partial removal of the clitoris and the prepuce, in very rare cases, only the prepuce (the fold of skin surrounding the clitoris) (Parekh 2006:275).

2) Excision: partial or total removal of the clitoris and the labia minora, with or without excision of the labia majora).

3) Infibulation: narrowing of the vaginal opening through the creation of a covering seal. The seal is formed by cutting and repositioning the inner, or outer, labia, with or without removal of the clitoris.

4) Other: all other harmful procedures to the female genitalia for non-medical purposes, e.g. pricking, piercing, incising, scraping and cauterizing the genital area (WHO 2010).

The Excision and Infibulation are banned in all western countries, much to the distress of some Muslim immigrants. However the practice is considered to offend deeply basic human and universal values. Parekh writes:

It inflicts irreversible physical harm, is sexist in nature, violates the integrity of the child, makes irreversible decisions for her, endangers her life, and removes an important source of pleasure. It therefore deserves to be banned unless its advocates offer compelling reasons that measure up to its enormity.... the fact that it is sanctioned by a religion or a culture is a reason but never a conclusive one for allowing it (Parekh 2006:276).

Supporters claim that the procedure of female circumcision is done for religious and cultural reasons. In fact the reasons for female genital mutilation are many and include a mixture of cultural, religious and social aspects. Before we too readily condemn those who practice FGM we should remember that many who perform this act on their daughters believe that they are doing the best for their daughters. Waris Dirie under went this procedure aged five. In her thirties she wrote in her book *Desert Flower*:

I don't blame my parents. My mother had no say so in my circumcision, because as a woman she is powerless to make decisions. She was simply doing to me, what had been done to her, and what had been done to her mother, and her mother's mother. And my father was completely ignorant of the suffering he was inflicting on me; he knew that in our Somalian society, if he wanted his daughter to marry, she must be circumcised or no man would have her. My parents were both victims of their own upbringing, cultural practices that have continued unchanged for thousands of years (1998:238).

The World Health Organisation gives the following outline of reasons for female genital mutilation (FGM):

- As a social custom, the practice is maintained because there is a strong pressure to behave like everyone else in order to be acceptable.
- FGM is often deemed to be the correct way to raise a young woman and prepare her for marriage. In some rural communities a young woman cannot marry unless she has been circumcised (Goodwin 2008:175).

- FGM is connected to beliefs that there is an acceptable sexual behaviour and that by reducing a women's libido she will be better able to resist 'illicit' sexual acts.

- It is often considered to be a cultural tradition that should continue. It is thought of in connection with the cultural ideas of femininity and modesty which comprise the notion that girls after FGM are 'clean' and 'beautiful'.

- Many of the women who perform this operation believe it has a religious foundation.

- There is no one religious viewpoint towards FGM. Some leaders try to eradicate the practice, while others stress it is irrelevant to religion. Still others continue to encourage FGM.

- At times the practice is actually supported by the local structures. Tradition can be very strong in these areas and some men believe the folklore which says they will die if their penis touches a clitoris. Others believe that the baby will die if the child's head touches the clitoris during birth (Goodwin 2008:175).

- Some societies have adopted the practice of FGM as they copy the customs of their neighbours. In some places the practice has started as part of a wider religious renewal movement (WHO 2010).

Female circumcision is usually carried out between infancy and 15 years but can be performed on adult women. It has no health benefits, in fact it often has complications which can include severe pain, shock, haemorrhage (bleeding), tetanus or sepsis (bacterial infection), urine retention, open sores in the genital region and injury to nearby genital tissue. Ayaan Hirsi Ali (2007), aged five, was circumcised by her grandmother against her parents' wishes. Her account makes harrowing reading:

> She (my grandmother) caught hold of me and gripped my upper body in the same position as she had put Mahad (my brother aged 6) Two other women held my legs apart. The man who was probably an itinerant traditional circumciser from the blacksmith clan, picked up a pair of scissors (...)
>
> A piercing pain shot up between my legs, indescribable, and I howled. Then came the sewing: the long, blunt needle (...) when the

sewing was finished, the man cut the thread off with his teeth. (...) it wasn't until much later that I realised my legs had been tied together, to prevent me from moving to facilitate the formation of a scar.

(My sister) Haweya was never the same afterward. She became ill with a fever for several weeks and lost a lot of weight. She had horrible nightmares (...) my once cheerful, playful little sister changed. Sometimes she just stared vacantly at nothing for hours. We all started wetting our beds after the circumcision. In Mahad's case it lasted a long time (2007:32-3).

Female circumcision can be life threatening and many women suffer from long term health problems after the operation. These problems include infertility; an increased risk of childbirth complications and newborn deaths; bladder and urinary tract infections; cysts and the need for later surgeries. Obviously a woman who received Type 3 circumcision which seals or narrows a vaginal opening often needs actually to be cut open to allow for sexual intercourse and childbirth. So strong is the tradition that she often is re-stitched after giving birth, maybe several times which naturally adds to the risk to her health (WHO 2010).

Opponents declare that it is 'an extreme form of oppression of women.' Female circumcision practised by many immigrant parents on their daughters causes great concern to UK society. It is also known to take place among immigrant communities in the USA, Canada, France and Australia. In all of these countries it is illegal' (BBC 1998).

In the United Kingdom, female genital mutilation is regarded as a form of child abuse. Female circumcision has been a specific criminal offence since the *Prohibition of Female Circumcision* Act was passed in 1985. The child could be removed from her home where this is the only way her protection can be guaranteed. This was superseded by the *Female Genital Mutilation Act 2003* The Scottish Parliament passed the *Prohibition of Female Genital Mutilation (Scotland) Act* in 2005. The tradition remains prevalent in certain east African states and there are reports of the practice happening in the UK in specific migrant communities. While Scotland Yard is understood to have made investigations into female circumcision in the UK, and offered a £20,000 reward for information, no one has been successfully prosecuted for carrying out the procedure' (Kerbaj 2009).

A multicultural society faces conflicting demands and needs to devise a political structure that enables it to reconcile its members in a just and collectively acceptable manner. It should foster a strong sense of unity and common belonging among its citizens, as otherwise it cannot act as a united community, able to take and enforce collectively binding decisions and regulate and resolve conflicts (Parekh 2006:196).

5.3.2. Newham College Students' Views

In the question: Male circumcision is allowed in the UK but in many countries female circumcision is also practised. Do you think the UK law should allow female circumcision? - 12.0% of Christians and 20.0% of Muslims opted for the answer 'Yes, Definitely.' 'May be' was chosen by 46.0% of Christians and 47.3% of Muslims. It would have been interesting to know the reason so many thought that perhaps female circumcision should be allowed. Possibly some of the young people were giving that answer because they knew very little about it and thought it was similar to male circumcision and therefore harmless, while others might have been considering the fact that we are a democratic society and that people should be allowed freedom of choice. 'Definitely not' was voted for by 42.0% of Christians and 32.7% of Muslims.

Figure 5.3 Position taken on allowing female circumcision (%)

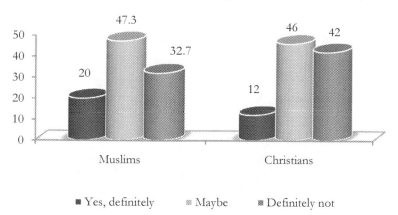

- Yes, definitely   Maybe   Definitely not

5.4. Conclusion

In this chapter we were trying to answer the question whether the young Muslim students' attitudes towards polygamy, divorce, and female circumcision are very different from British society's viewpoint. Polygamy is not allowed in the UK, but Muslim men can marry another wife or wives provided they meet the Islamic conditions of marriage. It means that our question whether UK Law should allow immigrants to have more than one wife? – was not an abstract question for the Muslims. It is true that not a very high percentage of Muslims would support that law - just sixteen percent of Muslim students. However, forty-one percent of them were unsure. Less than forty-three percent would definitely not support the law compared with sixty-six percent of Christian students. As we wrote above the interviews revealed that the majority of the Muslim respondents, especially female students, were definitely against polygamy. It is important to add that our research on the subject of attitudes to polygamy showed that Western society does not need to be afraid. The attitude of the younger generation regarding polygamy is not very different to Western society.

A more difficult subject is equal rights for men and women regarding divorce. In Islam a man can divorce his wife without the necessity of going to court. Nearly fifty-four percent of Muslims thought that men and women should have equal rights and a woman should be able to divorce her husband. Almost sixty percent of Christians agreed with them. It is significant that as many as seventy-five percent of Muslim females born in the UK strongly support women's rights to instigate divorce. This is twenty-five percent more than Muslim females born abroad. Muslim males are less inclined to agree.

The students' answers to the question: Do you think the UK law should allow female circumcision? were surprising. Only thirty-two percent of Muslim students chose the answer 'definitely not'. A high percentage of the students were unsure. Perhaps the young people knew very little about the subject. After all, although female circumcision is practised in a number of Asian countries it is not as prevalent as in some African countries.

CHAPTER SIX

Dress

In this chapter we will consider the whole area of perceived Muslim dress. In the first part we present the debate on Muslim women's dress in the UK. We are showing Muslim culture and tradition regarding dress and afterwards we give the opinions of the students in Newham College.

6.1. UK Society

The UK would like to claim to have very liberal attitudes towards dress and there are a number of dress conventions and dress codes. Until the end of the Second World War these codes were more transparent. Labour is still referred to as either 'white collar' work or 'blue collar' work to differentiate office from manual work. The experience of military conscription led to the propriety of men having short hair called 'short back and sides'. The societal and cultural changes in the last decades have made these codes less obvious, but there are still conventions for men wearing a suit for job interviews and formal social events. The garish fashions of the 1960s have been replaced by designer labels and the growth of the creative industries has increased an awareness of fashion. The recent increase in the availability of cheap clothing has made new clothes more affordable for more people. This is not to say that the UK population is well dressed, but the options are there.

There are still many uniforms related to status and role. Judges and barristers wear wigs and gowns, and the clergy wear black cassocks and white clerical collars, while newly designed school uniforms have been reintroduced into many schools. Other less formal traditional uniforms such as bowler hats and rolled umbrellas have disappeared.

There is no UK national costume, so national costumes from other states are generally regarded within the context of liberal dress codes, but can be questioned in practice if they are perceived to be making a political statement. Migrants who wear religious clothes have become a matter of public debate. We might note that this problem of dress is not a new issue. For example we can read in the Catholic Relief Act in 1829 that Roman Catholic clerics were still prevented from wearing clerical dress in public places and could be fined £50 for a breach of that law[7]. The law was not repealed until 1926.

In the UK fewer than 10% of the population are from ethnic minorities although the percentage is higher (approximately 33%) in London. Approximately 3% of the British population are Muslim. What Muslims consider to be religious dress, is widely worn in public, including in schools. The *Hijab* is worn by Muslim women. It is a scarf that covers their hair and neck and is commonly seen in some UK cities. While the *niqab* is visible less often, in some parts of London, it is far more noticeable, in Birmingham and some northern UK cities.

So why has there been so much debate about the wearing of the *hijab*? McGoldrick in his book *Human Rights and religion: The Islamic Headscarf Debate in Europe* clarifies this for us:

> There are complex and multidimensional reasons why women do or do not wear the headscarf-*hijab* veiling can have symbolism for the wearer and for the observer. It is invested with meaning by social construction and power relations. For the wearer it could be an act of free, individual, informed, rational choice and agency. Or it could be done under coercion from spouses, family, communities, religious leaders or state.
>
> Veils can also be problematic for observers. Some people are offended by the practice of veiling at all, at least in western societies, because whether she feels oppressed or not, the condition oppresses her and it should not be seen in the streets of a liberal modern country. It can be seen as a rejection of the idea of equality of women. Others argue that specific categories of women should not be able to veil in certain circumstances, for example, teachers or

---

[7] The Catholic Relief Act, 1829 XXVI. And be it further enacted, that if any Roman Catholic ecclesiastic, or any member of any of the orders, communities, or societies hereinafter mentioned, shall, after the commencement of this Act, exercise any of the rites or ceremonies of the Roman Catholic religion or wear the habits of his order, save within the usual places of worship of the Roman Catholic religion, or in private houses, such ecclesiastic or other person shall, being thereof convicted by due courses of law, forfeit for every such offence the sum of £50.
http://members.pcug.org.au/~ppmay/acts/relief_act_1829.htm.

other public servants or officials. There is also concern that the veil necessarily hides any evidence of physical violence or abuse.

For some (...) the headscarf-*hijab* is a visible indicator of religious extremism and is associated with religious fundamentalism and proselytism (McGoldrick 2006:14-15).

Niqab means covering up completely with only a slit or mesh for the eyes. This is a less common but growing phenomenon in the UK. In 2006 the Cabinet Minister Jack Straw said that he would prefer Muslim women not to wear veils which cover the face. He added that although he didn't want to be 'prescriptive' he believed that covering people's faces could make community relations more difficult. He asked Muslim women at his Blackburn constituency surgeries if they would mind removing veils. While some Muslims said that they understood his concerns, others called his remarks insulting (BBC 2006c).

So why does the covering of one's face make community relations more difficult? We have to remember that all people not only live out of a present culture but come from a culture and tradition. This past history naturally influences their thoughts, feelings and reactions.

In the European past 'the covering of the face is charged with all varieties of negative associations: ghosts, burglars, prisoners, masked figures, Halloween pranks and untrustworthy disguises of various kinds' (Tarlo 2010:134).

More recent events may also affect how Europeans view the *niqab*. For some Europeans seeing the *niqab* brings:

associations with covered faces - Hamas militants on TV or in the newspapers. Such images might suggest....that the *niqab* is linked to radical interpretations of Islam and to the possible threat of terrorism (Tarlo 2010:134).

Consequently other ideas come to mind that the person is 'alien', 'a troublemaker', 'brainwashed,' or 'oppressed' etc. Therefore when a European sees someone with her face covered, all sorts of association come into subconscious play and culminate in a sense of unease, concern and sometimes even anger. When two strangers in Europe come into contact with each other, say on a bus, they send out a non verbal but visible message: 'okay, safe.' But when someone gets on who is so covered she emits no message but a patent desire to be closed to all interaction. It is a cause for many people in Britain to think immediately: 'that someone who has so much to cover up just must have something to hide' (Tarlo 2010:134). Far from the woman becoming invisible, she attracts more attention and usually negative feelings. Because she looks different she is more visible. People look more closely. They look surreptitiously but they take her in. She becomes a target of curiosity. Her long black garments attract and repel at the same time (Tarlo 2010:132-134).

In Britain, the controversy over wearing headscarves in school dates back to the late 1980s. One dispute began in 1988, when the town authorities in a school near Manchester decided that wearing headscarves can be dangerous in the school laboratories, or during physical education lessons.

On December 21, 1989, two Pakistani sisters, Fatima and Aisha Alvi, came to Altrincham Grammar school, near Manchester, dressed in white headscarves. They were told either to remove them or to go home. The situation was repeated every day for a month. At that time, the older sister began to give interviews to the reporters. She told them that the school had three male teachers and according to Islam, Muslim girls should cover their hair in the presence of men. Fatima said: 'We'd like to show the strength of our religious beliefs'. Eventually, the Altrincham authorities concluded that the ban only created a rise in religious tension. The dispute reached a compromise, acceptable to both parties. They allowed the girls to wear the headscarves in class with the exception of the laboratory and the gymnasium. Muslims were satisfied with the result (AlSayyad 2002:12).

Another incident took place in 2003 in another school. A 14-year-old, Shabina Begum was sent home from school, for wearing a full-length gown, called a *jilbab*. The case went to court, which ruled in favour of the school. The ruling was based on the opinion, that the school already made appropriate concessions for Muslim pupils, who were in the majority, allowing them to wear special trousers and tunics. However, in March 2005, Shabina's family went to the High Court, which ruled that the school had violated her religious rights (BBC 2006a). The school endeavored to resolve the issue. In 2006 they consulted the local Muslim community, which suggested an alternative uniform, taking into account the cultural and religious sensitivities of

Shabina. Once again, however, the family went to court, now the Court of Appeal which ruled, that Shabina's rights had been violated. In March 2006, this ruling was reversed by the House of Lords, which stated that the claimant's rights were not violated due to the fact, that in her area there were two other schools with permission to wear a *jilbab* so she could easily transfer to one of those schools (Knights 2007:118).

Another case involved a 23-year-old Muslim teaching assistant, dismissed from work after wearing a face veil during lessons. In November 2007, the Anglican school in Dewsbury, West Yorkshire, suspended Azmi, after a quarrel regarding her wearing the *niqab*. The school authorities had ordered her to remove the face veil during lessons, because some students had difficulty understanding what she was saying. The Employment Tribunal dismissed her complaints about religious discrimination and harassment. However, Azmi received 1100.00 pounds in compensation for opinions 'hurting her feelings' (BBC 2006b).

In August 2006, Prime Minister Tony Blair announced that the discussion on veils worn by Muslim women was part of a major debate on how to integrate the Muslim community into British society. He also described the wearing of the veil by Muslim women as a 'mark of separation', that could make people outside that community feel uncomfortable (Tristam 2008).

Another case took place in 2007, where a student from school in Buckinghamshire, failed in a legal bid to overturn her school's *niqab* ban. The school had argued that the veil made communication between teachers and pupils difficult and thus hampered learning (Guardian 2007).

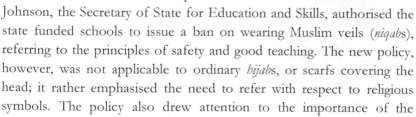

In March 2007, the UK government published new guidance for schools on school uniform policies. Alan Johnson, the Secretary of State for Education and Skills, authorised the state funded schools to issue a ban on wearing Muslim veils (*niqabs*), referring to the principles of safety and good teaching. The new policy, however, was not applicable to ordinary *hijabs*, or scarfs covering the head; it rather emphasised the need to refer with respect to religious symbols. The policy also drew attention to the importance of the students' welfare and effectiveness of teaching, with the importance of teachers and pupils being able to make eye contact. The guidelines stated that schools must be able to identify individual pupils in order to maintain order, and spot intruders. Furthermore it was added, that if a student's face is obscured for any reason, the teacher may not be able to judge their engagement with learning or secure their participation in discussion and practical work (BBC 2007b).

Although some groups of Muslim were not satisfied with that decision, others, for instance Dr Tag Hargey of the Muslim Education Centre, welcomed this guidance. He said:

> When you conceal the face, that actually not only dehumanises the person involved, but also creates a chasm, a gap, a bridge of non-understanding between communities and I think the sooner we can get rid of this veil, this face veiling, this face masking in Muslim societies across Britain, so much the better (BBC 2007b).

Until 2007 there was no legal policy in the UK, banning the wearing of headscarfs or other forms of Muslim clothing in schools. In fact there was still an atmosphere of tolerance for students and school staff who chose to wear the *hijab*. Each school usually had its own dress code, which the young people were expected to abide by. However, after considerable controversy that ended in litigation, the British government decided that there was a need for an unambiguous solution and introduced certain restrictions in school dress codes. However it was stressed in the manual for school uniforms that schools should not discriminate on the ground of sex and advised them to be sensitive to other cultures, races and the religious beliefs of their pupils. It was announced that schools were expected to meet the different cultural and religious needs of their students, under the uniform state policy (Knight 2007:117).

The wearing of headscarves in British schools, unlike the policy in French schools, has never been a great problem, in common with a more liberal approach to Islamic dress in the workplace in the UK. However, in the UK, where police officers have the right to wear headscarves (Cherribi 2003:196), it looked quite strange when during the elevated threat of terrorism, a staff member of the security at Heathrow Airport, wore a green scarf, identical to those worn by Palestinian suicide bombers.

There are many isolated incidents that catch the attention of the media when they occur, as did the 2006 British Airways incident with one of its staff losing her job through wearing a cross. Although BA had banned crosses on chains the company allowed its employees to wear *hijab*s and turbans. In 2007 BBC news reported that BA was changing its uniform policy:

> to allow all religious symbols, including crosses, to be worn openly. BA announced a review last year after a row erupted when Heathrow check-in worker Nadia Eweida challenged a ban on her visibly wearing a cross necklace. The airline now says it will allow religious symbols such as lapel pins and 'some flexibility for individuals to wear a symbol of faith on a chain' (BBC 2007c).

One might wonder why we have included this incident as it involves a Christian not a Muslim. However it caused considerable distress amongst the Christian community who saw that 'foreigners,' that is the Muslim and Sikh communities, were receiving preferential treatment in the UK. They were allowed to display their religion while Christians were prohibited. It had potential to be quite an explosive situation.

Incidents like these show an underlying tension in the UK. However, the debate is far less central than it is in France where headscarves and all religious symbols are banned in schools:

> The problem of the *burka* is not a religious problem, it's a problem of liberty and women's dignity. It's not a religious symbol, but a sign of subservience and debasement. I want to say solemnly, the *burka* is not welcome in France. In our country, we can't accept women prisoners behind a screen, cut off from all social life, deprived of all identity. That's not our idea of freedom (Sarkozy reported in The Guardian 2009).

There has been an argument that Catholic nuns wear similar dress in the UK and no one has a problem with them. In actual fact while Catholic nuns never completely covered their faces, most Catholic nuns in the UK modified their religious dress (habits) substantially in the late 1960s and many gave it up completely in the late 1970s as they found that their dress had become a counter sign. It separated them from other people. Some non Catholics thought they were 'odd', 'strange' and some people were even a little fearful of them. Dressing like everyone else, in ordinary clothes, while still dressing modestly made them more approachable. Therefore they were able to reach out to help more people. They believe that dress does not signify the depth of one's faith or give any indication of one's relationship with God. The religious dress they wore for many years just happened to be the type of clothes their foundresses had worn in the 16th - early 19th centuries. It set them apart as being committed to Jesus Christ and belonging to a particular group – nothing more. It was tradition.

In 2010 the Islamic veil and in particular the *niqab* became a topic of fierce debate in many European countries. In July 2010 Belgium was the first European country to legislate against the veil or *niqab*. It was closely followed by the lower house of the French Parliament which overwhelmingly approved a ban on *burka*-style Islamic veils (Nesrine 2010). Italy, Switzerland, Austria and the Netherlands are also considering a ban.

It was not only European parliaments who were beginning to question whether the veil was problematic. In June 2010 Syria transferred hundreds of primary school teachers who were wearing the veil, at Government run schools, to administrative jobs. A month later the Syrian government legislated against Islamic veils, banning the *niqab* from all public and private universities. Directives were given to the universities to ban *niqab*-wearing women from registering. A government official stated that the *niqab* contradicted university ethics (Gardner 2010).

In the UK the Sunday Telegraph reported that the immigration minister, Damian Green, had declared that Britain would not follow France and introduce a law banning women from wearing the *burka*. He stated that he thought it was 'rather unBritish and ran contrary to the conventions of a tolerant and mutually respectful society' (Hennessy 2010). Caroline Spelman, one of the Government's most senior female ministers, agreed with him and gave her opinion, declaring that she thought the wearing of the *burka* was empowering and dignified for Muslim women (Prince 2010). While some agreed with her, many disagreed. Michael Nazir-Ali, the former Bishop of Rochester, while supporting freedom of expression and belief for all, reminded us that:

> Such a principle does not exist in isolation and has to be balanced against other considerations of the common good and of public order. As far as the wearing of the *burka* is concerned, there are, first of all, questions of safety. Naturally, it would be quite inappropriate for the *burka* to be worn while driving or operating certain kinds of machinery. It is dangerous even while crossing the street (Nazir-Ali 2010)!

He added that for reasons of security it was inappropriate where identity has to be established – in airports, immigration control and access to public buildings. He thought it was also appropriate to ban the *burka* wherever a high degree of social interaction was required. He found it difficult to understand how a teacher or nurse or GP could adequately perform wearing a *burka*. He went on to state that he supported Jack Straw's pleas that the *burka* should be removed in the context of one-to-one interviews. He reminded his readers that Stephen Timms, a Labour minister in Newham, had been stabbed by a woman wearing a burka who had come for an interview at his constituency surgery. He declared that he was not:

> in favour of an outright ban. Women could be free to wear it in domestic contexts, while visiting friends and colleagues and elsewhere but only if not compromising public or personal safety, endangering national security or impeding professional or social interaction (Nazir-Ali 2010).

In 2006 UK citizens were asked their view on whether veils are a visible statement of separation and difference or whether Muslim women are segregating themselves by wearing a veil. They were also asked their view on Muslim women's right to wear the veil. We can see by the results that while 77% strongly defended a Muslim woman's right to wear a veil (Figure 6.2), a large number of respondents 58%, felt that wearing the veil was a sign of separation and difference (Figure 6.1).

Figure 6.1 UK Society's view on whether veils are a visible statement of separation and difference or whether Muslim women are segregating themselves by wearing a veil (%)[8]

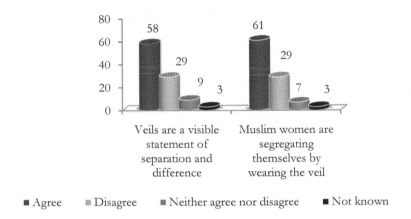

Figure 6.2 UK Society's view on Muslim women's right to wear the veil (%)

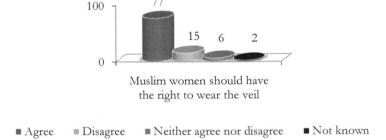

However even some Muslims would agree that the veil has the potential to be a sign of separation:

> The wearing of the *hijab*, that ostensibly mild statement of cultural difference, is, Adonis (Ali Ahmad Sa'id, Syrian-Lebanese poet) argues, harmfully socially devisive; 'It is, in fact, the symbol for a desire for separation: it means we refuse integration.' Moreover as he reminds us, such overt demonstrations of difference may have nothing to do with religion (Bennett 2004:62).

---

[8] Ipsos MORI interviewed 1,023 British adults aged 18+ on 11th October 2006e. Fieldwork was conducted by telephone. Data are weighted to reflect the national population profile.

In fact many pro-*hijab* supporters would agree with Adonis that the *hijab* is in fact meant to be a sign of separation:

> that it is a requirement of the Islamic way of life based on the separation of sexes and submission to God...in emphasising this aspect, *hijab* activists build on the original Arabic meaning of *hijab* – which is concerned with screening and separation rather than a particular form of dress. It is of course precisely such potential separating effects that many European governments are anxious to diminish (Tarlo 2010:64).

When the respondents were asked in 2006 if they agreed with women wearing a veil at work (Table 6.1) the majority of people preferred a Muslim woman not to wear a veil. In relation to TV newsreaders, 59% would prefer they didn't wear a veil. 54% would prefer a teacher and 61% a police woman not to wear a veil. The main exception to this general feeling was in relation to GP's. Perhaps because there is a shortage of GP's in the country 52% of respondents were willing for their GP, if she was a Muslim woman to wear a veil. Regarding politicians the respondents were quite evenly split: 46% disagreed with them wearing a veil and 42% agreed while 9% didn't agree or disagree. As we can see from these findings the majority of people have a definite view with only 6-9% of each group questioned being indifferent.

Table 6.1 UK society's opinions regarding the Muslim veil being worn in various occupations (%)

	Agree	Disagree	Neither agree nor disagree	Not known
TV newsreaders should be allowed to wear a veil when reading news	32	59	6	3
I would be happy to be seen by a GP who wears a veil	52	40	6	2
Teachers should be allowed to wear a veil at work	35	54	8	2
Police women should be allowed to wear a veil at work	29	61	7	1
In an election, I would be less likely to vote for a candidate if she wore a veil than if she did not	42	46	9	4

Source: *Muslim women wearing veils,* http://www.ipsos-mori.com/researchpublications/researcharchive/poll.aspx?oItemId=315.

We should add at this point that not all Muslim women in Britain support the *hijab*. While most uphold the right for women to wear the *hijab* if they wish, many find its increasing popularity disturbing and regard it as a backward and divisive step. They are also concerned because the *hijab* wearers often give the impression, through criticism and appearing over-pious, that they consider the non-wearers lesser Muslims. The non-wearers are concerned that the 'they also emphasise the extreme sexualisation of the women's body implied by the idea that she must cover, and complain that it is not up to women to cover but up to men to exercise self-restraint and stop viewing women in a sexual way (Tarlo 2010:62).

In July 2010 a YouGov Survey discovered that 67% of 2205 voters wanted the wearing of full face veils to be made illegal, with 42% feeling strongly. Only 9% felt strongly that the *burka*[9] should not be banned (Hennessy 2010).

The Kettering MP, Philip Hollobone, tried in late July to bring a private member's Bill to ban women wearing the *niqab* or *burka* in public. Legal rights campaigners warned him that he faced legal action if he refused to see any of his constituents on those grounds, as he would be breaching the Equality Act (Mail on Sunday 2010).

6.2. Immigrants' Culture and Traditions

There has been considerable debate over the last ten years over what is and isn't an Islamic dress code. In 2001 Glasse in his book: *The Concise Encyclopaedia of Islam*, wrote:

> In many Muslim societies, for example in traditional South East Asia, or in Beduin lands a face veil for women is either rare or non-existent; paradoxically, modern fundamentalism is introducing it. In others, the veil may be used at one time and European dress at another. While modesty is a religious prescription, the wearing of the veil is not a religious requirement of Islam, but a matter of cultural milieu.
>
> In India the introduction of the use of the veil among Muslims, which happened comparatively recently amounted to a

---

[9] Drawing by Regina Baltrukowicz.

great liberation. Purdah the separation of women from men, meant that women of the classes that could afford to practice purdah could not leave their homes. The introduction of the veil amounted to a portable purdah and allowed women a mobility they had not previously enjoyed (2001:38).

It might be well to mention here that the concept of purdah is cultural. The purdah is known by different names – *niqab*, *burka*, *chador*, *jilbab* – in different countries. According to the Women's History Resource Site, Kings College, London it is thought that the purdah developed in Persia and later spread to Middle Eastern lands. Purdah also flourished in ancient Babylon and ancient Assyria and was practised in India by Hindus as well as Muslims. Some Arab women who are not Muslims also wear purdah. By some people, purdah is seen as a practice that has:

suffocated the rights of women and perpetuated male chauvinism. Critics see women who practice purdah as having no voice or free will. Others, mostly believers in Islam, see purdah as a very positive and respectful practice that actually liberates women. It is viewed as liberating because it brings about an aura of respect. Women are looked at as individuals who are judged not by their physical beauty but by their inner beauty and mind. By covering themselves, women are not looked at as sex objects that can be dominated.

   The role of purdah in any culture has become more controversial since the rise of the women's movement. Purdah has almost disappeared in the Hindu practice and is practised to greater and lesser degrees in many of the Islamic countries. Either way the practice of purdah is looked at, whether in a negative or positive light, it stills remains an integral part of everyday life for some peoples and marks a part of their culture (Women's History Site).

It is important to remember that while the full *niqab* can be a free choice, that is not always so and it can also cover up serious abuse. Yasmin Alibhai-Brown writing in the Evening Standard expressed her concern about hidden abuse:

Domestic violence is an evil found in all countries, classes and communities. Millions of female sufferers hide the abuse with concealing clothes and fabricated stories. But this total covering (*niqab*) makes it completely impossible to detect which is why...victims of family brutality are forced to wear it. I now have

twelve letters from young British Muslim women making allegations
(of brutality) all too terrified to go public (Alibhai-Brown 2005).

While leaving aside for the present, the debate on purdah, let us
concentrate on the *hijab* which is a more common sight in the Muslim
world. Many Muslims see the *hijab* as a religious requirement of Islam
and even among Muslim scholars and journalists there is considerable
debate. Some defend it ardently, as intended by the Prophet and others
claim that it originated in the 14th century while still others claim that it
is a recent invention. It is, however, a known fact that women in all
societies, on every continent, have covered their head with a variety of
head-dresses over the centuries. These had such names as lachak,
chador, rusari, picheh, among many others and all had tribal, ethnic and
traditional origins and were never associated initially with religion,
(Taheri 2003:6) apart from the wearing of a head-covering for prayer.

Maqsood defending the value of the veil in 1997, explained that
Arab dress at the time of the prophet was very free. Women often fed
their babies in public and even bared their breasts completely when
leading armies into battle. The prophet expected Muslim women to act
differently, to cover their bodies appropriately, and to dress modestly
(Maqsood 1997:26-27). The Koran states:

> Say to the believing men that they should
> Lower their gaze and guard their modesty...
> And say to believing women that they should
> Lower their gaze and guard their modesty.... (Qur'an 24:30-31)

The eminent Islamic scholar Dr Zaki Badawi (1994) explained in Jan
Goodwin's book *Price of Honour* that:

> This section of the Koran also states that women should not show
> 'their adornment except what normally appears.' This means it is left
> to custom. There has never been an Islamic obligation for women to
> cover at any time. In fact veiling the face is an innovation that has
> no foundation whatsoever in Islam. Even in Saudi Arabia the
> covering of women is recent (Goodwin 1994:1).

The Muslim veil appears to have originated in Persia where it had come
to symbolise the elite and distinguish them from the common people
(Goodwin 1994:2). In 1991 Armstrong wrote in her biography on
Muhammad that the veil was originally only worn by Muhammad's

wives to give them some privacy from the constant stream of visitors who came to ask Muhammad for advice:

> It (*hijab*) is often seen in the West as a symbol of male oppression, but in the Quran it was simply a piece of protocol that applied only to the prophet's wives... women are not told to veil themselves from view, nor to seclude themselves from men in a separate part of the house. These were later developments and did not become widespread in the Islamic empire until three or four generations after the death of Muhammad (...). It seems that later other women became jealous of the status of Muhammad's wives and demanded that they should be allowed to wear the veil too. (...) thus many of the Muslim women who first took the veil saw it as a symbol of power and influence, not as a badge of male oppression (1991:36-37).

Other scholars think that the *hijab* is a more recent invention. In 2004 Allam declared:

> The *hijab* an invention of the 14th century and it has no real basis in the Koran. In the Koran, '*Hijab*' comes from the root 'hjb' which refers not to an object, but an action: wearing a headscarf, pulling down a curtain or screen or reducing light so as to prevent others from prying or looking in. The jurist, Ibn Taymiyya was the first to use the word '*hijab*' to mean 'headscarf.'....It came to distinguish a woman's identity and religious association (2004:11).

In 2003 Taheri made an announcement which many will consider startling. He wrote an article in the New York Post in which he stated that:

> the *hijab* has nothing to do with Islam as a religion. It is not sanctioned anywhere in the Koran, the fundamental text of Islam, or the *Hadith* (traditions) attributed to the Prophet. The headgear was invented in the early 1970s by Mussa Sadr, an Iranian Mullah who had won the leadership of the Lebanese Shi'ite community (2003:6).

Taheri claimed that he had interviewed Mussa Sadr in Beirut in 1975. During that interview Sadr declared that he had invented the *hijab* and that it came from an inspiration, having seen the headgear of Lebanese Catholic nuns. Sadr claimed to have designed the head dress for Shi'ite women as a visible sign that they were Muslim to protect them from

Palestinian gunmen. In 1977 the *hijab* took on political significance when Iranian women adopted the *hijab* as a symbol of Islamic-Marxist opposition to the Shah's regime. However in 1981 the role of the *hijab* changed yet again:

> Abol-Hassan Bani-Sadr, the first president of the Islamic Republic, announced that 'scientific research had shown that women's hair emitted rays that drove men insane.' To protect the public, the new Islamist regime passed a law in 1982 making the *hijab* mandatory for females aged above six, regardless of religious faith. Violating the *hijab* code was made punishable by 100 lashes of the cane and six months imprisonment (Taheri 2003:6).

Nancy Dupree, an Islamic studies specialist, of Duke University described these developments as follows:

> At the time of national movements against colonial powers, it became a symbol of resistance against alien politics that were generally viewed as a move to encourage female over-permissiveness. After independence was won and governments embarked on their indigenous Western-oriented paths, the veil was discredited as an emblem of enforced orthodoxy and suffocating social control, an archaic social institution similar to slavery (Taheri 2003:6).

If we look at history we can see how at the beginning of the 1980s, as Islamic radicalism became more prominent, the pendulum for Muslim women swung away from liberalism and once more they were hidden behind veils. The *hijab* had become a distinct symbol of Muslim identity which declared a separation between the sexes and created a gender barrier in public spaces. That development appeared to legitimise and institutionalise inequality for women. In some countries that step was taken even further, creating a focus on sexual discrimination, with demands by Islamic organisations for Muslim women to stay at home, deprived of education, to stop working, and to resign from positions of authority and increasingly be forced to dress in a specific way, in particular to wear the purdah (Goodwin 1994:2).

Badawi, however was adamant that the above is not a requirement of Islam. He stated 'According to our religion, women have a perfect right to take part in society' (Goodwin 1994:2).

It might be noted at this point, in 2003 Taheri wrote that fewer than 1% of Muslim women wear the *hijab*[10] and that the whole Western debate regarding whether it should be allowed or not in the western world comes at a time when Iran (the only country that has a law stating that women must wear the *hijab*) is actually reconsidering its position (Taheri 2003:6). In fact over the last 74 years many young women in Iran have fought for the human right of choice over their dress code. In recent years while keeping the letter of the law 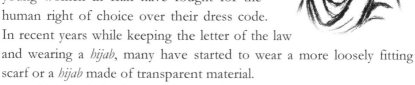 and wearing a *hijab*, many have started to wear a more loosely fitting scarf or a *hijab* made of transparent material.

To conclude, the *hijab* is a complex issue worn for many different reasons. Allam and Taheri both regard the wearing of the veil to have no religious basis but is sometimes given a religious connotation. Allam declares:

> Whoever wears it (the *hijab*) especially in the west, does so because they are coerced or conditioned to do so or are claiming their rights and asserting their free choices. There are many opinions, but they all defer to a series of unsolved conflicts: between Islam and the West, with Islam itself and between law and culture (Allam 2004:11).

The UK is a democratic society which values freedom of speech and of action as well as tolerance for difference but it still has to have laws. Naturally any State has the right to have a considered dress code. No country allows its citizens to walk around completely naked because it would offend many of the citizens' sense of decency and proprietary. In many countries it is acceptable to wear a bikini on the beach but not in the centre of town. And in some countries there are beaches were it is acceptable to be naked but not on every beach. Likewise in the UK it is proper to have a dress code that doesn't offend its citizens.

As mentioned earlier only 3% of the British population is Muslim (Muslim Council of Britain 2010). If the full *niqab* or *jilbab* causes offence to the majority of citizens because of the message it evokes in non Muslims (ie. women are oppressed), or causes separation

---

[10] Drawing by Regina Baltrukowicz.

and discord in communities (because it creates a barrier and gives the message that Muslims wish to be segregated from other citizens) or if it causes fear of terrorism (through hidden identities) and could also endanger the Muslim women themselves, perhaps the UK should consider whether this dress code is appropriate in the UK?

Regarding the *hijab*, it is education that is needed by both the non Muslim population and the Muslims – a clearer understanding of why the young women are wearing the veil and the effect it can have on others and then a moderation in the dress code. As Hisham al-Zoubeir suggests:

> What is needed is the traditional, moderate Islamic balance; maintaining one's Muslim identity whilst adopting the best practice and culture which the land has to offer. An application of this traditional balanced approach will see the development of an authentic self identity and culture, in which there is no tension between being both Muslim and Western.[11]

And perhaps as Emma Tarlo (2010) suggests in her book *Visibly Muslim*, it is the fashion industry and the desire of young women of all religious persuasions to be fashionable that will in the end help integration as fashion breaks down barriers and people become more approachable. Sofia Kara of Imaan Collections agreed saying:

> Why can't we take advantage of both cultures, fuse them together, and create something different which is us after all? It's our identity….Modest dress doesn't have to be intimidating. Let's face it, we do judge a book by its cover and I can see why black can be intimidating and off-putting. I don't want to set up barriers; I want to break them down, help women integrate better, look nicer, more appealing and attractive (Tarlo 2010:198).

Zeena Altalib of Primo Moda expressed it in a similar way:

> The fashions that I offer can help break down the barriers between Muslim women and Western society (Tarlo 2010:199).

---

[11] Extract from Anas Sillwood's responses to an on line interview with Hisham al-Zoubeir for Deenport, a popular Muslim Web site based in Britain as quoted in Tarlo, E., (2010) *Visibly Muslim – Fashion, Politics, Faith*, Berg, Oxford:198.

6.3. Newham College Students' Views

To discover how the students in our survey viewed the law regarding wearing Muslim dress, we asked them three questions. We began with one concerning French law. In early 2004 the French government passed a law for schools which banned any clothing that clearly indicated a student's religious affiliation. The law was worded in a very neutral way but it was understood by everyone that it was the state's way of preventing Muslim girls from wearing the *hijab* in school (Bowen 2007:3). So we asked:

1. Do you agree with the French government's secular law that prevents Muslim women from wearing their *Hijab* (headscarf)?

2. Most UK schools have a school uniform. Do you think that UK schools should allow young women to wear the *Hijab* (headscarf) and young men the turban if the young person also wears his/her school uniform?

3. Do you think that UK schools should allow young women to wear the *Burka/ Niqab* (garment that covers the entire face and body)?

In response to the first question: 15.4% of Christians and 7.8% of Muslims chose the answer 'Yes, definitely'. 'May be' was chosen by 38.5% of Christians and 17.2% of Muslims while 46.2% of Christians and 75.0% of Muslims chose the answer 'definitely not'. Unsurprisingly the Muslim students felt more strongly about this issue than the Christians (Table 6.2).

Table 6.2 Agreement with the French government's secular law that prevents Muslim women from wearing their *hijab* (headscarf)

Religion		Yes. Definitely	May Be	Definitely not	Total
Christian	N	8	20	24	52
	%	15.4	38.5	46.2	100
Muslim	N	9	20	87	116
	%	7.8	17.2	75.0	100
Total	N	17	40	111	168
	%	10.1	23.8	66.1	100

(Chi2=13.376;df=2;p<0.001;Vc=0.282)

However when we compared answers to the same question of Muslims born in the UK with those outside the UK, some interesting differences (Figure 6.3) were shown: 90% of Muslim males born in the UK disagreed with the French government's secular law that prevents Muslim women from wearing their *hijab* (headscarf) while Muslim males born outside of the UK felt less strongly about it with only 61.5% disagreeing with the French law on this subject. The differences expressed by the females were less pronounced but those born outside the UK felt more strongly 79.3% disagreed while 72.4% of females born in the UK disagreed with the law.

Figure 6.3 Muslim Students' position in relation to the French government's secular law that prevents Muslim women from wearing their *hijab* (headscarf) %

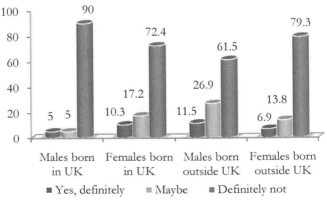

In the second question: Most UK schools have a school uniform. Do you think that UK schools should allow young women to wear the

Hijab (headscarf) and young men the turban if the young person also wears his/her school uniform? once again Muslims felt more strongly about this topic than Christians, with 69.6% of Muslims and 38.9% of Christians choosing the answer 'Yes, definitely.' 38.9% of Christians and 23.5% of Muslims chose the answer 'May be'. 22.2% of Christians and 7.0% of Muslims chose the answer 'definitely not' (Table 6.3).

Table 6.3 Position of students regarding acceptance of permission to wear religious symbols in school

Religion		Yes. Definitely	May be	Definitely not	Total
Christian	N	21	21	12	54
	%	38.9	38.9	22.2	100
Muslim	N	80	27	8	115
	%	69.6	23.5	7.0	100
Total	N	101	48	20	169
	%	59.8	28.4	11.8	100

(Chi2=16.094;df=2;p<0.001;Vc=0.309)

Figure 6.4 Students' attitude to UK schools allowing young women to wear the *hijab* (headscarf) and young men the turban if the young person also wears his/her school uniform (%)

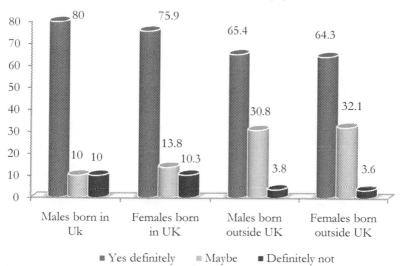

Once more Muslim males born in the UK (80%) felt more strongly about this than Muslim males born outside the UK (65.4%). Muslim

females felt slightly less strongly. Of those born in the UK 75.9%, agreed that UK schools should allow young women to wear the *hijab* (headscarf) and young men the turban if the young person also wears his/her school uniform while 64.3% of Muslim females born outside the UK also agree.

On the third question: Do you think that UK schools should allow young women to wear the *Burka/ Niqab* (garment that covers the entire face and body)? - 32.1% of Christians and 66.4% of Muslims chose the answer 'Yes, definitely'. 34.0% of Christians and 26.9% of Muslims chose the answer 'May be'. 34.0% of Christians and 6.7% of Muslims chose the answer 'definitely not (Table 6.4). Thus while two thirds of Muslims agreed, only a third of Christians agreed.

Table 6.4 Opinions on whether UK schools should allow young women to wear the *burka/niqab* (garment that covers the entire face and body)

Religion		Yes. Definitely	May be	Definitely not	Total
Christian	N	17	18	18	53
	%	32.1	34.0	34.0	100
Muslim	N	79	32	8	119
	%	66.4	26.9	6.7	100
Total	N	96	50	26	172
	%	55.8	29.1	15.1	100

(Chi2=25.364;df=2;p<0.001;Vc=0.392)

From Figure 6.7 we can draw the conclusion that the second generation Muslims are more radical than young Muslims born abroad regarding their views on wearing the *burka*. We see that Muslim females born in the UK felt most strongly on this topic with 82.8% agreeing that UK schools should allow young women to wear the *burka/niqab*. Only 48.3% of Muslim females born outside the UK agreed with them. Muslim males born in the UK felt slightly less strongly with 71.4% agreeing. It is interesting to note that while only a few Muslim females (3.4%) born in the UK felt that the UK government should not allow young women to wear the *burka/niqab* in school 13.8% of Muslim females born abroad agreed with them (Figure 6.7).

Figure 6.5 Students' attitude on UK schools allowing young women to wear the *burka/niqab* (garment that covers the entire face and body) (%)

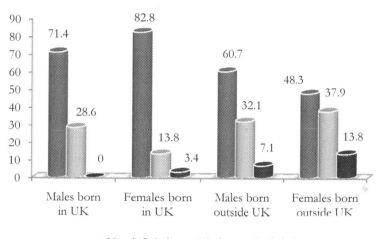

■ Yes definitely   ▨ Maybe   ■ Definitely not

Some of the young Muslim women interviewed expressed their thoughts and feelings regarding wearing the *hijab*. Let us look first at the attitudes of those born in the UK.

A nineteen year old born of mixed parentage, whose mother was from Malawi and her father from Pakistan, said: *It depends on my age. At present I want to learn, have plans for future. After having children, after 10-15 years, when I'm old enough and I think I'm ready. Putting on a hijab is not like just putting it on every day, it's related to the religion and I think in my opinion I should respect the religion and when I'm ready for it (at present not practising). I would talk to my husband and explain I'm not ready yet.*

Many of the young women we interviewed expressed the thought that they were not ready yet to wear the *hijab*. This feeling among the students is confirmed by Tarlo's research. Tarlo (2010:64) writes in her book *Visibly Muslim*:

(…) the pressure of living up to the virtues and expectations of *hijab* – 'of being worthy of it' – is a common theme in many women's accounts. Some who do not wear it speak of 'not yet being ready to adopt it'; many see it as a stage in their spiritual development.

Another young Muslim woman born in London who describes her identity as British Cypriot told us: *Sometimes I think - why do they cover their faces. They have good faces but sometimes I think possibly the family brought up the daughter like that.*

A young woman aged 19 born in London, who describes herself as British Pakistani told us that she: *wears hijab in Pakistan because of 'perverts' over there but chooses not to generally. Doesn't experience much discrimination (here). She has only been wearing the scarf (in UK) since August (10 months) and feels that since then people regard her as a terrorist.*

A seventeen year old born in London who described herself as Bangladeshi and British told the interviewers: *I've never worn the hijab. My mother does but it's my choice. They won't force me. The only man who should look at you is your husband. (It is) to keep unwanted attention away.'*

An eighteen year old whose parents had come to the UK also from Bangladesh described her identity as British Asian declared: *Niqab not necessary.*

Some of the young Muslim women who are first generation immigrants and were born overseas expressed their thoughts and feelings regarding wearing the *hijab.*

A Bangladeshi aged 19 told the interviewers that she is a British Bengali and would like to marry a Muslim. She doesn't: w*ear Hijab at the moment but would like to in the future. Mum wears it.'* Another young Bangladeshi who came to the UK eight years ago aged nine, described herself as a *strong practising Muslim,* who would like to marry someone from her own community. She said: *Wearing of the hijab is up to the individual.* She chooses not to wear it.

A young woman aged 19 born in England to Pakistani parents told the interviewers: *My mother does not wear a niqab (face veil), she had unpleasant experiences. Sisters do not wear it either.* She told us that she wears a niqab herself and: *is against the way English girls dress.*

A seventeen year old Iranian who had arrived in the UK just seven months before she was interviewed stated: *In Iran I wore hijab.* She went on to explain that she had to because in Iran you have to wear a *hijab* by law. She came to London because that law does not exist in the UK. There is freedom.

An Afghani who arrived in London a few months before she was interviewed declared that she was: *Not going to cover my face.* Another

Afghani aged eighteen who came to the UK in 2005 told the interviewers: *In Afghan I wore hijab but don't wear it here. It is not Islam that you have to wear niqab. Some countries wear it but it is cultural.*

Some of the young Muslim men interviewed expressed their thoughts and feelings regarding their wives wearing either the *hijab* or *niqab*. Let us look first at the attitudes of those born in the UK.

A British Pakistani aged 17 and born in London reflected: *wouldn't expect wife to wear niqab ever but maybe headscarf when she is about 40 or 50.* Another young man aged 19 whose parents were born in Pakistan said he: *would allow wife to choose headscarf or niqab. It is a traditional thing to do with respect.*

A twenty year old born in the UK who described his identity as Muslim, British Bangladeshi said he: *would like wife to cover her hair but not her face.*

Now let us consider the views of some of the young Muslim men interviewed who were not born in the UK regarding their wives wearing either the *hijab* or *niqab*.

A nineteen year old Nigerian man who came to the UK in 2003 said: *women should cover their bodies so they are not a temptation to men.* He added that he also thought they should cover their faces. A young Somalian aged 18 who came to the UK in 2006 said it was important for him for his wife to be a Muslim and he would: *prefer her to wear the niqab.* A Tanzanian who came to the UK eleven years ago aged nine said that his: *wife will be Muslim, regardless of the country. She has to be traditionally dressed. Niqab is up to her.*

A nineteen year old who came to England from Bangladesh aged five asked if he would expect his wife to wear the hijab declared: *intention is more important than what you wear.* An Asian British man aged 19 whose parents came to England from Bangladesh just before he was born said that he thought girls should wear: *headscarf outside but not niqab.* However it would be his wife's: *free choice. Wouldn't force her to. It's what's inside that counts.*

A nineteen year old from Afghanistan who came to the UK sixteen years earlier declared: *doesn't matter how wife dresses, as long as family is OK with it (...) In Afghanistan they are forced to wear hijabs (...) otherwise they wouldn't want to.* He added that he felt girls had a harder life than boys as they had more restrictions placed on them. An eighteen year old Afghani who had just arrived in the UK having lived in Holland for fourteen years told the interviewers: *Many more people in Afghanistan wearing headscarf because they are scared.* Another man aged nineteen came to the UK in 2006. He described his identity as British Afghani. He said: *Wife can wear whatever she likes as long as she is covered.*

A Turkish man aged 19 who came to the UK in 2004 emphatically said: *Woman should cover their heads and bodies. It is what men want. They do not need to cover their entire face. There are ten students in my class who are female and seven males. I do not speak to the girl students.*

6.4. Conclusion

Muslim dress is a hot topic in Europe. In this chapter we wanted to hear the point of view of the Muslim students from Newham College regarding the *hijab* and *niqab*. We began by asking them if they agreed with the French government's secular law that prevents Muslim women from wearing their *hijab*. Unsurprisingly the Muslim students felt more strongly about this issue than the Christians with seventy-five percent of the Muslims saying 'definitely no' while only forty-six point two percent of the Christians felt as strongly.

The results from our research appear to be a contradiction to the common British point of view that Muslim women are forced by their families to dress in a particular way. However there are some signs that Muslim students are divided in their opinions. Ninety percent of Muslim males born in the UK disagreed with the French government's law while Muslim males born outside of the UK felt less strongly with only 61% disagreeing. The women felt strongly with nearly 80% of those born outside the UK disagreeing and just over 72% of females born in the UK disagreeing with the law. The students are against a law that forces them to dress in a particular way. However that does not mean that they necessarily support wearing the *hijab*. From our experience only a small percentage of girls we observed in the college dressed in a *hijab* and many seemed to view it as much as a fashion accessory as a religious symbol. Some of the girls who were not wearing the *hijab* believed it was a religious requirement but they believed one has to be prepared and ready to wear it.

Our last question connected with Muslim dress was linked to the *burka* and *niqab*, the subject of debate in many countries in Europe. As we know there is a gap between the opinions of British society and Muslims. In our research we looked at the question whether schools should allow young women to wear the *burka/niqab*. Nearly 66.5% of Muslim students agreed while only 32% of Christians felt the same way. Muslim females born in the UK felt most strongly on this topic. Muslim males born in the UK felt slightly less strongly. No Muslim males and just a few Muslim females felt the UK government should not allow young women to wear the *burka/niqab* in school.

It would be interesting to know whether these young people support the wearing of the *burka* in school because they believe in freedom of expression or because they believe in the actual action of wearing the *burka/niqab* in itself being a good thing. Certainly none of the young women we interviewed actually wore it and we were not aware of any college dress code that said it could not be worn.

CHAPTER SEVEN

Identity: Religion - Culture and Nation

In this chapter we will reflect on the identity of the Muslim students in British culture. We want to discover what kind of influence religion, culture and nationhood have on identity.

7.1. UK Society

British society seems confused about its identity. A number of different concerns have recently led to a somewhat confused and unsatisfactory debate about British identities. These different concerns include political devolution and the establishment of new parliaments in Scotland and Wales, and the restoration of a parliament in Northern Ireland. This has been accompanied by a rise in internal nationalism and a new debate on the identity of being Scottish, Welsh or Northern Irish. Less attention has been given to the nature of English identity, except by far right politicians. This internal debate has been further fuelled by debates over the EU Constitution and European citizenship, and has spilled over into discourses about migration and integration.

There are perhaps two dominant ways of addressing identity. The first is from an ethnicity perspective where identity is dependent on ancestry and cultural assimilation, while the second approach is focused on an approach to civil society dependent on respect for civil institutions, having national citizenship status and being fluent in a national language. Attempts to describe a single identity as a definition or even as a description are unhelpful. The UK has long been populated by those who have self-selected multiple identities, for example Anglo-Irish and Anglo-Indian. Now more and more complex identities are constructed based on geographical location, specific ideologies and a sense of belonging. 'I'm a bit of a mixture, I was educated here and I have lived here most of my life. I would not have had such a good job or quality of life, but in a sense my home is where my parents came from,' is a frequently heard description of multiple identities.

The British, and particularly the English, are unclear about the nature of their identity. Political descriptions are little more than a list of stereotypes or an agenda of moral qualities, with exhortations about pride and patriotism, with which few would disagree anyway. It would, however, be wrong to paint a picture of a plural society where anyone can make up their own identity. Identity difficulties are reflected in the usage of the English language itself. The iconic campaign for recruitment in the First World War announced in stark letters that 'Your country needs you'. It did not say '*Our* country needs you', nor did it say '*Our* country needs *us*'. The popular press today describes the war casualties from Iraq and Afghanistan as '*Our* heroes', without explaining exactly who is implied in the 'Our'. This often contradictory use of language reflects on-going confusion over identity and deeper divisions in the UK that have direct relevance for integration.

In recent years the education authorities in the UK introduced the subject of 'Identity and Cultural Diversity' into the National Curriculum for students in secondary schools, in an attempt to develop a programme that promotes community cohesion:

> Community cohesion refers to a society in which there is a sense of belonging across all communities, where diversity is appreciated and valued, and where there are similar life opportunities for all (UK National Curriculum).

Obviously a cohesive society is a fairer and happier one. Many people would agree that the educational establishments have a duty to promote community cohesion. The UK government decreed that from September 2008 Ofsted would be expected to inspect and report on the contributions made in this area.

Hellyer (2009) in his book *Muslims of Europe the 'other' Europeans*, wrote of the impression held by large sections of the UK society that there is something fundamentally different about Islam which makes the integration of Muslims into UK society complicated:

> Some of these segments of society are non–Muslim, and are reluctant to allow such integration to take place; others are Muslim, as represented by a Muslim father's advice to his son: 'you're Muslim, remember; you'll never be English.' (...) These sentiments

raise a number of issues relating to plural identities and their compatibility with modern-day Europe and Islam (Hellyer 2009:143).

However not all immigrants have a problem with identity. Umara Hussain stated in *Gloucester Voices: Our Untold Stories* - Asian Stories:

> A half of me is Pakistani and half of me is English. I have found out that I must take the best from the Pakistani way of life and culture and also of the English. When these fit together, they make me a British Pakistani Muslim. I love England from the depth of my heart. It is my country, my birth country (BBC 2003).

The UK held a citizenship survey in 2007-08 on the subject of identity and values. The report published in 2009 came to the following conclusion: most people, in fact 93%, declared that they felt a part of British Society. It might surprise one to read that while 84% of white people felt strongly that they belonged to Britain, 89% of Pakistani and 89% of Indian people also felt they strongly belonged. Over two thirds (68%) of those questioned agreed that it was possible to belong to Britain and have a separate religious or cultural identity. Christians (66%) were less likely than Muslims (89%) to think it possible to belong to Britain and have a separate religious or cultural identity.[12]

In the United Kingdom there are some features about the organisation of religion that have specific relevance for migrants. The usual division in Western Christianity between Catholic and Protestant is not particularly helpful in the UK context. The Church of England broke its ties with the papacy in 1534 and is the 'established' national church. It claims to be both catholic and reformed and is often described as a 'broad church' in which both catholic and protestant practices are found. It is part of the worldwide Anglican Communion, but as the established church in England, the reigning monarch is the secular head of the church and its bishops are crown appointments and are appointed on the advice of the prime minister who in turn depends on nominations from the church. 26 bishops sit in the House of Lords, the upper house of the UK parliament. The Church of Ireland, the Church of Wales and the Church of Scotland are not established.

---

[12] UK (2009) *Citizenship Survey: Identity and Values Topic Report* – national representative sample of 10,000 adults with an additional sample of 5,000 adults from ethnic minority groups.

The relationship between church and state is contentious and complex, but it does provide a geographical network of parishes across the UK and there are legal rights, which are not dependent on belief for all residents living in those parishes. Other Christian Churches in the UK are more congregation dependent, and so belief dependent, although some are organised on a parish system. As such their pastoral care is more to their congregation. Migrants have ready access to the churches, usually through identifying with their belief or through their geographical residence. Many migrants coming to the UK have strong links with either the Roman Catholic Church or Pentecostal churches.

Perhaps a more useful way of describing the differences of formal Christian structures in the UK is to look at the varied way in which the many different denominations emphasise the importance of the authority of the church and its traditions against the way they understand the authority of Scripture.

In larger cities there is a plethora of different churches and a growing number of mosques, temples and other meeting places for worship. The first mosque in Britain was built in 1889. Since then many migrant minority communities have established places of worship for their own community. Public policy now refers to working partnerships with 'Faith Communities'.

Dialogue between different churches has been underpinned by the 'Ecumenical Movement' which promotes greater unity among different Christian churches under the banner of 'Churches Together'. This is more recently seen in a broader concept of 'Multifaith and Interfaith Dialogue' that is focused on shared global concerns, for example, peace, cultural understanding and the environment. In this context perhaps the most significant feature has been the attention that organised religious bodies have paid to migrants and refugees. There is significant concern for 'the stranger in our midst' and at local community level religious bodies have been active and effective in providing support services and interventions to meet the needs of migrants. There is also a strong political lobby from faith communities about many integration issues. This is an important resource for migrants.

Formal religious practice in the UK is in decline. There is a popular debate about whether the UK is still a Christian country, but there is little consensus about what people actually mean by being 'Christian' or being 'religious'.

> With over 170 distinct religions counted in the 2001 Census, the religious make-up of the UK is diverse, complex, multicultural and surprising. Less than half of the British people believe in a God, yet about 72% told the 2001 Census that they were Christian, and 66% of the population have no *actual* connection to any religion or church, despite what they tend to write down on official forms. Between 1979 and 2005, half of all Christians stopped going to church on a Sunday. Religion in Britain has suffered an immense decline since the 1950s, and all indicators show a continued secularisation of British society in line with other European countries such as France (Crabtree 2007).

It is more than a simple rise in secularism that this complex picture presents. There has been a cultural change in religious practice that now no longer sees formal practice of religion as relevant. It has been said many times that much traditional religious practice in the past was based on social mores and habit rather than articulated belief. The decline represents disengagement between formal religion and the population, and individual identity no longer has a need to include religious practice. It is important to remember that the lack of numbers in British churches on a Sunday does not necessarily indicate that the British don't really care about religion. The British pay their government to support their churches and expect their church to be there when they need it. Many go to church for baptisms and funerals although less and less for confirmation and marriage.

Yet, there is a growth in the informal house church movement and a growth in the number of Pentecostal churches and this is very evident in the London boroughs where there is a high percentage of immigrants. The Roman Catholic Church is overflowing with thousands attending masses every Sunday. There is a particular growth in the number of undergraduates reading Theology, despite negative reports of the failure of Religious Studies in schools.

By far the most significant religious issue facing migrants, and especially Muslim migrants, is the rise of Islamic fundamentalism, often referred to as Islamism. It has been described as a movement to regain the earlier purity of Islam. Its contemporary rise has been linked to perceived nationalist failures in the Middle East and the failure of Arab States which were caught between the post-war struggle of power blocs in the West and the East, and amid ideologies of capitalism and communism. A growing number of fundamentalist Islamic groups call for the restoration of the caliphate as a way of uniting Islamic nations while the more radical see acts of terror as a way of triggering revolution to achieve the restoration of the caliphate and Sharia law. Al-Qaeda ideology declares a complete break from the foreign influences in Muslim countries. Different enemies are identified: America, Israel, Christian-Jewish conspiracies. Killing such enemies is justified as jihad-Holy War.

In 2001, the 9/11 Al Qaeda attacks on the United States led to backlash and a sudden growth of negative attitudes towards Islam. The events of 9/11 turned the implications of the Islamic fundamentalist ideology into a real threat to the United States. The UK is more used to bombing and terror attacks. London was bombed in both the First and Second World War and the UK was repeatedly bombed by the predominantly Catholic IRA and affiliated nationalist organisations in the 1970s and 1980s. The British see themselves as more resilient to attack, but this changed with the London bombings in 2005. The bombers were themselves British, educated in the British system and working in the mainstream labour market. This represented an internal terror threat which generated a popularist negative attitude towards the Muslim community as a whole and this spilled into discrimination and quasi-racist comment. This phenomenon has been dubbed 'islamophobia'.

The issue of fundamentalism has proved divisive. Fundamentalism's basic tenet is that it is unquestionably right. The implication is that those who do not agree are then demonised and in a political context become the enemy. This has been articulated in different ways, for example 'unscientific', 'non-Christian', 'death to America'.

This demonisation of all who do not subscribe to the tenets of a particular fundamentalism militates against social cohesion. In public policy, the concepts of a tolerant multicultural approach have been largely dropped in favour of pursuing a poorly developed concept of integration. Faith communities in the UK face an urgent challenge to develop a new understanding of the complexities of integration and need to address a more sophisticated critique of their societal role.

7.2. Immigrants' Culture and Traditions

It is not easy to talk about immigrants' culture and tradition in the context of identity because people arrive from so many different countries and traditions. The immigrant's identity is very much dictated by the traditions and culture of their perceived home nation.

We all realize of course that Islam and Christianity are both religions not cultures but sometimes the boundaries between religion and culture and even identity can become blurred. As Tariq Ramadan (2004) wrote in his book *Western Muslims and the Future of Islam*:

> The Muslim women and men who emigrated from, for example, Pakistan, Algeria, Morocco, Turkey, or Guyana brought with them not only the memory of the universal principles of Islam but also, quite naturally, the way of life they followed in those countries. Moreover, to remain faithful to Islam meant, in the minds of first-generation immigrants, to perpetuate the customs of their countries of origin. They tried, without really being aware of it, to continue to be Pakistani Muslims in Britain or the United States, Moroccan or Algerian Muslims in France, Turkish Muslims in Germany, and so on (2004:215).

This combining of religion and culture was not generally a problem for the first generation migrants. However it emerged as a problem for many of the second and third generation migrants who became unclear about many issues: what is essentially Muslim and what is part of my parents' home culture? Where are the boundaries? What is my own identity? For example: Am I a Pakistani first or British or am I a Muslim? Can the two be separated? In their parents' eyes it is probably even more difficult to discern between the two. As Ramadan writes:

> It is with the emergence of the second and third generations that problems appeared and the questions arose: parents who saw their children losing, or no longer recognizing themselves as part of, their Pakistani, Arab, or Turkish culture seemed to think that they were losing their religious identity at the same time. However, this was far from being the case: many young Muslims, by studying their religion, claimed total allegiance to Islam while distancing themselves from their cultures of origin (2004:215).

However as Ramadan explained at the same time converts were coming to Islam, and finding themselves having to choose between 'becoming' Pakistani or 'becoming' Arab rather than being Muslim. They slowly began to be aware of their mistake and realised that there was a clear difference between Islam and the cultures of origin. Ramadan went on to explicate:

> This awareness and the birth of a new understanding of Islam marks the period of transition we are experiencing today, and it is inevitably difficult, even impossible, for parents of the first generation to cope with (2004:215).

According to Ramadan what the younger generations see as a sign of hope, is for the first generation the opposite. They see the end to any respect for the traditional rules of Islamic morality. They look at western society and see that everything appears to be acceptable. For example alcohol seems to be allowed in the name of freedom. Naturally their reaction is to isolate themselves, either as individuals, as families, or as communities. They try their best to protect themselves by trying to live parallel lives to the surrounding dominant culture which they consider morally and culturally dangerous:

> The equation, itself usually imported, was put in simple terms: less Western culture naturally equals more Islam (2004:217).

Islam does not have one central authority like, for example, the Roman Catholic Church, or the Anglican Communion. The dogma of Islam is very simple. Allah is God and Mohammed is his Prophet. This allows people from different parts of the world, to feel they are members of the same community, but when they come to the application of the Koran to everyday 21st century issues, it creates problems because there is a big difference in interpretation.

Mondal in his book *Young British Muslim Voices* explains the dilemma faced by second generation Muslim immigrants:

> Young British Muslims are turning to Islam as part of a wider strategy of empowerment against the cultural restrictions imposed upon them by older generations of migrants from the Islamic world. While such mores and practices may have offered a sense of comfort to earlier generations they are increasingly seen by their offspring as an unnecessary and unacceptable suppression of their

personal and social development. They have absorbed, and now take for granted, the freedoms that surround them in Britain, and they want to experience them for themselves (2008:29).

Shah's book *The Imam's Daughter* gives many insights into the tradition and culture of the Pakistani Muslim community she belonged to in the north of England. Many of Shah's Pakistani neighbours, like her parents, came from rural Pakistani villages and had little education. They lived with the hope of returning to Pakistan for good and therefore tried to maintain their village life, right in the centre of a large British city. She wrote that her father, the Imam, got most of his sense of British culture from what his children were watching on TV, the 'soaps'. He called the English 'gora' meaning white, although when he said it, he was expressing it in a derogatory way. She wrote:

> If people were drinking alcohol in a pub and flirting, he'd remark: 'Typical goray! That's all those English people ever do – drinking alcohol and sleeping around!' As he had no direct experience of English culture, he chose to believe that the TV programmes were true to life (Shah 2009:102-103).

He spoke no English and her mother very little so at home the children spoke Punjabi to their parents but often English to each other. Hannah spent her teenage years trying to fit in with her white friends. She found that her home experience had no relationship to her friends' home life so she tried to find common ground by watching British TV with her older brothers and listening surreptitiously to pop music when their father thought they were praying. Her home was a place with no music as her father had declared it haram (forbidden). Shah related:

> Like most people on the street, my parents feared 'outsiders' coming in and upsetting their ways. The police were seen as outsiders, not as people who would protect you if things went wrong (Shah 2009:118).

As a teenager Hannah found non-uniform days in school very embarrassing and difficult. Her father insisted that she wore the clothes she would normally wear at home, the traditional Pakistani dress – a dull *shalwar kamiz* and a headscarf (*hijab*). Hannah started to borrow Western clothes from a Hindu friend. She wrote:

I wore the skin of a subservient Muslim girl, and the Imam's daughter, whereas in reality I was dying inside (…) I was trapped in a culture I neither liked nor related to (Shah 2009:138).

Sanghera wrote in *Daughters of Shame* about many young women who were afraid that they would be forced into marriage and in writing about the young women's backgrounds she gave many insights into their Asian culture. One young woman -

Yasmin grew up in awe of her father. 'If he was to walk into a room and I was sitting down, I would stand up. It wouldn't matter if there were fifty seats for him to sit on, I would still stand.' At home they only spoke Pushto and life was very strictly regulated; in fact, she said, she grew up feeling torn between two worlds. At school she was a boisterous and popular English girl; at home she was quiet and submissive, the dutiful Muslim daughter.

Yasmin found growing up in the UK really challenging. She longed to go swimming or shopping with her English friends but knew her family wouldn't allow her. Apart from four hours every weekend when she was expected to help in her father's shop, her weekends were spent at home. Her parents stressed the importance of a good marriage CV and nearly everything she was expected to do was aimed at that purpose, preparing tea for visitors, playing with their children, showing what a good wife she would make. Even her GCSE choices were made by her father with marriage in mind. She knew that at some stage while still a young teenager, like her sister, she would be expected to spend a year in Pakistan because it 'looked good on your marriage CV'. A good marriage to maintain the family honour was all that mattered (Sanghera 2009:118-119).

Sanghera's mother was her inspiration. Although she lived for forty years in England her mother never learnt a word of English and 'died a stranger in the land she lived in but never called home' (2009:8).

In 2005 a group of 466 Muslim students attending universities across the UK, took part in a survey entitled *The Voice of Muslim students*. They were asked to define 'being British'. The answers given included questions of citizenship, nationality and geography.

Most views fell under four main categories: to be born or to live in Britain, to have a British passport, to have values of justice and democracy and to live in a multicultural society.

The largest proportion of respondents defined 'being British' as being born in Britain, growing up with British culture, or holding a British passport. For others, 'being British' was a nationalistic idea that went against the bonds of faith that a Muslim shared with other Muslims around the world. Notably despite the overwhelming emphasis on the diversity of Muslim communities in the UK, many respondents attempted to overcome fragmentation by describing a common Muslim experience. Simultaneously, individual attitudes towards Islam also affected people's response to the question. Some felt that to be a Muslim here your faith must become a very personal experience that doesn't infringe on others, while others spoke of Islam enriching British society in a very outward manner (FOSIS 2005:15).

The survey showed that 55% of the Muslim students valued most the freedoms available here, in particular the freedom of speech and freedom of faith in the UK (FOSIS 2005:17).

7.3. Newham College Students' Views

7.3.1. Identity and Belonging

Analysing the students' answers to the question: How would you describe your national identity? (Table 7.1) we see that the results are different from our expectations. It is true that more Muslims (8.5%) than Christians (2.2%) referred to their religious identity and more Muslims (39.6%) than Christians (26.7%) made a religion's connection with being British, but far more Christians than Muslims referred to their country of origin. However, that could be caused by the fact that there are fewer second generation students who are Christians than Muslims. It becomes clearer if we look only at the second generation of Muslims, because it gives us an idea about the percentage of young people identifying with the country where they were born.

Table 7.1 Position of students on their identity

Religion		Identity				Total
		Referring to religion	British and religion or nationality	Only British	Only Country of origin	
Christian	N	1	12	8	24	45
	%	2.2	26.7	17.8	53.3	100
Muslim	N	9	42	19	36	106
	%	8.5	39.6	17.9	34.0	100
Total	N	10	54	27	60	151
	%	6.6	35.8	17.9	39.7	100

(Chi2=6.340;df=3;p=0.096;Vc=0.205)

In Table 7.2 we can see that many of the second generation Muslim males (20.0%) appear to identify more strongly with their country of origin than do Muslim females (3.8%). Both males 60% and females 61.5%, identify fairly strongly with a combination of identities, being British and Muslim or being British and identifying with their country of origin. However Muslim females (26.9%) were more inclined to just call themselves British than males (6.7%).

Table 7.2 Identity of the second generation of Muslims in the UK (%)

Identity	Muslim males	Muslim females
Referring to religion	13.3	7.7
British and religion or nationality	60.0	61.5
British	6.7	26.9
Country of origin	20.0	3.8

This makes the following table very interesting, for when we compare the same students' answers on the question: How strongly do you feel British? (Table 7.3) - we see that Muslim males claim that they feel more strongly British than Muslim females. Table 7.2 would indicate the opposite.

Table 7.3 Position on feeling British (%)

Feel British	Muslim males (%)	Muslim females (%)
Very	50.0	48.4
Quite	40.0	25.8
Somewhat	10.0	19.4
Not very	-	6.5

There is some difference between Christians and Muslims regarding the question: How strongly do you feel British? (Table 7.4). The option 'Very' was chosen by 44.6% of Christians and 34.5% of Muslims with 'Quite' by Christians 26.8% and Muslims 29.3%; 'Somewhat' by 8.9% of Christians and 15.5% of Muslims; 'Not very' by 7.1% of Christians and 12.1% of Muslims; 'Not at all' 12.5% of Christians and 8.6% of Muslims.

Table 7.4 Comparison between Christians and Muslims regarding how strongly they feel British

Religion		Very	Quite	Some-what	Not very	Not at all	Total
Christian	N	25	15	5	4	7	56
	%	44.6	26.8	8.9	7.1	12.5	100
Muslim	N	40	34	18	14	10	116
	%	34.5	29.3	15.5	12.1	8.6	100
Total	N	65	49	23	18	17	172
	%	37.8	28.5	13.4	10.5	9.9	100

(Chi2=3.793;df=2;p=0.435;Vc=0.149)

Regarding the question: Do you sometimes feel that you belong nowhere? (Table 7.5) – the results were different to what we had expected. Usually one tries to explain the frustration of the second generation of Muslim immigrants arising from a feeling of being suspended between two cultures, not really belonging to either. However our survey showed that Christians are more likely to feel that they do not belong anywhere. The Christians response was 'often' 17.0%, while only 8.1% of Muslims agreed with them; 'Sometimes' was stated by 28.3% of Christians and 16.2% Muslims; 'Rarely' was chosen by 15.1% of Christians and 14.4% of Muslims, and 39.6% of Christians and 61.3% of Muslims said 'Never'. Possibly the difference can be explained by the fact that Muslims have stronger bonds with their community.

Table 7.5   Position of students on belonging nowhere

Religion		Yes. often	Some-times	Rarely	Never	Total
Christian	N	9	15	8	21	53
	%	17.0	28.3	15.1	39.6	100
Muslim	N	9	18	16	68	111
	%	8.1	16.2	14.4	61.3	100
Total	N	18	33	24	89	164
	%	11.0	20.1	14.6	54.3	100

(Chi2−8.283;df=3;p=0.041;Vc=0.225)

If we look at the answers from the Muslim and Christian students born in the UK, we see an even stronger reaction. The Christians are far more likely to express the feeling that they belong nowhere than their Muslim colleagues. 37.5% of the Christian males born in the UK and 25.0% of the Christian female students who answered this question stated that they often felt they belonged nowhere. Only 5% of Muslim males agreed with them and none of the Muslim females felt able to agree (Figure 7.1).

Figure 7.1 Sense of not belonging - students born in the UK (%)

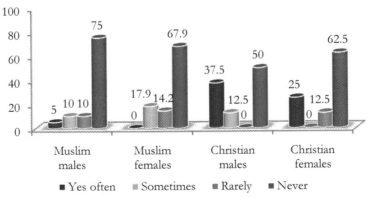

However, it also appears that the Christian students are surer of themselves, with only 12.5 % of both male and females saying that they 'sometimes' or 'rarely' felt they belonged nowhere. 20% of Muslim males feel they 'sometimes' or 'rarely' belong nowhere, and 32.2% of Muslim females feel they 'sometimes' or 'rarely' belong nowhere.

7.3.2. Religion

Looking at religious practice it is difficult to compare Muslims and Christians because these two religions have different obligations. Christians are expected to go to church on Sunday (in our survey 30.4% of respondents stated that they did so). Some of them go more  often (23.7%), not regarding attendance at a Sunday service as obligatory. Christians pray at home and the majority of Muslims do likewise. Only the Friday prayer, *juma*, is obligatory for Muslim men to attend, a sin only accruing if they miss three consecutive Fridays. The desire to go to the mosque for daily prayers is due to receiving more reward from God for doing so, in the hereafter. Perhaps it is more helpful to look at the percentages of respondents who chose 'sometimes' and 'never'. 'Sometimes' was chosen by 28.6% of Christians and 30.6% of Muslims, while 17.9% of Christians and 13.7% of Muslims chose 'never' (Table 7.6).

Table 7.6 Religious practices of Christian and Muslim students

Religion		I attend					Total
		Every day	A few times a week	Once a week	Some-times	Never	
Christian	N	3	10	17	16	10	56
	%	5.4	17.9	30.4	28.6	17.9	100
Muslim	N	33	24	12	38	17	124
	%	26.6	19.4	9.7	30.6	13.7	100
Total	N	36	34	29	54	27	180
	%	20.0	18.9	16.1	30.0	15.0	100

(Chi2=19.498;df=4;p<0.001;Vc-0.329)

Male and female Christians have the same obligation regarding religious practices but not so in Islam. Additional difficulties are connected with the different obligation between different Christian denominations. We must remember that Christian immigrants are not representative of national Christians because they are not as secularized as the Christians who are UK nationals.

Because we are interested in the process of integration of Muslim immigrants in the UK it is very important for us is to compare religious practice between first and second generations of Muslims in the UK. As said earlier, it is difficult to analyse the practice of Muslim females so for this question we look only at the results from Muslim males born outside the UK, comparing them to Muslim males born in the UK. We can see very little difference until it comes to the number born in the UK who never practise, 9.1% while only 3.3% of males born outside the UK make the same claim (Figure 7.2).

Figure 7.2 Religious practices of Muslim males born outside and inside the UK (%)

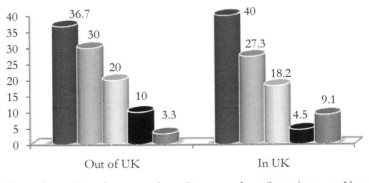

Similarly in the question: How often do you pray at home/at work? it is difficult to make a comparison between Christians and Muslims because Muslims are obliged to pray five times a day, while Christians usually feel an obligation to pray only twice - in the morning and in the evening. In our survey 34.5% of Christians were praying several times a day and 12.1% once a day. 55.5% of Muslims pray several times a day while only 9.2% pray once a day. The percentage of respondents who pray only sometimes is very similar between Christians and Muslims, respectively 20.7% and 19.3%, but it is very significant that 22.4% Christians never pray while only 1.7% of Muslims never pray.

Table 7.7 Frequency of prayer

Religion		Several times a day	Once a day	A few times a week	Some-times	Never	Total
				I pray			
Christian	N	20	7	6	12	13	58
	%	34.5	12.1	10.3	20.7	22.4	100
Muslim	N	66	11	17	23	2	119
	%	55.5	9.2	14.3	19.3	1.7	100
Total	N	86	18	23	35	15	177
	%	48.6	10.2	13.0	19.8	8.5	100

(Chi2=24.120;df=4;p<0.001;Vc=0.369

It is important to remember that Christian immigrants are usually much more religious than people of their age who are UK nationals.

If we compare Muslim males born outside the UK with those born inside the UK, we can see that the former are more likely to pray every day. While 62.1% said they prayed every day, only 33.3% of Muslim males born in the UK said that they did so. No Muslim male admitted to never praying. The results can be seen in Table 7.8.

Table 7.8 Prayer patterns - Muslim males first and second generation (%)

Muslim males prayer patterns		
	Born out of the UK	Born in the UK
Every day	62.1	33.3
A few times a week	6.9	23.8
Once a week	10.3	23.8
Sometimes	20.7	19.0
Never	-	-

The young people were asked about the faith of their parents. Only 178 were either able or willing to respond to questions about their parents' faith. We can see in Table 7.10 that well over half the mothers (114) are Muslim and 47 declared their mothers to be Christian. A few belonged to other faiths or Christian sects. Even fewer of the students, only 168, were able or willing to state their Father's faith revealing that 113 of the fathers were Muslim and 39 Christian.

Table 7.9 Parents' faith

Religion		Mother		Father	
		N	%	N	%
Christian	Church of England	11	6.2	12	7.1
	Roman Catholic	21	11.8	14	8.3
	Methodist / Baptist	3	1.7	2	1.2
	Greek / Russian Orthodox	1	.6	2	1.2
	Pentecostal	3	1.7	3	1.8
	Christian	8	4.5	6	3.6
	Total Christian	47	26.5	39	23.2
Muslim	Muslim	114	64.0	113	67.3

When we asked if their parents practised their faith by going to church or mosque fewer students were able to answer. It would appear that Christian mothers attend church more often than Muslim mothers but that will largely be down to tradition. Women have always been more likely to attend church than men and in Muslim culture it is traditional for the men to go to the mosque and the women to pray at home. Christian mothers (61.4%) attend church at least once a week or more whereas 45.1% of Muslim mothers go to the Mosque.

Table 7.10 Showing attendance at church/mosque for mother

Religion		My Mum attends					Total
		Every day	A few times a week	Once a week	Some-times	Never	
Christian	N	5	11	11	8	9	44
	%	11.4	25.0	25.0	18.2	20.5	100
Muslim	N	27	8	6	29	21	91
	%	29.7	8.8	6.6	31.9	23.1	100
Total	N	32	19	17	37	30	135
	%	23.7	14.1	12.6	27.4	22.2	100

(Chi2=19.829;df=4;p<0.001;Vc=0.383)

More than half of the students' fathers (53.3%) attend the mosque every day. If however we look at the percent who attend at least once a week or more the total is considerably higher at 83.3%. Christian men are less likely to go to church to pray. Thus it comes as no surprise to find that only 4.9% of Christian men go to church every day and only 46.4% go at least once a week or more (Table 7.11).

When it comes to how often their parents pray, many of the young people were unable to answer. Half of the Christians (51.1%) who responded said that their mothers prayed several times a day. With Muslims the result was even higher with three quarters of the respondents (77.5%) saying that their mothers prayed several times a day.

Table 7.11 Showing attendance at church/mosque for father

Religion		Every day	A few times a week	Once a week	Some-times	Never	Total
				My Dad attends			
Christian	N	2	7	10	13	9	41
	%	4.9	17.1	24.4	31.7	22.0	100
Muslim	N	48	12	15	12	3	90
	%	53.3	13.3	16.7	13.3	3.3	100
Total	N	50	19	25	25	12	131
	%	38.2	14.5	19.1	19.1	9.2	100

(Chi2=34.121;df=4;p<0.001;Vc=0.51)

It is important to remember that traditional ways of praying vary for Muslims and Christians. For Muslims there are set time periods to pray and they pray often using set prayers and a prayer mat, so obviously it is noticeable when they are at prayer. For Christians, however, there is a great stress on praying in secret and many mothers pray as they wash the dishes or walk down the street to do their shopping. It is not obvious that they are praying, so perhaps we should not take the Christians too seriously when they say that 11 of their mothers never pray. All we can state is that as far as they are aware their mothers do not pray.

Table 7.12 Mothers' prayer pattern

Religion		My Mum prays					Total
		Several times a day	Once a day	A few times a week	Some-times	Never	
Christian	N	23	2	3	6	11	45
	%	51.1	4.4	6.7	13.3	24.4	100
Muslim	N	79	11	8	4	0	102
	%	77.5	10.8	7.8	3.9	.0%	100
Total	N	102	13	11	10	11	147
	%	69.4	8.8	7.5	6.8	7.5	100

(Chi2=33.598;df=4;p<0.001;Vc=0.478)

Remembering what we have just said about tradition regarding the fathers, almost as many Christian students stated that they were not aware that their fathers ever prayed (30%) as those who knew their fathers prayed several times a day (37.5%), while all Muslims prayed at some time, with 68.8% of Muslim fathers praying several times a day.

Table 7.13 Fathers' prayer pattern

Religion		My dad prays					Total
		Several times a day	Once a day	A few times a week	Some-times	Never	
Christian	N	15	4	2	7	12	40
	%	37.5	10.0	5.0	17.5	30.0	100
Muslim	N	64	9	9	11	0	93
	%	68.8	9.7	9.7	11.8	.0	100
Total	N	79	13	11	18	12	133
	%	59,4%	9.8	8.3	13.5	9.0	100

(Chi2=33.926;df=4;p<0.001;Vc=0.505)

Freedom of Religion

In our research we asked the young people if they felt that everyone had a right to freedom of religion or whether the state should allow immigrant communities to punish someone who leaves their religion – we were touching on the so-called apostasy law in Islam. According to some scholars' interpretation of shariah law a person who leaves Islam deserves capital punishment. However we should state that not all Muslims believe that Islam states the necessity of killing an apostate.

Of course we are all aware that the Universal Declaration of Human Rights decreed in 1948 stated:

> Everyone has the right to freedom of thought, conscience and religion; this right includes freedom to change his religion or belief, and freedom, either alone or in community with others and in public or private, to manifest his religion or belief in teaching, practice, worship and observance (Article 18).

However not all Muslims believe that one has a free choice and in fact some Muslims who practise Shariah law insist on the death penalty for apostasy out of a concern to discourage apostasy. Others insist simply because they continue to cling to traditional views, no matter how much evidence exists against them (Shafaat 2006). Still others believe the Prophet called for the execution of Muslims who abandon their faith and that proof can be found in the sayings of the Prophet (*hadith*). In 2006 Abdelsabour Shahin, an Islamist writer and academic at Cairo University, in an interview with the BBC explained that although Islam in principle enshrined freedom of belief, there were severe restrictions on that freedom. He went on to say:

> If someone changes from Islam to Kufr (unbelief), that has to remain a personal matter, and he should not make it public.

He continued that if that person then went public he should be executed. There is considerable disagreement among scholars on this point. Abdelmouti Bayoumi of the Islamic Research Academy in Cairo disagreed with Shahin, saying that the particular *hadith* had been taken out of context and changing one's religion alone was not enough reason to be given capital punishment. One also had to be found working against the State (Abdelhadi 2006).

Perhaps we should reflect on what we mean by freedom of religion in Islam. Kadivar (2006) contributed a chapter entitled *Freedom of Religion and Belief in Islam* to the book *The New Voices of Islam. Reforming Politics and Modernity*, in which he explained his understanding of Freedom of religion:

> Freedom of religion and belief means an individual's right to freely choose any and all ideologies and religions he likes. It also means the freedom and the right to think, to have beliefs and values, to express one's religion and opinions, to partake in religious rites and

practices, and to freely teach religious values to one's children and to coreligionists. Similarly, freedom of religion entails the right to invite others to one's religion, to preach and propagate one's religion to other members of society, to build places of worship, to leave and renounce one's religion, and to be able to freely critique one's religion and religious teachings, freedom of religion means doing all these freely so long as others' rights and liberties are not infringed upon, and public order and morality are not disturbed. Freedom of religion and belief will become possible when, regardless of the beliefs that an individual may have, he is not persecuted for them and his civic and individual rights are not taken away because of them (119-120).

Kadivar (2006:120) goes on to explain that the Koran, while confirming Islam as the right religion, supports the plurality of religions and beliefs and recognizes people's rights to freely choose their own religion. Kadivar concludes by suggesting that Muslims bear in mind the verse in the Koran:

> No compulsion is there in religion. Rectitude has become clear from error. So whosoever disbelieves in idols and believes in God, has laid hold of the most firm handle, unbreaking; God is All-hearing, All-knowing (Koran 2:256).

He goes on to say that it is beyond any shadow of doubt that there is no compulsion in Islam. Islam does not sanction capital punishment for an apostate, nor does this verse agree with forcing infidels to choose between Islam and death. Judgment belongs to God (Kadivar 2006:133). Kadivar encourages all Muslims to embrace reason:

> The most prudent way to reform and correct people's beliefs is through reason not compulsion..... People change their beliefs and especially their religions very seldom. If they do change their religious beliefs, it is out of conviction rather than compulsion (...) Prohibiting religious freedom and the right to change religions, even denying coreligionists the right to change their religion, is ultimately counterproductive. In such a case, very few individuals

from outside one's religion are likely to become believers (2006:130-131).

In this section we first asked the students the question: Do you agree that religion is a personal choice and the State should have no say in that choice? There was just over 10% difference between Christians and Muslims - 76.4% of Christians and 65.0% of Muslims chose the answer 'Yes, definitely' and 18.2% of Christians and 25.8% of Muslims chose the answer 'May be' while 5.5% of Christians and 9.2% of Muslims disagreed.

Table 7.14 Christian and Muslim attitude towards choice of religion and state's non interference

Religion		Yes, definitely	May be	Definitely not	Total
Christian	N	42	10	3	55
	%	76.4	18.2	5.5	100
Muslim	N	78	31	11	120
	%	65.0	25.8	9.2	100
Total	N	120	41	14	175
	%	68.6	23.4	8.0	100.0

(Chi2−2.302;df=2;p=0.316;Vc=0.115)

In Figure 7.3 we see that Muslim males born in the UK (73.7%) were the group most likely to support freedom of choice of religion. Muslim females born in the UK were far less sure, with only 55.2% saying 'yes' and 31% saying 'maybe.' When it came to students born outside the UK, saying 'yes', the results for males (65.5%) and females (66.7) were similar. The majority of Muslim students supported freedom of choice with only 10.5% of males born in the UK, 13.8% of females born in the UK, 3.4% males born outside the UK and 10% females born outside the UK completely disagreeing. That is an average of 10.6% thinking that it is acceptable for the State to intervene.

Figure 7.3 Muslim (male and female) attitudes towards freedom of choice of religion (%)

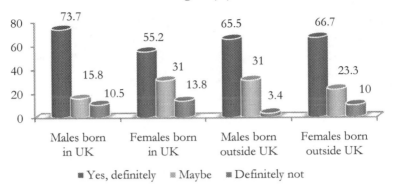

In the question: Do you think UK law should allow immigrant communities to punish one of their members if they change their religion? the students were not asked about specific punishment or capital punishment, but generally. Probably Muslims students had more knowledge about this than Christians. 7.5% of Christians and 13.3% of Muslims chose the answer 'Yes, definitely' and 22.6% of Christians and 28.3% of Muslims chose the answer 'May be'. 69.9% of Christians and 58.4% of Muslims chose the answer 'definitely not.'

Table 7.15 Opinion on whether UK law should allow immigrant communities to punish one of their members if they change their religion

Religion		Yes. definitely	May be	Definitely not	Total
Christian	N	4	12	37	53
	%	7.5	22.6	69.9	100
Muslim	N	15	32	66	113
	%	13.3	28.3	58.4	100
Total	N	19	44	103	166
	%	11.4	26.5	62.0	100

(Chi2=2.229;df=2;p=0.328;Vc=0.116)

In Figure 7.4 we can see that a high percentage of Muslim males born in the UK (73.7%) believe that UK law should not allow immigrant communities to punish one of their members if they change their religion.

Figure 7.4 Opinion regarding UK law allowing immigrant communities to punish one of their members if they change their religion (%)

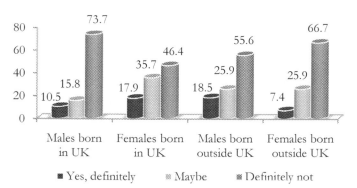

However females do not appear to feel so strongly, with only 46.4% agreeing with their male counterparts. Perhaps surprisingly when it comes to students born outside the UK, more females 66.7% believe that the UK law should not allow immigrant communities to punish one of their members if they change their religion, while only 55.6% of males agree with them.

7.4. Conclusions

The UK and in particular London is a multicultural society. Its members belong to different ethnic, cultural and religious groups and these identities naturally are very important to them. There is a tendency for people to believe that a nation has one identity or at least should have one. However there is no reason why a nation cannot have an internally plural identity and why a person cannot have multiple identities and still belong to a particular nation without causing a division of loyalties. For example a young Bangladeshi living in the UK can describe his/her identity as Asian Muslim or Bangladeshi or British Muslim. A young woman born in Somalia but living in Holland can describe herself as Dutch or Somali or Muslim, or may combine these labels in different ways. However as Parekh explains:

> Although there is no conflict in principle between ethnic, religious and other identities on the one hand and national identity on the other, it can arise in practice if either of them were to be so defined as to exclude or undermine the other. If being Muslim involves political loyalties and commitments incompatible with those in

Britain and its political way of life, then they cannot be accommodated within even the most capacious definition of British national identity. If national identity is to leave sufficient space for other identities, both need to be defined in an open and inclusive manner and brought into at least some degree of harmony.

National identity should be so defined that it includes all its citizens and makes it possible for them to identify with it (…).This identity should also accept all citizens as equally valued and legitimate members of the community (Parekh 2006:232).

Summarising the students' answers to the questions regarding identity we found that some of the results regarding the first generation students were not conclusive. The results were clearer for the second generation of Muslims. More than sixty percent of Muslim males and females identified with having a dual identity, being British plus being Muslim or British plus another nationality. Ninety percent of Muslim males and seventy-two percent of females felt very strongly or quite strongly British.

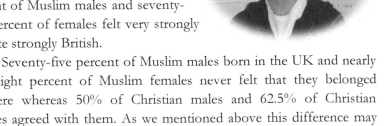

Seventy-five percent of Muslim males born in the UK and nearly sixty-eight percent of Muslim females never felt that they belonged nowhere whereas 50% of Christian males and 62.5% of Christian females agreed with them. As we mentioned above this difference may be explained by the fact that Muslims have stronger bonds with their community.

Regarding religious practice (going to the mosque) there is not a significant difference between Muslim males born in the UK and outside the UK. However more Muslim males born in the UK (9.1%) do not practise than those born abroad (3.3%). In the realm of private prayer there is an obvious difference between Muslims and Christians. Twenty-two and a half percent of Christians and 1.7% of Muslims said that they never pray. However 33% of Muslim stated that they prayed a few times a week or sometimes, not even once a day, with 40% of Christians agreeing. Therefore there is little difference in this respect between Muslims and Christians. Comparing Muslim males born outside the UK (62.1%) and those born inside (33.3%), we can see that the former are twice as likely to pray every day.

The majority of students agreed that religion is a personal choice and that the state should have no say in that choice. Muslim males born in the UK (73.7%) were the group most likely to support freedom of choice of religion. Muslim females born in the UK were far less sure, with a little above fifty-five percent saying 'yes' and just over thirty percent saying 'maybe.' 73.3% of Muslim males born in the UK believe that UK law should not allow immigrant communities to punish one of their members if they change their religion, while just over 55.5% of males born abroad agree with them. However Muslim females born in the UK are less sure about their feelings on this topic.

Perhaps we can conclude our reflection of the dilemma faced by immigrants regarding identity with two comments. The first, from Mondal's book *Young Muslim British Voices*:

> (…turning towards) Islam among the young generation of British Muslims is not in fact a turning away from Britain and Britishness but in fact represents an attempt to find their place within British Society (2008:66).

Our second comment is from Fauzia Ahmad's article: *Muslim Women and Higher Education Experiences in the UK*. Ahmad quotes a young Pakistani Muslim saying:

> If you put me in a room with a bunch of Pakistanis, I'm very 'English'. But if you put me in a room with English people, I'm very 'Asian' (2009:79).

This is the last chapter based on our quantitative research (217 questionnaires) supplemented by one hundred short interviews. Consequently, it is appropriate to consider how the students' navigation between the two cultures appeared in the previous four chapters. The last chapter (Identity: Religion – Culture and Nation) shows that the students strongly identify with their own religion, culture and their parents' country of origin. Chapter three shows that the attitude of immigrant Muslim students, regarding education and future work, is the same as in English society. The attitude of the female students also does not differ. However, when we look at the students' opinion regarding marriage (chapter 4 and 5) and dress (chapter 6) we see that they swing towards their parents' culture of origin. This tells us that 'ethnicity' is situation-specific, and that young members of ethnic minority communities are very well able to navigate the different categories and often to combine them.

CHAPTER EIGHT

Real Life Stories

The following are true stories as told by thirteen of the Muslim students who volunteered to tell the authors their own life stories. The students were asked if they were happy to have their own names printed in our book. The majority agreed although some chose a pseudonym. The authors were interested in their backgrounds and the topics related to their research. Most of the students, once they started, chatted away quite freely and were very open and honest about how they felt.

8.1. Sana

My name is Sana. I am twenty years old. Only my dad was born in Pakistan. My mum's background is Pakistani but she was born here and so were my two brothers and me. My mother's parents came to England in the fifties. My parents had an arranged marriage. They were not really related but the families knew each other. My dad came to the UK and then married my mum. I have a younger brother who is ten and in primary school and I have another brother who is also at this college and doing the 'Business' Course. I am doing 'IT' and I'm in my final year.

Neither my brother nor I are married yet. Arranged marriages are planned for boys and girls. I don't really have a problem with an arranged marriage, as long as you know the person you are going to get married to. I think it's important that you know your partner but that can be done with either a love marriage or an arranged marriage. I suppose, for us, it is more tradition. It's more of a culture thing. When my parents choose someone it could be a relative or it could just be someone from another family who shares our culture and tradition. My parents haven't anyone in mind for me at the moment. They just want me to educate myself, get to university which is really, really important. Society here is pretty different. Things have changed. I think education is very important for a good future. I'm not in a relationship at the moment. I just think it is more important to get your studies out of the way than find a partner because a partner could distract you from education. Education is more important. It comes first. To have a good education means you have a more successful future and you have an easier life rather than just struggling.

Before I started college I took a gap year from secondary school. After I did my GCSE's I thought... I've had enough of studying and want to go straight into employment. When I went into employment it wasn't what I really expected. I couldn't get a better job. I wanted to work in central London but you needed qualifications and I realised that education is important if you want to get a good job out there. So I came back to college and started off doing the IT course. Last year I did an internship with Ofcom and worked there for a month which was a really, really good experience in the IT field. I'm going into IT anyway so I enjoyed it. It was brilliant. It made me realise that education is more important..... That's just my personal opinion.

It's not all education. I have a social life as well. I have friends and family and we go out shopping, especially the sales at Christmas. I sort of balance my life out. You can't just do education. It's like the way you balance your diet. I go out with boys and girls. As you probably know my religion doesn't accept alcohol. In the holy book alcohol is forbidden. It is not really good for the body. I wouldn't like a partner who is drunk all the time. That would be an issue. It's not much of a relationship if your partner is drunk all the time. It's not forbidden to go and socialise in a pub. It's up to you. You can have alcohol. The choice is just yours. So there is nothing wrong in going into a building selling alcohol. It's just up to you, isn't it? You can go into a restaurant where they sell alcohol.

I practise my faith but I'm not 100% religious. Practising for me means keeping in contact with God by praying, by reading my holy book and by keeping Ramadan, fasting is important as well. In my country there is a lot of poverty. You don't always ....everyday.... think about someone not eating if you are always eating. But especially when you fast it makes you realise it's not easy. I mean it is easy to say but not easy to do, especially for eight hours or nine hours a day. It's very difficult and you realise there are people out there in the world not just my country but so many other countries where children just don't get food or water. It's not easy so you should always be grateful and thankful for what God has given you. You can expect more but never be selfish or greedy. During the time of fasting we have a charity collection to be sent home or to other countries where money is needed.

'Muslims can have more than one wife' people so often misunderstand that phrase. It's not really a cultural thing it is more religious. If you are going to have more than one wife you have to treat her equally. All the wives must have the same facilities. If you look at it it's not really easy. It's very, very difficult. I mean if you are going to give one, I don't know.... £10,000 ....you have to give the other three the same. Can that be done? I wouldn't want my husband to have another wife. To be honest I have a sister and I don't share my things at all. I'm the oldest girl and I'm spoilt rotten but I wouldn't share my husband. It's just my personal view. I think it is going to create more complications. It can be done it's not as if it can't but if there was a logic to it – I find it really, really difficult. 'Cos even to make a single marriage work it's not easy. It's hard work. It's not easy. I mean if you were a millionaire, why not? I think one of the reasons it happens is due to poverty but I'm not really sure on that issue.

I wouldn't mind a little family, why not? ... one or two children probably. I don't wear a *hijab* and nor does my mum. I don't think wearing a veil or a *hijab* makes you a proper Muslim. I think it is all to do with your intention and the way you think, your heart. You have to have a clean heart, mind and soul, to put yourself straight. There's no point just wearing it for the sake of wearing it, if you are not going to practise or be a good Muslim. There is just no point because at the end of the day God knows your intention. God knows what's really going on so you are just lying to yourself basically. There is no point in that. It's an identity because straight away people know you are a Muslim. People can make that out if she is wearing a veil or *hijab* means she is a Muslim. I don't have a problem with that. At the end of the day I respect them in that way. It is their choice. I respect every other individual, their beliefs, their rights. Everybody... you should respect every other person's beliefs. You can't go around saying people can't wear it because you don't like it. I don't have a problem with that.

I don't believe any one should be forced to wear the *niqab*. Covering your face and everything is not compulsory. When we go to do pilgrimage in Saudi Arabia the women do not cover their face. We are all equal, all one. That's the thing about it, it's not compulsory. There are men and women there from all different cultures and backgrounds but they are all one religion. Going to the pilgrimage you are all one. Everybody is equal but you are all doing the same activity and everything. You are all treated equally. You can't say to someone you are from this background so why are you here? Because you all have the same belief. It doesn't matter where you come from or where you were born. I haven't been on pilgrimage yet but my mum has. I'd love to go. I don't have an issue about covering myself.

One of my uncles married a Christian & his wife converted. My parents would expect me to marry a Pakistani but if I met someone else that person would have to convert. It wouldn't matter if the person was white or African if they converted. It doesn't matter who you are if you are converting, does it? The marriage wouldn't take place if the person didn't convert.

My parents made a good decision to come to England because in my country there are not a lot of facilities to educate yourself. It's difficult and people who do educate themselves deal with a lot of problems. There's a lot of poverty so that makes it very difficult for them to have a good future. They can only do farm work in the villages to just feed themselves. There's maybe not enough money to educate oneself which could lead to a not really good future and then it passes down, doesn't it, from generation to generation which makes it really difficult. My parents have come to this country. We get a good future and tomorrow our children will get a good future. As well as bringing us up and giving us what we need they are supporting other children by sending donations home.

A lot of the people I was at school with have applied to university or are going into higher education and everyone has a dream of being an architect or teacher or something. My class was pretty mature anyway and all had targets or aims.

My grandparents still live in Pakistan and I have visited them. I am not good at languages but my parents speak Urdu sometimes at home and I can understand them.

****

8.2. Abdul

I prefer to be called Abdul. I live with my mum and aunt. My dad broke up from my mum when I was just a baby, so I was brought up by my mum and my aunt. I was born in this country. My country of origin is Pakistan. My mum and dad and my aunt were born there. My dad married again and I have three stepbrothers and one stepsister. I grew up in Upton Park.

I am a Muslim but there's hardly a practising Muslim in this country because there are too many distractions and there's hardly any time. We are supposed to pray five times a day as a Muslim, but I don't do that because I don't have the time for that. As a Muslim I am supposed to go to the mosque on a Friday, but I am in college so I can't attend that so it's kind of tough following my religion. I know my roots. When I am not at college I go to the Mosque on a Friday but that's about it. I keep Ramadan. When you turn twelve you are supposed to keep Ramadan every year. But when you get older you can miss a few. I do try my best to keep every one but it is difficult. It is hard to wake up early in the morning and then wake up again for college, to eat after the sun sets and before it rises again. You can't eat or drink all day, nothing until sunset. I do try my best.

I am not thinking of getting married. I don't think I could handle the responsibilities, to discipline the child. First I want to stand on my own two feet, earn money and help my family as they have helped me. Then I'll think about marriage but right now marriage is at the bottom of my list. At present I'm working at becoming the man in the house.

I am hoping to become a network engineer. I've got a place at university for this autumn if I get the right grades and pass the entrance exam. I'm worried about that at present. It will be at the end of February but I am worried about my maths which isn't very good. When I was at secondary school my maths was brilliant but as I progressed with the years my maths started to go down. I don't know why. I am still trying to work it out. My English was bad but it is quite good now.

If I get married I will stick with one wife. The problem with being Muslim is if you get divorced you have to pay her to support the family and with a second wife it would not be easy. If I marry my wife will be a Muslim. My family would be against me marrying someone who was not a Muslim. I can't go against my family wishes. It would not be right. They don't mind me socialising with other religions but it can only be friendship, nothing more.

Talking about divorce, Muslims are allowed to divorce. In my religion the male has more power than the female that's how it is run. I think we should all be treated equally, inside all our blood is red whether we are male, female, white, black – our blood is red. We are all human. We should all have equal rights whether we are men or women.

Not all my friends are Muslim. I have Hindu friends and a few English friends. My best friend is a Hindu who I have been friends with since I was at secondary school. Our friendship is strong. We are like brothers, but he's at Uni and working at present so we don't have much time to socialise. I used to go to the gym. I do a lot of cycling and walking. I'm not happy to go to the pub with my English friends. I stay away from the pub because I know my roots. I might drink a soft drink outside the pub but I wouldn't go in. My English friends know I'm a Muslim and respect me.

[Authors: 'Do you think your family's decision to come to England was good?']

Yes and no, kind of both. I have been back to Pakistan but quite a few years ago. I lived in Pakistan for a while as a baby. I spent a year in Germany being disciplined when I was about ten/ eleven. I didn't have manners when I was young. I was wild. I studied in Germany and stayed with my aunt and uncle who disciplined me. It was a good experience. I can't remember any of the German I learnt and I can't speak Urdu. My grandma came to London and I used to speak Urdu with her but she has passed now.

I don't know anything about immigration. Gordon Brown has got some problems. He took over too quickly. If he tries I believe he can be a great Prime Minister.

I'd call myself an Asian, probably British Asian, maybe. I wouldn't say British Muslim. We haven't got a good reputation at present, have we? Our reputation is not as good as it was before. Some people think all this blowing up is right, but in the Koran you are not allowed to go killing and killing yourself. You are throwing your life away. The life God gives you is like a gift. If you bought a gift for, say, your grandson and he threw it right back in your face, you'd be upset, wouldn't you. That's what it is like when you commit suicide or kill yourself. You are throwing the gift right back in God's face.

The hard thing is to help other young people who don't think like this. Everyone has freedom of choice. If they want to do it they will even though it's the wrong thing. Many are completly blinded by what George Bush has done and they will believe anything anyone says.

Regarding the *niqab*, *hijab* etc. if women are really religious they have no choice especially if their family are very strict. But they should somehow reveal themselves now and then because how can you survive without a full face. It would be my wife's free choice what she wears. I would prefer if she was covered a bit but not the whole face. She can go out without the scarf. It would be her choice as long as she doesn't go too far. I would give her a choice.

When I was 16 I had some trouble with some bullies. I got mugged & messed around a bit but I realised it was the way I walked with my head down, dragging my feet. I realised I shouldn't be doing that. I was letting them do what they wanted. I could have gone after them, eradicating them from the face of the earth but if you are always making trouble it is just unfair to people. When my parents were my age you could leave your car door open, you could leave your bedroom door open but you can't do that now. I mainly had trouble with Bengalis but if I was a Police officer I wouldn't be biased even if my friend was causing trouble, I couldn't be biased. I'd take him in if he was causing trouble. My main problem has always been the Bengalis. I don't know the reason. I don't know if there is any problem in my own country between Bengalis and Pakistanis. I know there is a problem between Hindus and Muslims.

****

8.3. Isma

I have three older brothers and we were all born in England. My parents were brought up in this country but they were born in Bangladesh. I have been to Bangladesh about three times in my life that is in 16 years. I'll be 17 next week.

Bangladesh is actually quite similar to this country. There are lots of issues, arguments and debates over there. There is a prime minister in both countries. There are similarities but it doesn't have the riches we have. One thing I did realise while I was there visiting a poor area of Bangladesh I saw lots and lots of orphans, lots of poor children and mothers who are pregnant but live on the streets. Some of these people are not poor, they have a home, they are stable. They haven't got all the good things of life – toilets, education but they do have a home but they are still on the streets, still asking for money. One thing I realised that over here you can claim benefits, no matter how bad a state a person is in, there is always help. There's lots of services out there for people who are homeless. There are no facilities in Bangladesh. It upset me quite a bit. As I entered that part of the country all these children came to my feet, begging for money, calling me in Bengali, their language - their sister. It upset me. Obviously what I had in my purse I handed it out. But you hand out something to one person and others see what you have and more come. And obviously I can't give it to everyone. It did upset me quite a bit and it made me appreciate things more. Here I have to have the latest shoes. Over there they will be grateful for a bowl of rice and a glass of water. It did make me appreciate things much more.

My parents' decision to come to England was good. Sometimes I have an argument with my mum when I ask my parents for something expensive and my mum hasn't the money to buy it. She will say to me 'If my parents didn't bring me to this country then you wouldn't be where you are now. You would be living in a house made of hay or straw and you wouldn't have the clothes you are wearing now. You should be grateful.' Now I am older, I have matured and I understand. Maybe a couple of years ago I wouldn't have understood and I would have argued with my mum. Some of my relatives are in Bangladesh. My dad's family are still over there and because he is working he sends money and so they are living somewhat similar to us. They can get doctors when they want to and they can go to school and college. They've got education. Whereas there are some people there who haven't got anything, so it makes me appreciate more. One thing I would like to achieve in my life is to go out to one of these countries and hopefully build up and fund raise so that people can give money. I would like to help.

My parents' marriage was a love marriage. They went to the same school and the same college. It wasn't so much love as it just happened and they were happy with it because they knew each other. I want to get married but not anytime soon. I want to finish college and go to university but I would like to get married one day. I'd like to have kids. I want to have thirteen kids. I want nine boys and four girls. I like big families. I come from a really big family. My aunts, uncles, nan, grandpa, everyone has really very big families and I enjoy a big family.

I want to go to university. At the moment I am doing beauty therapy. It's not what I really want to do. I want to do nursing but basically the course I want to do, the nursing course is not available until May so I am doing beauty therapy just until May. So it passes away some time. I am doing it just to build some experience. I hope to go to Uni and hopefully do a nursing degree and hopefully I can be a nurse one day.

I don't know if I will have a love marriage. I haven't a boyfriend at the moment. If later on if I do have a boyfriend and he's a good guy and my parents agree to it. At the end of the day my parents' opinion means the most to me. If my parents were to say that person is not the right one for you, I'd accept it because my mum and dad know best but obviously if I did come to an age where it was time for me to get married and I did have a boyfriend and my parents were okay with it, and accepted it then I would go along with it. I know my parents wouldn't choose someone for me who wasn't good looking or wouldn't look after me. They would choose someone suitable. They don't mind me waiting. My dad is very strict about education. He says that to all of us. My little brother is 8 years old. My dad never got to do anything with his life and says he regrets it now. At the time he was mucking about with his friends. I didn't understand I'd need education in life. Obviously now I do because now I am struggling. He'd say to us. 'No matter what, you need education in life otherwise there isn't a bright future.' That's my dad's motto – 'No education – no future.' My dad's really strict about education. He wouldn't let me get married without finishing my education. Even if I wanted to, he wouldn't let me.

My family are not as religious as some Muslims are. But we have limits and we have our boundaries. We have morals and values. If I was to fall in love with an African, and maybe he wasn't a Muslim, obviously I would want him to participate in all our family cultural celebrations. Obviously it would be totally different for him. He wouldn't be used to it. For example we have Ramadan and we have to fast and obviously I would want him to fast with me. But he wouldn't be able to do it because he wouldn't be used to it. In our religion we are not allowed to marry a non-Muslim unless he converts. He has to convert not for his wife, not because he loves me but for the sake of our God. If he converted for the right reason and put his original religion behind and started to follow the Muslim faith then my parents would probably consider it, but I'm scared what my dad would say. My dad would rather I married a Bangladeshi. A Pakistani's culture is similar to ours so I think my dad would cope with a Pakistani but not an Indian Muslim. Their culture is quite different. There were a lot of wars going on between Bengalis and Pakistanis. Obviously it's not just about me and him. I would have to think about whether we could have a life together.

I'm a real family person. My mum and dad wouldn't allow me not to be there for a special occasion. They would want me to be there so if we say wanted to celebrate Eid his family could come over to our house but if they were Indian they wouldn't know what to do. They wouldn't communicate in a way that they would do, if they were Bengali so there are issues there definitely.

I would probably accept it if he wanted a second wife but he would have to let me go first. I don't think I could cope with my husband and then another person. If for example he was to want my best friend it would just be wrong in my eyes and everyone else's. When he married me, my best friend would have become like a sister to him. If he was to have a second wife, I would have to tell my mum and dad. I don't keep secrets from my mum and dad, so it would be quite embarrassing. I would have to tell my parents my husband wants a second wife. My husband wants more children. I am not enough for him. It is quite embarrassing.

In Bangladesh it is not acceptable for a man to have more than one wife. Obviously there are exceptions. For example my uncle's wife passed away and he had four children. Every child has the right to have a mum and dad so obviously he had to get married again and he did. He got married again and everyone agreed to it because the lady seemed nice and she said she could cope with four children. They seemed happy and they got married but it lasted about 9 months. At first she was grateful for whatever she got and she did take the children on and she looked after the children as if they were her own but after nine months, she got a bit bored. We don't know what the situation was but she stole money, gold and stuff from my uncle and she left. Obviously that was my uncle's second marriage and he was back to square one again. He had no wife and four children. His youngest son had got used to the mother and she left him, so obviously it is going to affect him mentally. Now it has been about a year or more and they are looking for another wife. Obviously a father always wants the best for his daughter and he is going to be wary. He will say to his daughter you will be this man's third wife. You are going to be the third best. They are not your children but you will be taking these children on and it is a big responsibility. Are you going to be able to cope with it?

If it happens, it happens. If someone has to get divorced for financial reasons or if they have been abused, then obviously it is acceptable but in my family if my dad was to get bored of my mum and just leave and get a divorce and he had no actual reason. If he just said, 'I am getting bored.' but he wanted to see the children, personally I wouldn't let my dad see me because he didn't have any reason. It would not be acceptable. My family would accept it in certain circumstances.

Many people have different views about Muslim dress. Many people have a totally wrong view of what Muslim dress is or what it stands for or what it should be worn for. Fashion is such a big part of life these days. Everyone cares about fashion and some girls do wear the *hijab*, headscarf or the *burka* not because it is a religious item to them, but because it is a fashion item. You should keep yourself covered so that no one can look at you or judge you. When you walk down the street no man is able to say that girl is quite nice. It should keep you covered whereas some girls do wear the *burka* or a headscarf but in a fancy way, and they wear bright colours whereas it should not attract attention.

My family are religious but not religious to that extent. I do not have to wear a headscarf. My dad accepts that. There are some people out there who say you have to wear the headscarf no matter what. Some parents because they are really strict with their daughters insist their daughters wear a headscarf so the daughters go out wearing one but as soon as they are out they take it off and shove it in their bag and it is not very good because you can hide it from your parents but you cannot hide it from God and at the end of the day we will all be judged on what we have been doing. I should be praying five times a day and I should have a headscarf on my head but I don't. I know every day I am doing a sin. I shouldn't show my hands and I shouldn't be wearing tight trousers but I do it and obviously I accept the fact that one day I will be judged on it and what I am doing is wrong. I believe it is wrong.

I went with my parents to Saudi Arabia when I was about 14. My dad said this is the stage when you are grown up. I don't want to go the wrong way, take drugs and stuff. You should be covered. I do believe you should be covered. Personally I wouldn't wear a skirt and I wouldn't wear a short skirt showing my legs. Obviously I have to wear trousers because I am not allowed to wear a skirt in my lesson. It is part of the uniform. It is acceptable. My parents have taught me to cover myself that you mustn't just put yourself out there. I personally do believe that it is wrong because what is said in the Koran our holy book, people have completely turned it around. Now there are so many religious priests, imams in Islam that everyone tends to come out with a different opinion. There are different imams. One or two are down to earth who are very strong on their religion and they believe the basic things, but there are others who completely turn it around and will say, well, you don't have to do this. You can wear a headscarf if you need to. Others - Yes, you should wear it. In the Koran it doesn't say that you have to wear the *hijab*. Other imams would say you have to cover your face and you have to wear gloves etc. In my family my dad realises that I am a teenager and I am going to want to wear makeup and want to wear flash shoes and what not, but don't put yourself out there. Boys these days tend to take advantage of girls because there are girls out there who are vulnerable and don't understand and are misled. Some people do argue that if you are covered men wouldn't approach you but it does happen even if you are covered. No one knows what is underneath. There could be a very nasty and horrible person underneath. Just because they have the *hijab* on or are wearing a *burka* it doesn't make them an angel. You never know. Many terrorists wear a *burka* and *hijab* and they give such a bad name to the people who are genuinely wearing it because they have a strong faith, because they are religious and believe in God. But Terrorists give such a bad name so that when we go to airports and are going on holiday when we go through security if you are wearing a *hijab* they will check you on purpose. They will bodily check you whereas if I were to go there in jeans and a top they wouldn't check me so much even though I am a Muslim. My grandmother went to Bangladesh 3 months ago and she was wearing a *burka* and they checked her, whereas my auntie was with her in plain clothes and they didn't check her so much. We were saying she is my nan and she was just going on holiday like any normal person, not doing anything bad but obviously they had to check her. She had paracetamols and what not in her bag and they got everything out and she had to explain what everything was for which was a bit odd. But obviously security has been very tight.

When I'm old I will probably wear a *burka*, maybe when/ if I am a grandmother. It would be my duty to be covered, to have my head covered at all times, to do my five daily prayers. If I have children and grandchildren I have to set a good example to them. They say the older you get the wiser you are. I will get to a stage in my life when I will wear a *hijab*. If you are working and it gets in the way like if you are nursing then you can take it off but as soon as you go out into the street you should cover yourself. It is allowed if you are working. You don't have to keep the *hijab* on. In some work places you do see people with the *hijab* on.

I can have male as well as female friends. Obviously I come to a college of boys and girls but I went to a sixth form of just girls. I have boy mates but not boy friends. I am very close to some of my friends and I know they won't see me in a different way. They will see me just as a friend. My parents accept me having boy mates as long as it is friendship and nothing more. As long as you are not sleeping with any boy that you are friends with my parents accept it. Personally I wouldn't go swimming with boys because I'm not confident enough with my body to go swimming with boys. I've been swimming with my girl friends. We go bowling and to the cinema, stuff like that. I wouldn't go swimming with a boy. I wouldn't wear a swimming costume because I wouldn't show my arms and legs to a boy unless he were my husband. It's not acceptable. He might for example say I had nice legs which is absolutely wrong. It wouldn't be his fault. I'd be allowing him because I'm showing him my legs.

Even though I am a Muslim if I were sitting here with you and all I could see were your eyes, I wouldn't be...um....feel comfortable, you know and I would prefer it if I was sitting there and could see your whole face, not because I want to look at your face to see how pretty you are, but because it makes me feel more comfortable. I think if someone was sitting in a classroom with a *niqab* on for example and you could only see their eyes she might not communicate with the class very well because the class isn't communicating with her, not because she has a *niqab* on but because people feel a bit uneasy with her and feel a bit offended. They're not going to talk to her because they can't see her face so they're not going to feel comfortable. Obviously she is not wearing it because she wants to make other people feel uncomfortable. She is wearing it for her own benefit but it does happen. Even I would feel a bit uneasy, uncomfortable if I can't see their face, can't see their lips moving. They are saying words but all I can see are their eyes. For all I know I could be sitting next to someone with a *niqab* on, all I can see are the eyes. I don't know if it is a man or a lady. Some terrorists at war wore a *niqab* and they were Somalian boys and obviously some people might be racists and they might not talk to the person because of racist issues, because they are against Muslims in *niqabs*. Generally people, I wouldn't stop talking to a person because of what they were wearing. I would go talk to them if I have to but I would still prefer to see their face.

****

8.4. Sultana

I was born in Pakistan. I came here with my mum when I was a couple of months old. I have got three older sisters and two older brothers, well I have actually got one younger than me. They are working. One sister is married. She had a love marriage. She knew him for 4 years. My parents knew about it and were so cool. He used to come around the house, go to each other's house, a nice family, parties and things like that. He is also Pakistani, obviously. My dad came to England when he was 17 ...16 I think he was. Obviously they got married back home. They were quite young when they got married.

One of my sisters is studying at this college, two are working, doing Diploma level 3. I have an older brother who is working as well and a younger brother in year 11. Hopefully God will give me kids and I will have two or three. Well it depends, I am not going to say I want three and then have six later on when the time comes. I am not going to speak too soon. I am allowed to have a love marriage. Society has changed now, things have changed. I might be allowed to marry anyone as long as he converted to Islam. Not for my sake but for Islam. If he was not willing, to convert then obviously I wouldn't get married to him but obviously I wouldn't let myself get into that situation. I would have to go out of my way just to marry a Hindu or a Christian. I am a good girl, I would think about my parents, think about Islam. To be honest with you, my personal opinion, I would want whoever I marry to be a Pakistani. He could be a Somali, Muslim, but the culture is different. There are things we would do differently - a certain type of food that we eat and they don't eat, certain ways of living and language, too different. We would believe in the same God but social life would be a problem. I've got nothing against Somalis.

[Isma interrupted Sultana] — Is it alright if I speak? My uncle fell in love with a Spanish lady who was quite religious. She was Christian so she didn't want to convert to a Muslim. And his mum and dad and brothers said we are not going to accept it. We are not going to accept this marriage. She is not going to be able to follow our rituals and our values because she is a Christian. So he said you know what if it comes to a stage where I am going to start my own life now. She is my life and if you are not going to accept it then I have no other option but to separate myself from the family. So he left home and we haven't seen him for a very long time. They're still together. They married and they have a daughter. Obviously she didn't convert. About a year ago she offered to convert for him but he said I don't want you to convert. I only want you to convert if you convert properly. We haven't seen them for about 3 years now. They are still together but it came to a stage when he had to separate from his mum and dad because they said 'we are going to disown you. If you are not going to follow our generation's values you are just going to have to go,' so he went.

[Sultana continued] - I know a white girl whose boyfriend is Pakistani. She has been with him for 2 years. She told me that she was going to convert for him because obviously 'his mum won't accept our marriage unless I convert'. She has tattoos on her arm, still drinks and eats haram. Tattoos are not acceptable and obviously drinking is not and eating haram — pork and things like that. I was telling her there is no point in converting. You are only converting for him. You will end up regretting it, saying why did I do this? There is no point converting unless you have the right intentions for yourself or your loved ones or sacrifice but she just wants to do it for him because she loves him and I think that is totally wrong. Either you believe in Islam or not. You have gone through the Koran. There's an English version now, isn't there?

My family is a very religious family. I don't wear a headscarf but I do pray 5 times a day. Obviously I am in college and miss some of the prayers but when I get home I go over it again. God tries to make things easy for us. Mum says there are different levels of prayers. The one early in the morning is very short. You can do it in less than 5 minutes. Mum says 'look how easy it's made for us. When we have to wake up at 6 o'clock in the morning and we are not feeling up to praying we have a very short time of prayer. He's made it easier for us. It's very short. He has understood. God has given us the opportunities. Sometimes we don't take it, sometimes we do. Prayer is 5 times during the day there is one at 6, one at 12, one at 3. Do you know what I mean there's a good three hours between. There's a five minutes prayer and that's it. Obviously sometimes in college you have to do some of the prayer at another time, but it's good to do it at the right time.

Hopefully I will do something in beauty therapy. Last year I was doing level one but hope to also do level two and three.

In Islam it is alright for a guy to get married again but that's obviously only if his wife is allowing him and not just because he wants to have another wife for the sake of it. A woman who has kids and no husband and is not capable when it comes to money matters and food and everything and she has to marry… obviously I know you are going to say….why does he have to marry her and she can't even help us but as far as Islam goes you have to marry her. I wouldn't mind if he would only be marrying her to help her. He wouldn't have sex with her. It's not acceptable. In Islam you are only allowed to have sex with one person and one person throughout your life even if you are married to more than one person. You marry her to help her. You are not supposed to be married to two people at the same time. If you marry a person and it doesn't work out, then you have to let that person go and then get married again. That's acceptable. Obviously if you were to have sex with this lady again, that person you had sex with is no longer your wife. This lady is your wife now. Say I was to have two husbands. I can't have sex with one on Tuesday and the other on Wednesday. It's not allowed, it's just not allowed. It's not right. In our religion you are not allowed to have sex for pleasure, it is meant to be to make children. To spread Islam is to make more children. Condoms, protection is absolutely forbidden in our religion. It's not allowed. Before you go through menopause you have to stop having sex. It's age as well. Obviously a man shouldn't have sex with two ladies at the same time during his life time.

Your husband has to ask you if he can get married again. If the first wife says yes then he can if she says no he won't. A wife wouldn't agree to a husband marrying again. You wouldn't like it. It's like getting cheated on, isn't it? A wife wouldn't accept getting cheated on. She would probably have a divorce. She would probably stop the husband seeing the children, if there were children involved. It's not acceptable. A wife would not be able to live under the same roof with her four children of one husband if she has another husband. She is doing things with the father of her children on Monday, Wednesday and Friday and she is giving the rest of the time to her other husband the rest of the time – a Tuesday, Thursday and Sunday. It is not acceptable. In our religion it is not acceptable. It shouldn't be allowed. But if a husband was to go and ask his wife and say 'I am not happy in our relationship and I want to get married again,' then she will say 'okay, fine.' Then we have to come to an arrangement. We have to get divorced, whatever. We have to let all our family members know that you and I are no longer an item and we have to let the kids know. And you have to arrange something so that you can see the kids. You can't come to me. You are going to get married again. She will be your wife and you are going to get all your physical activities from her, not from me.

[Sultana continues]

I've never had any racism problems but I'll be honest with you, I have had problems with being a Muslim. The whole terrorism thing that went on you do see people from different, cultures, race looking at us as if we are some kind of terrorist. Obviously I see it because my mum wears a headscarf and everything. I see the way they talk, when I went shopping with my mum. You just get the vibes when they think something is up especially with the police. I think they are racist, to be honest with you.

The media has sort of put Muslim people in a different perspective, a different light. I would blame the media for everything and not just that. There are a lot of girls out there suffering anorexia, suffering from illnesses like that, that just do not need to happen, girls who put their bodies through it because of the media because they see Jennifer Lopez looking all nice and slim. Stuff like that. You tell the media the truth and the media twist your words. You hear different things especially when it comes to race and that…. they say terrorists…

[Sultana becomes quite animated]

…not everyone's a terrorist. We are not all like that, you need to understand that. I am not a terrorist nor is she. I am a Muslim but what my Muslim brothers and sisters did or whoever did it. It is not right. It is wrong. It is not right for people to look down on you just because you are a Muslim, just because you wear a headscarf. I think that is totally wrong. We are not blowing up buses, blowing up trains. We are Muslims, yes, but we are not terrorists going around bombing.

[Isma intervened on a calmer note]

It is the media's fault because they put Muslims under a different light. They will say –'terrorists…blah…blah..' and they will show a picture, they could easily show a picture of one of the terrorists, just a picture of his face but they will show a picture of him wearing a headscarf or her wearing a headscarf, or her wearing a *burka*.' They will purposely show a picture where it is the wrong image completely. Maybe the journalist who sold the story is racist, maybe not, maybe he didn't realise that his story would have the effect it would have on the community, on the public, but obviously he sold the story to the papers for money. What he doesn't realise is if it's in the news we believe it. People will ask 'how is the weather going to be tomorrow?' We can hear things from people hearsay but when we see it on the news we say okay we will prepare for a rainy day tomorrow. It is the media's fault, personally I think it is. If we hear it from another person we won't prepare. I know racism has always been around. There has never been a stop to it and I think there will never be a stop to it. It will just carry on. Obviously the media have to come out with stories. They have to make the newsletter look interesting to sell the newspaper. Obviously we have Islamic newspapers but they don't have anything on terrorists. They have general issues of what has been happening in Bangladesh. You don't pick up a Islamic newspaper ... I don't know some people may think it is going to have all stuff like issues on terrorism, the *hijab* and issues and just religious stuff. It's not. It just has general news, just like the Sun has general news on what's happening in England. It's stuff like that. It's just the same.

I used to go to an Islamic Youth Club before I went to college. I went every day and every weekend, trips and everything, just to get myself off the streets and keep myself out of trouble. It was mixed – boys and girls and there was a man for the guys and a woman for the women. I think these terrorists – why are they bombing the trains? As Muslims we should have love. We don't know why they are doing it. I think they are doing it because they have so much hate and anger. Maybe it is something in their past life that went wrong, whatever. They have a different perspective of non-Muslims, non-Islamic believers. They have a different life. They have so much hate and anger. They are so bitter it comes that they have to do something about it because they want to get noticed. They want to make themselves known. I think the government should do something about it. If we were to open an institution maybe where people......obviously they are not going to say all terrorists are welcome here. If we were to have a club and the title could be 'Is terrorism right or wrong – what are your views, your opinions?' We could have one or two terrorists among us. We don't know. We could get all opinions on the table and with professional help, say a psychiatrist. These people might have something wrong with them mentally, something wrong in their past life and now they are taking it out. Thinking now I can do this and now I can do that to get myself noticed.

****

8.5. Maya

My family background is Indian. My parents were obviously born in India but they came here at a young age probably when they were about twenty, early twenties. Obviously they got married. That was an arranged marriage. My dad's dad, my granddad, he knew people who knew my mum, they were friends. They got in contact and they discussed and everything. Then they got along, enjoyed it and so they said yes we'll get married. So then after they got married they had six children, three boys and three girls. I'm 17 and the youngest in the family. None of them are married yet. My eldest brother is only 23. He thinks that's a young age for a boy. Hopefully within the next couple of years two of them will be married. It will be an arranged marriage, but in our town the definition of 'arranged' means my dad will look for a girl or maybe my brother himself will look for a girl and will tell my dad about it. My dad will look into it, like their family background, how the person is herself then they will probably arrange a meeting from there and if they are still not sure arrange another meeting and if they want to go for it say 'yes' If they want to say 'no' they look for someone else but nothing like forced. Nothing like that comes into it. It mainly comes down to the person who is going to get married. If I met a nice lad here, as long as he was my sort of Indian I could introduce him to my dad. By my type of Indian I mean - Gujarati. My language is Gujarati. In India there are different castes of Gujarati and each caste speaks a slightly different Gujarati and the way I speak is more like slang Gujarati but that would be okay as long as he was a Muslim. Initially there would be meetings so I could get to know him. Then if I wanted to I could go out with him to get to know him better as long as I took a third person with me, a family member or friend. I'm not looking for a boyfriend. Of all my brothers and sisters I rely more on my mum and dad. They can do all of it. What I want my dad and mum might not like but I don't mind their choices because I know what their choices are like. I have already told them: 'look, I want this and I want that and don't want that,' in them.

If my husband wanted more than one wife it would be pretty tricky….. obviously I would want everything for my husband to be happy, but then it will just not be the same for me, like my husband is not mine then. He is someone else's so for me it's more of a no, that's basically it. I don't think I would be able to do that.

In Islam girls are very, very precious like diamonds so if anything was to happen to the girl like, say for example the girl was seen doing the wrong thing it would be a real big issue. But if boys were to do it, obviously it would be big but not so much as for a girl because it is the girl that families respect. The boy is taking the girl home. The husband is given money when he marries his bride but the money/jewels really belong to the girl. If she gets a divorce at the end the money comes back to her family.

I'm not very Indian myself but from what I have seen and what I have heard so far and what I know is that many years ago Indians used to bury their daughters alive. Now I don't know why they used to do that but from rumours I have heard they even killed baby girls at birth. They wanted boys to carry on the second name. Girls don't carry on the second name, so they want more boys than girls, but now it is different. From what I have heard they used to do all sorts just to kill their daughters, but I don't think they actually realised that girls are precious. Some people started questioning: if you don't have daughters how are you going to have kids and how is Islam going to go on?

My plans are probably to pass through college with good grades, go on to Uni and complete my studies and then hopefully get a job. One or two years into the job when I have enough money for myself then I would probably want to get married and settled down and carry on with my job. Right now I have got my heart set on being a social worker because I love children but seeing them in trouble, I hate it. It would be better for me because if I become a social worker I can help some of those kids get into families and be happier. it's obviously not the same not having your own parents, but doing the best I can would make me feel good.

I visited India exactly 11 years ago. My dad's uncle was living there at that time. I definitely saw differences between the situation of women in families in India and in the UK. The main thing was religion. Over here probably a good 60-75% of Islamic people, Muslims, they don't act upon their religion, no way. I believe it is probably because of the society and the people they meet. People are becoming more like the society. But back home in India religion is very, very strict. People know, and it's not that they have been forced into it, but they know their rights and their wrongs in religion. They know when the limits are to have fun, when the limits are to have friends, like it is probably up to the gender or something. Over here…being friends….well it just depends if you can control yourself well you'd be alright but if you let friends come in the way of your life and your religion you just end up going along the wrong way.

I'm less religious than my parents because my dad is like a priest in a mosque, an Imam and he is a mosque teacher as well. So he's full on to everything. So is my mum. She didn't use to be but obviously once she got married she became like that. I'd say I'm far less religious than my parents though obviously I try my best to do what I can. My five times prayer a day is there anyway, but it's like I'm not very strict on them still. But I'm trying my best to carry on as I'm getting older.

I wear a *hijab*. My scarf is a family thing really but it's not that my dad said if you don't wear a scarf this or that. It's nothing like that. He said 'Look I would prefer it if you wore a scarf because you are my daughter. If you didn't wear it, think about what the people would say and think about yourself. You're losing respect. And you know what there is nothing wrong with wearing a scarf, to be respecting our religion and practising. We've all worn it. The *niqab*, veil is mainly your choice. I mean people who are really, really strict on religion they will probably say that it is necessary to wear it, but Islamically it is not necessary. It is like saying it is good if you do wear it, but it's not at all bad if you don't. If you do wear it obviously it is good because you are covering your face but if you are wearing it and doing the wrong thing it is not good. Personally I do not think it is necessary, but if you are ready to wear it and are hoping to act upon what you are wearing then that's fine. My mum doesn't wear it.

Regarding identity I think of myself as British Indian but obviously I am a Muslim but mainly I am British Indian for myself I think it comes down to be able to practise religion in every single area of the country you live in because I have experienced being called all sorts. I have seen people looking at me funny like and no offence to anyone, but they have always mainly been white and some give me this bad look and I always wonder 'What have I done?' Okay, terrorism might be from my sort of people, but not all of us are the same. I think racism comes down from every single background, culture, religion and all sorts of people no matter what age or whoever you are. Racism needs to calm down. If racism was to calm down this place would be a much better place. It's racism that causes these arguments. It's because people are not being heard. If the problem is people of our age I think youth clubs should open up in local areas. People all over that area could go and get to know each other and know that everyone is not the same. The message would spread - you know I have got this friend here and they are so not like the people they show on the news. News spreads a lot like sometimes even friends break up. I think for me it would probably be youth clubs. People don't really listen. I know people who have experienced really bad racism but they are angry. They are showing anger.

I think it is possible to resolve the conflict between the Jews and Palestine. I believe that since George Bush became president there has been more war in the world between different religions and different races. It's just all gone down the drain. He blew up every single thing. What he did when he became president was absolutely atrocious. Okay he may not be a bad man but from what everyone has seen over many years and all these innocent people. It's not just about Muslims, it's about all sorts of people. The way people have been getting tortured is absolutely disgusting and that's why racism has spread so much. And it's like people hating the Americans. What have the Americans done. It is their president. They are not all the same, you know. I blame him, definitely. He hasn't thought about anything. He just became president.

Regarding Palestine and Israel, I think both should have their own state. If I had a say I would speak to the most understanding person on the opposite side. They are killing kids, women, mothers. It's disgusting because....we see it all on the news....the news doesn't even show all the pictures of the killed babies and things. They should realise that they are killing all those people. How would they be feeling? The kids that have lost families, babies have died. What do they care?

****

8.6. Fuzia

I am Pakistani Muslim, aged 17. My dad came here when he was 10 and he went back home when he was about 28 and that's when he met my mum. She was living in Pakistan. They saw each other and got to know each other and their families met. They got married and then they came here. My mum had me quite late. I have a brother who is 2 years younger than me.

I would like to have 3 children. I would like to go to Uni and get a good job. I'd like to become a teacher, maybe a nursery teacher. I don't mind.

All my family, my cousins finished their education and then they have got married. Most of my friends are Muslim. Speaking of marriage I expect my marriage will be arranged. My parents' choice would be very different to mine. They would want someone... not that I'd mind someone... religious....but they would want someone really, really religious and strict. I would want someone religious, but not so strict. My mum is very strict. She just covers her head. My parents don't force me but they tell me they would prefer I marry someone strict. I don't think my husband will come from Pakistan. I think my husband will come from East London. My parents are more religious than I am, especially my mum. I try praying five times a day but I mainly pray my Friday prayers and I keep Ramadan. I have kept the fast since I was thirteen. Most people start at seven years old.

I have non-Muslim friends. I keep contact with them but I don't go with them to the pub.

I wouldn't agree to my husband having another wife. 'Definitely no.' I would want him for myself. In the past when people were poor they needed providing for, so it was okay for a man to have more than one wife. In Saudi some of the Arabs may have more than one wife even now. The man has to treat every wife equally.

****

8.7. Moonisah

My name is Moonisah. I was born here and so was my mum, but my dad was born back home in Pakistan. He was brought to this country when he was 11 to join his older brothers. One was newly married in this country. My uncle brought my dad into this country so that he could work and earn money and make a life. He stayed with his brother and then he got married. My mum and my dad are related. They are like cousins but not close cousins so it's complicated. My mum's aunty's husband's brother is my dad. When they got married my mum was 25 and my dad was 9 years older than my mum. I've got an older brother because my dad was married before. Afterwards my mum had me and my brother. My dad didn't really get on with his first wife, so he brought my older brother back to this country with him so my mum brought him up when she got married to my dad.

My dad isn't a strict Muslim. He doesn't pray but as he is getting older he is starting to pray and reading the Koran and stuff like that. Even though my mum was born in this country she still prays five times a day but she doesn't cover her hair. She doesn't wear a scarf or anything. I'm not religious at all. I do follow my religion but I don't pray as often as they do.

I would like to go to university and get a nice job and have a family, but sometimes you find if you get married to someone, like an arranged marriage, they wouldn't want you to work. They would want you to stay at home and look after their parents. You have to go to their family after you get married but I would like to work. I would like three children, two boys and one girl because if I have the boys before the girl they will control their sister and she won't go along the wrong track and become more westernised. Sisters are more scared of their brothers than they are of their dad. My brother is far stricter with me than my dad. He told me to cover my head when I am talking to a boy. If we are walking together he doesn't like me screaming or talking loud. He gets really angry and starts hitting me. My brother does it because he wants me to follow my religion, to be respected. I don't see it as control but rather care and respect. People talk a lot and news gets spread around everywhere. Every Muslim on the street will know.

Regarding marriage my dad told me that if I educate myself and get a good job that I can have my own choice, because at the end of the day I am going to be the one living with the person not them, but he has to be Muslim and Pakistani. Some Pakistani families allow you to marry another Muslim who is a Bengali Muslim or Gujarati Muslim or Arab but my family won't allow that. It used to be really strict and you had to marry someone in your own caste. It's not so strict now but they find it hard because the higher the caste the more strict whereas the lower castes are more wild. The lower castes would marry like Bengalis, but not the higher castes, they want the respect still there. The respect comes more from our culture (rather) than religion. Our culture sometimes takes over. The culture is all about castes.

I have a friend who about two years ago would have been forced into a marriage if she hadn't spoken up but now she is happily married with that person, obviously a cousin and now she is saying she loves him a bit and as time goes on she is getting to know him. Their personalities do not clash. They get on and she is saying that if she were to stay with him a few more years I would probably be a much better Muslim than I am now because he is very strict on his religion but he doesn't say to her - you have to wear a scarf being my wife. He says to her 'if you want to be my wife that's fine and I would love to be your husband but I would prefer my wife to do certain things'. Now she said, 'I would want my husband to love me. He loves me anyway but if I want him to love me it would be better if I wear a scarf for him and myself and my religion.' She had a tough time for two years, but now she is happily married.

I had an Afghan friend who after school... when she turned 16, after a time... she had to get married even though she was really good in her education. She got really high marks, but she had to get married. For them it was like tradition. They are brought up to know they have to get married to who their parents say. So she married him and now she has a baby. She is only seventeen. She's happy but I think that is really out of order because she could make something of her life. Her husband, coming from back home...he has no experience of anything. She could work and earn so much money. But she has to sit at home and look after the baby.

I have a friend who is a boy and my brother knows, but he hasn't told my parents. I think he is okay with it and he wouldn't be violent towards me. If he found me somewhere with a guy - like holding hands and just walking with him, if my brother saw me, that's it - he would beat me up. I know he would. He would beat me up. That's the respect gone if my dad loses respect for me that's the end. He wouldn't trust me again. He wouldn't talk to me. I can only talk to boys if I'm in a group. I can't talk to a boy if I am on my own. You can be friends in college. That's a different story, but outside of college you can't count them as a friend and walk down the road with them. If a lad you are with in college walks up to you and asks you to lend him your notes that's okay.

I have three brothers who are terribly strict and I would be scared to do anything wrong, but still I have a best friend who is a boy. He lives a way up north. My sister knows about it. I talk to him on the phone. I have only ever seen him once. He's only ever come down once. Here our parents let us have a bit of freedom and they will let us go out but in Pakistan they won't let us girls go out. We have to stay at home. You can only go out with, say, your older brother. If I was back home I wouldn't be educated, I wouldn't be in college. You would just finish school and that would be it. If I were back home I would probably be preparing for my wedding.

When I get married I will go and live at his house with his parents. I will be doing what I normally do in my own house but for my second parent. We call them our mother and father-in-law but Islamically they are now our parents. It's not that we forget our family. They are still our family, but my mum and dad would say to me: 'Don't think of us as your proper parents - all of you must go to them. You have to start impressing them in that family.' If something went wrong in our marriage I could still go back to my parents and say 'mum or dad, this is what is going on. What can I do?' or 'Can I come and live with you for a time, until he picks himself up' They can talk to the parents and say 'obviously this man has always been bad but you obviously don't know about it. But we care about our daughter and we don't want her to get into that kind of life where she is totally disgusted with your family. We still want them to live together. If they still want them to live together and still be seen as a married couple with the children and happy, then you will need to do something about your son. But if you don't stop him and he doesn't care about the marriage then we will take her back and you will lose the children, your grandchildren and you are losing (your) daughter-in-law.' One of them, the man or woman, has to say 'divorce' three times and then that's it. The Islamic marriage is over. You don't have to sign a paper or anything. It's just over.

Even if the family has a few sons all the wives go to live there. You would start treating your husband's brothers as your brothers. They would all live close together, maybe buying the house next door where you perhaps all go for dinner. Sometimes the man you are going to marry already has his house. Your parents and your in-laws are happy with you going and moving out.

****

8.8. Usman

My name is Usman. I was born in Pakistan. I have been in the UK four, nearly five years. I came to the UK before my first birthday and started primary school here. We went back to Pakistan when I was five and stayed eleven years. Aged sixteen I came back to England to start college. I have experienced both cultures, but I would prefer to live here. It depends on the lifestyle - if you have a good business, a good way of life then you can live in Pakistan or anywhere else but these days the condition of the world is changing. In Pakistan most of the people know what is going on there. I prefer to live here.

I have just one older brother. I live with my mum here. My dad lives in Pakistan taking care of my grandmother.

My future plans are to be an architect and to do designing as well. Also when I finish the course I might go to work because I don't believe in going to universities these days. I have heard rumours. I know someone who went to Uni who is still looking for a job while another who went to the same college got a better job. I think it is all about your own abilities, basically.

I'm not thinking about marriage at present. Twenty-four or twenty-five is my target. I am twenty-one now. Because of my background I will leave the choice of my wife to my parents. However my parents have told me that if you find anyone you like, tell us and we will talk about it. At present I am not looking. These days I want to improve my skills and perhaps open my own business. I want to stand on my own feet. I will be concentrating on getting a good job. I don't want to have to depend on anyone. I want to be able to do for myself.

The boy's family has to give to the wife a certain amount of money, but some of the Indian cultures will say that you have to give all the money to pay for the furniture, television etc. to the girl's family but I don't think this is right. It is not according to Islam. I only want one wife. It would be very hard to have two or three as you have to give equal time to each of them. We are allowed to have four at a time providing you give her equal rights, equal opportunities.

I think I am probably as religious as my parents. They are quite religious. I think it is possible to solve the problem between Palestine and Israel. I think they should have equal rights. Instead of blaming each other they need to look at the main source of the fighting. You have to look at the fight from both sides, to see who is telling the truth.

Some of the time I am happy with what the media says about Muslims and sometimes I am not. I have been at this college for more than four years and we tried to get a prayer room for people who want and need to pray and this college is saying 'we are a secular institution and we are not allowed a permanent prayer room for one single faith but we can't see why we can't have a multi-faith room. After all Newham Borough is a multicultural society and this college is multi cultural. We are allowed to use a room for prayer but we have to wait for Sabi to let us in and sometimes we are running late and our classes have started.

Most religious people still prefer to wear the veil. Many females still wear veils because according to them all the beauty of the person should be seen in the face. My mum doesn't wear a veil.

I see myself as a Muslim. My faith comes first and then I should have a nationality. I am a Muslim British.

****

8.9. Imran

My name is Imran. I was born here and my parents were from Bangladesh. I'm second to last with 3 brothers and 2 sisters. The oldest brother and sister are married and live in another part of London. My sister has a boy and a girl. They both had 'love marriages'. I'm expecting a love marriage. I haven't a girlfriend at present. I am not really bothered whether she comes from Bangladesh. I will marry whoever I fall in love with. My parents won't really mind who I marry as long as it is the right person. The person may have to be a Muslim, I'm not sure. Either my mum or dad will be on my side. One will feel more strongly that I must marry a Muslim. I would like two or three children, maybe four, two of each, 2 boys and 2 girls. I only want one wife. More than one would be 'too much hassle'.

Considering I was born here I could say I am British. I think of myself as British. I feel British. I grew up in south London and had more English friends than Asian and Black. When I moved here I discovered this area is more mixed. I like everything in Great Britain. There's nothing really to hate. Well, it's changed now people are drinking at 8 or 12, at 13 and 14 and getting pregnant and stuff. When I was 12, 13, 14 it wasn't like that. It was different. I am 21 now. I still have British, English friends who are not Muslim. I have no problem with my friends going to pubs for a drink. I wouldn't obviously drink, but I'd have an orange or lemonade. To be honest, my friends don't really go to the pub. They are always playing football or going out to the cinema or whatever.

I think my parents probably made the right decision to come here. You get a better education in Britain and more opportunities. I rarely go to Bangladesh. My plans for the future are to go to university and get a degree in business and law and see what happens in the future.

****

8.10. Jabz

My name is Jabz. I was born in this country but my ethnic background is Bangladeshi. My parents came to the UK after they married. I have three brothers and two sisters. They are all older than me. I am eighteen and the youngest. My oldest brother is married. It was an arranged marriage. I'm not sure if I will have an arranged marriage. I think my parents would prefer to arrange it but I really don't mind. You can't predict the future so I am not sure whether my future family will be big or small.

I hope to do something in corporate management. I have one more year to go before I will go to university. I would like to go to Greenwich University.

Regarding marriage - one wife would be enough. As my wife gets older she would probably wear a *hijab*. It's up to her really, isn't it? My mum wears a headscarf.

I'm not as religious as my parents. My parents pray five times a day but I don't because I am at college.

I don't go into pubs at all. Some of my mates might go in to play pool but I don't go there. It is not my thing. I have got quite a few friends who are not Muslim. We just mess around, hang around and chat. We also play football.

I can't see any possibility of the conflict being solved between Israel and Palestine because there are enough people willing to die for it. They have killed so many people now. The Israelis have gone too far. Loads of people died in that area. Palestinians will remember. I think 9/11 was wrong because that has given us a bad name. People look at Asians and say they are probably terrorists. But it's not right. The

British media tend to be biased. They don't present Muslims correctly all the time.

In Bangladesh, on the wedding day, the parents of the groom pay some money to the parents of the bride. The same thing happens when we get married here. There are negotiations about amount and the money goes to the bride. When my oldest brother got married the same thing happened. He had to pay up. If they split up she keeps the money and there is some kind of arrangement where the man has to give her more money or something like that. He has to give her an extra payment.

****

8.11. Waheeda

My name is Waheeda. I was born here. My family came from Bangladesh. They married there. I have two brothers and two sisters. There are five of us all together. I am 20 years old and the youngest. Two sisters and one brother are married. My parents' marriage was arranged but at this time our parents do allow us to have love marriages. But they do kind of arrange it so it is a mixture of arranged and love. They would want me to marry a Muslim, definitely and myself I would rather marry a Muslim as well. If I did want to marry someone who wasn't a Muslim my parents wouldn't be very happy with it.

I have come across others who have married someone who wasn't a Muslim and some parents cut the relationship, but then others forgave the child. I haven't met anyone where the husband was brought from Bangladesh although it did happen with my sister. My parents showed her a few guys that were from the same country but she didn't quite like them. But they were okay with it. It was her decision.

My parents are obviously more religious than me. I'm not that religious but I do pray sometimes. My mother wears a headscarf. I don't although when we are praying we do sometimes and if we go to funerals, stuff like that. No one in my family wears the *niqab*, but I have relatives that do wear it. I think it is more connected with religion than culture.

I wouldn't want my husband to have any other wives. I would like to have four children. I am studying health and social care and still

197

have two years here. After that I will probably get a job. I think of myself as British Bangladeshi.

My parents are okay with me having boy mates as long as I don't go too far. They will tell me to keep it at friendship. They know I am at a mixed college, so they know there are boys around. However if I wanted just to go out with a boy for a lunch, they wouldn't allow it.

Girls do go swimming but it has to be females only if you do go swimming. If there are any males around girls are not allowed. We do go to the beach but Islam says where there are males, women should be covered. They shouldn't show their beauty. That's temptation, so we wouldn't be allowed to go in the water and that if there are males around.

****

8.12. Manna

My name is Manna. I am nineteen now. I will be twenty in April. I was born in Bangladesh and I came here when I was seven months old. I came here in December 1990. We came for family reasons. I had a heart problem and the doctors said: 'if you go to the UK it will help her health,' and it did. We made our family here - me, my mum and my grandma, my dad. At first we lived in a hotel then we rented a house and then a flat. That's how much I can remember. Then at the age of two we got our first proper house. Now there are three of us - me and my two brothers. I am the eldest.

I went back at the age of seven. Whereas I hadn't any memory of when I was young I found out how much I missed my own country. I have been back three times. The last time I was there was five years ago.

I am studying child care. My passion when I was six was I wanted to be a doctor. My dad asked me aged eleven - 'What do you want to be?' I answered 'A Doctor' He replied …..'You want to be a doctor!' it was a shock to him. I replied 'Okay, what is wrong with being a doctor?' When I was in year seven and eight my options changed. I had to look after my two brothers while my mum was away. Later I had to look after my nephews and that's how I became interested in child care. Now I am enjoying every minute of it. It's hard work, but it's worth it.

My one dream is that by the time I am thirty I will have travelled the world. It's the only dream I have got left. I am getting married in two years time. It is an arranged marriage. He is my cousin. We get along with each other. He's okay. I don't really believe in this 'love' relationship and all that. It's too complicated. He is in England. He came to England two years ago. He wants to travel too. He is twenty-five now. Age difference doesn't really matter.

I told my parents when I was sixteen 'if you are going to get me married I will do it when it is right for me.' So now I think when I am twenty-four or twenty-five will be right for me. I feel as if I am still fifteen. I am not ready, I am not a woman yet. I haven't the understanding yet. I am still like a teenager wondering about this and that. I do understand certain things but for me it is going to take time to understand a bit more. But I don't want to rush it either but another few years and it will be right. If I am going to get a family I want to be twenty-four or twenty-five.

My brothers are thirteen and fifteen. They were born here and they love England more than Bangladesh because they were born here. If you were born in a country you love that country. They don't understand their mother tongue or how it feels to be Bangladeshi. If you ask them if they would like to go to Bangladesh they say: 'I don't want to go.' They say they don't know anyone there. They have met them. They know who they are. They are their own family. There own flesh and blood.

I came here last year doing level one. People looked at me and said 'Are you from Pakistan?' '...from India?' I said 'No, I'm from Bangladesh.' They reply 'You don't look like Bangladesh. Are you from Iran?'

[she became agitated]

'How can people judge you just because of your skin colour? It's so annoying, ridiculous.' My dad is white and my mum is brown. That's the only colour I see. That is why I am fair.

My parents are more religious than me. I don't understand religion as much as they do. At the moment I am trying to understand it by reading books. I went to Saudi Arabia once, two years ago. I haven't done the haj yet. When I went there I felt different. Now I know my Muslim identity in life. I'm a Muslim but not a pure Muslim. Pure Muslim like Sufi worship every part of the day. I pray when I feel like praying. I pray if I have to pray. At home I get bossed around 'Go and pray… go and pray.' If I feel like it I will go and pray. I believe in one God. Prayer sometimes works, sometimes it doesn't work. The Koran I read every day and understand it, but there are certain things I question and I get the answers from praying to God.

I have chosen how I dress. I went to a Madrasah, Islamic school. I was required to wear the prescribed *hijab*. It was okay. It was part of the school uniform. At age twelve I got more understanding of my religion and was covering my hair, praying and all that. Wearing a scarf has always been up to me. I wasn't forced into it. If it's your culture go along with your culture. Okay I understand you are in Britain. You are young and you grew up as a London or Essex girl whatever. Be modest. A guy doesn't just look at you because you are pretty or ugly. A guy looks at you because you are a girl.

****

8.13. Rabiah

My name is Rabiah and I am 25 years old. I work in a primary school. I was born in Bangladesh. I came to this country in 1997 with my family - three sisters and my dad. My mum came here in 1995. My eldest sister is married and she has got a son. I'm the second one in the family and I have got three younger sisters, one studying in University and another one at 6th form college doing her 'A' levels at the moment.

My sister had an arranged marriage. It was organised within the community. It comes through your family and friends. You come to meet each other and that is how it is arranged. Usually the preference is for the couple to come from the same community. It depends on the individual whether the person goes home and marries someone from back there or if they marry someone from here. My sister got married here to a man who was already here. As for myself I don't see myself as going home and getting married. My parents and I am looking at the moment for someone. My home is quite different, to be honest and we are allowed to find someone for ourselves. Obviously he has to be a Bangladeshi Muslim. For me, even if my parents arrange it I am allowed to meet the person and make my own mind up. I hope to meet someone through friends who know friends within my social group. If I was to fall for someone who wasn't a Muslim I don't think my parents would be very happy about it. If I met a married Muslim who wanted a second wife - I wouldn't go for that. If I was married and my husband wanted a second wife I would file for a divorce. I can't accept that. For me it is not right. Some women might be able to accept that but I think it is a personal thing. I don't think any woman would like her husband to be married twice. I don't think it has anything to do with society or being Westernised. If you are forced into something you have to accept it or how are you going to go around it? Do you have the independence to get around it and what happens next? It's up to individuals really and how they cope with it. I suppose it helps here because women are more independent. They know their rights and they are more open about it. They grow into their religion as well whereas back home they are not educated. Back home, poverty definitely has an influence. If you are a young widow and you have nowhere else to go.

I would like a small family about two children. I don't mind if they are boys or girls. Children are a blessing from God.

I see the *hijab* as a religious thing. I see myself as dressing modestly but that wouldn't mean I would necessarily wear a *niqab*. You are only asked to dress modestly. I would like later on to maybe wear a *jilbab* but I have to come to that, be ready to do that. There would be no pressure from my family. My mum wears a *hijab*. My sisters and I just wear a *hijab*, the headscarf we don't wear the *jilbab*. I can't see myself ever covering my face up with a *niqab*. It's just a personal preference. I just can't do that. I'd wear a headscarf and *jilbab*.

Regarding the practice of my faith I think my parents' practice and my own are very similar. My dad is more into religion than I am. Obviously I am building up on it as I get older. I am going more into religion, I suppose and that's the aim. Nobody is perfect.

My life would be very different if I was living in Bangladesh. The culture there is different and people see things in different ways. For me I have my cultural background and my religious background and I am Westernised. I have got the three in one. I think I'm quite independent as well whereas if I were at home (in Bangladesh) I probably wouldn't be with women's rights and stuff.

I feel I'm Westernised because I'm allowed to work and to study , I'm allowed to wear a *jilbad* if I want to, but I want my independence, I still want to work and then obviously I still do my religious duties as well. In the end the way I dress is different. I think my thinking is quite open. I am more open minded. If I was back home I would never think like that. For me, I would be happy to marry any Muslim person. He doesn't have to be Bangladeshi. He could come from another country as long as he was Muslim whereas if I were back home I would never be thinking of that. He would definitely be Bangladeshi. My parents would prefer if he were Bangladeshi, but my time and their times are changing now. It's the 21st century isn't it, everybody changes. Religious tradition is not against it. It's rather a cultural thing where parents would say 'I want a Bengali man for you' because you are in the same boat, aren't you, regarding culture. But religiously I can marry anybody, from any other country as long as they are Muslim. So my parents would come around anyway as long as they are Muslim. At the end of the day that is what matters. My way of thinking is if I married someone from Bengal, his way of thinking would be different. So I want to marry someone from here because I would get on better with him. Because he was brought up here as well, his way of thinking would be similar to mine. He would be more open about things.

To me I practise my own faith and I don't see any problem with working in a catholic school. It's up to individuals how you feel about it.

8.14. Conclusion

Analysing the interviews of the Muslim students in this chapter it is crucial to stress that the students appeared very open and glad to share their stories. They were chosen randomly, if they happened to be available, and in the area, at the time we were interviewing. We asked them to talk firstly about themselves and their family, going on to encourage them to talk, with a few questions related to our research - questionnaires and short interviews. We tried not to interrupt them when they started to speak and generally only had one student at a time. We wanted to find out how the students' points of view towards culture, values and traditions differed from that of their parents and Western society. That means where they stand between these two cultures. Do they lean towards one rather than the other, or do they swing between the two?

We interviewed thirteen students, nine girls and four boys. They were all Asian Muslims whose parents were born either in Pakistan, Bangladesh or India. Nine of the students were born in the UK. However two came to England as babies and two came as teenagers.

Regarding the desire to complete their education, to get a job or to go on to further education we could find no difference between the male and female students, in spite of the fact that in their parents' country of origin, many of the females would have expected to be married by their age. What is very important is the fact that they all stated that their parents valued the need for education. One of them (Isma) put it in this way:

> (Dad) says to us: 'No matter what, you need education in life otherwise there isn't a bright future.' That's my dad's motto – 'No education – no future' My dad's really strict about education. He wouldn't let me get married without finishing my education. Even if I wanted to he wouldn't let me.

The interviewed students were very conscious of the difference between their life in the UK and the life possible in the country of their parents. Many had visited and none of them wanted to live there. The gap in the standard of living shocked them. Sana told us:

> My parents made a good decision to come to England because in my country there are not a lot of facilities to educate yourself. It's difficult and people who do educate themselves deal with a lot of problems. There's a lot of poverty so that makes it very difficult for them to have a good future. They can only do farm work in the villages to just feed themselves. There's maybe not enough money to educate oneself which could lead to a not really good future and then it passes down, doesn't it from generation to generation which makes it really difficult. My parents have come to this country. We get a good future and tomorrow our children will get a good future. As well as bringing us up and giving us what we need they are supporting other children by sending donations home.

Isma agreed:

> My parents' decision to come to England was good. Sometimes I have an argument with my mum when I ask my parents for something expensive and my mum hasn't the money to buy it. She will say to me: 'If my parents didn't bring me to this country then you wouldn't be where you are now. You would be living in a house made of hay or straw and you wouldn't have the clothes you are wearing now. You should be grateful. (…)' Some of my relatives are in Bangladesh. My dad's family is still over there and because he is

working he sends money and so they are living somewhat similar to us. They can get doctors when they want to and they can go to school and college. They've got education. Whereas there are some people there who haven't got anything so it makes me appreciate more.

Imran said:

> I think my parents probably made the right decision to come here. You get a better education in Britain and more opportunities. I rarely go to Bangladesh. My plans for the future are to go to university and get a degree in business and law and see what happens in the future.

We can conclude that these young immigrants from Muslim countries, males and females, have the possibility of being well integrated with the rest of society on the socio-economic level. The results of these interviews corresponded to the results from the questionnaires and the short interviews, giving the students a very strong base for a promising future in the UK.

Regarding the cultural integration of these young students the situation is more complex. We can be optimistic that the majority of the students felt they were British, even though some of them also referred to their religion (Muslim British), or referred to their country of origin, for example British Pakistani, British Bangladeshi. We had the impression that they treated the UK as their own country, even when they were not happy with the way the British media presented Muslims. Sultana stated:

> You tell the media the truth and the media twist your words. You hear different things especially when it comes to race and that.... they say terrorists that ...not everyone's a terrorist. We are not all like that, you need to understand that. I am not a terrorist nor is she. I am a Muslim but what my Muslim brothers and sisters did or whoever did it. It is not right. It is wrong. It is not right for people to look down on you just because you are a Muslim, just because you wear a headscarf. I think that is totally wrong. We are not blowing up buses, blowing up trains. We are Muslims, yes, but we are not terrorists going around bombing.

A second generation immigrant expressed very well, the feeling of belonging to the UK, in the following text. Manna stated:

> My brothers are thirteen and fifteen. They were born here and they love England more than Bangladesh because they were born here. If you were born in a country you love that country. They don't understand their mother tongue or how it feels to be Bangladeshi. If you ask them if they would like to go to Bangladesh they say 'I don't want to go.' They say they don't know anyone there.

The interviews in this chapter have elements that do not always lead to optimistic conclusions. Some issues clearly showed that there is a significant gap between Western society and Muslims regarding the position of women in Muslim society and cultural expectations. In European society there is a strong emphasis on the equality of the sexes with an individualistic approach. Islamic society is very patriarchal with a paternalistic approach. We can see it in Maya's and Moonisah's descriptions:

> In Islam girls are very, very precious like diamonds so if anything was to happen to the girl like, say for example the girl was seen doing the wrong thing it would be a real big issue. But if boys were to do it, obviously it would be big but not so much as for a girl because it is the girl that families respect. The boy is taking the girl home. The husband is given money when he marries his bride but the money/jewels really belong to the girl. If she gets a divorce at the end the money comes back to her family (Maya).

> I would like three children, two boys and one girl because if I have the boys before the girl they will control their sister and she won't go along the wrong track and become more Westernised. Sisters are more scared of their brothers than they are of their dad (Moonisah).

This approach has a strong influence on the relationship between the two sexes in Islam. In Muslim countries girls usually are educated separately from boys. In Newham College young people are together, and as we heard parents tolerate it, they even allow a very limited friendship between their daughters and boys from College, for example sharing notes from a lecture.

The relationship between parents and children in the Muslim community is different from the general UK society. Parents expect their children to be respectful, even submissive. This can be observed in the tradition of arranged marriages. More than eighty percent of the Muslim students in our questionnaire survey and almost one hundred percent in the short and long interviews, accepted arranged marriage as the norm. Muslim children usually respect their parents' choices of marriage partners. In Muslim culture individuals and families have high regard for the opinion of their community and their standing in the community. Consequently family honour is very important and influences the way one lives one's day to day life.

Arranged marriage is a matter involving parents taking the initiative to find a husband or wife for their child, but this is not a 'love marriage'. A 'love marriage' is something essential and indispensable in contemporary European culture. Arranged marriages in the immigrant's culture, are logical when we remember that the boys and girls are kept separate once they reach puberty. Therefore how can young people find a husband or wife when they are not allowed to meet with potential candidates?

Many people in UK society see the specific dress, in particular the *niqab* or *burka*, of Muslim women as a sign of submissiveness to their patriarchal culture. However the young women concerned see the covering as firstly a religious duty. Secondly, they cover themselves because they believe the only person who should look at them is their husband. Their form of dress automatically separates them from Western society. From the interviews it is possible to get a clear idea about the conflict which is going on in the heart of young girls between their need to express themselves as individuals in how they dress and the expectation of their family and community to follow tradition and rules. Isma told us:

> Many people have a totally wrong view of what Muslim dress is or what it stands for or what it should be worn for. Fashion is such a big part of life these days. Everyone cares about fashion and some girls do wear the *hijab*, headscarf or the *burka* not because it is a religious item to them but because it is a fashion item. You should keep yourself covered so that no one can look at you or judge you. When you walk down the street no man is able to say 'that girl is quite nice.' It should keep you covered whereas some girls do wear the *burka* or a headscarf but in a fancy way and they wear bright colours whereas it should not attract attention.

However it is clear that the majority of students treat Muslim dress as a religious obligation, something like giving the testimony of God's presence in the world. Conversely, some of them find it very difficult to follow that obligation. They talk about wearing the *hijab* when they consider themselves to be a 'better' Muslim. This applies even to the *niqab* or *burka*. Isma went on to tell us:

> I should be praying five times a day and I should have a headscarf on my head but I don't. I know every day I am doing a sin. I shouldn't show my hands and I shouldn't be wearing tight trousers but I do it and obviously I accept the fact that one day I will be judged on it and what I am doing is wrong, I believe it is wrong. (…) When I'm old I will probably wear a *burka*, maybe when/if I am a grandmother. It would be my duty to be covered, to have my head covered at all times, to do my five daily prayers. If I have children and grandchildren I have to set a good example to them. They say the older you get the wiser you are. I will get to a stage in my life when I will wear a *hijab*.

Regarding the *burka/niqab*, it has become the subject of much political debate in Europe due to women's rights and for security reasons. The majority of the students, both male and female, were not in favour of it. They expressed the opinion that it is not a moral obligation and depends on an individual's decision. Abdul declared:

> It would be my wife's free choice what she wears. I would prefer if she was covered a bit but not the whole face. She can go out without the scarf. It would be her choice as long as she doesn't go too far. I would give her a choice.

Sana gave her opinion:

> Covering your face and everything is not compulsory. When we go to do pilgrimage in Saudi Arabia the women do not cover their face. We are all equal, all one. That's the thing about it, it's not compulsory. There are men and women there from all different cultures and backgrounds but they are all one religion. Going to the pilgrimage you are all one. Everybody is equal but you are all doing the same activity and everything. You are all treated equally. You can't say to someone you are from this background so why are you here? Because you all have the same belief. It doesn't matter where you come from or where you were born. I haven't been on

pilgrimage yet but my mum has. I'd love to go. I don't have an issue about covering myself.

Our research showed that at least in the case of educated young Muslims polygamy is unlikely to become a problem in Europe. We met very few students who would consider a polygamous marriage. One student, a girl, said that she would agree to her husband choosing another wife if she was sick or had problems with fertility. We met a lad who was thinking of polygamy because he wanted to have many children. The majority thought that even though their religion allows for it, it is not practical. As Sana explained:

> If you are going to have more than one wife you have to treat her equally. All the wives must have the same facilities. If you look at it it's not really easy. It's very, very difficult. I mean if you are going to give one, I don't know.... £10,000 ....you have to give the other three the same, can that be done? I wouldn't want my husband to have another wife. To be honest I have a sister and I don't share my things at all. I'm the oldest girl and I'm spoilt rotten but I wouldn't share my husband.

Maya told us:

> If my husband wanted more than one wife it would be pretty tricky….. obviously I would want everything for my husband to be happy but then it will just not be the same for me, like my husband is not mine then. He is someone else's so for me it's more of a no, that's basically it. I don't think I would be able to do that.

Looking at the above interviews it is possible to conclude that in some areas of the UK society's culture and the culture of young immigrants there are no significant differences. However in other areas there are considerable differences. The existence of these differences does not mean that integration cannot take place. The UK has come very far from the time when it was attempting to assimilate all immigrants from different cultures. European culture has its strengths but also its weaknesses - like secularisation, extreme individualism, the undermining of family life, the questioning of the sacredness of human life, individuals putting themselves before the happiness of even their own children (cohabitation, divorces). Immigrants bring with them values we had as a nation and have lost. Their presence can enrich our society and bring healthy nourishment to present day Europe. Nonetheless Europe has come a long way in how it sees itself as a democratic, fair, tolerant society with equal rights for men and women. We need to beware of the parts of immigrant's culture that can and might deny what we hold as essential.

Even today, in the 21st century, the majority of the young immigrants told us that they did not even think about the possibility of marrying somebody outside their own ethnic group. All of them were sure that it would be impossible and at least extremely difficult to marry a non-Muslim. It would be the end of their relationship with their family. This, surely, is a sign that being in Europe they will be in some sense always a separate group, similar to the Jewish people who remained as a distinct community throughout many centuries in Europe. These predictions are supported by the fact that the Muslims are a very religious community living in a secular society. There are significant differences which would not be easy to overcome.

On the other hand, it was possible to see in the students' views some signs of changing and creating of new values, in a sense a new culture - a balancing between the culture of their parents and Western culture. Rabiah explained:

> My life would be very different if I was living in Bangladesh. The culture there is different and people see things in different ways. For me I have my cultural background and my religious background and I am westernised. I have got the three in one. I think I'm quite independent as well. Whereas if I were at home I probably wouldn't be with women's rights and stuff. I feel I'm westernised because I'm allowed to work and to study, I'm allowed to wear a *jilbad* if I want to but I want my independence, I still want to work and then obviously I still do my religious duties as well. In the end the way I dress is different. I think my thinking is quite open. I am more open minded. If I was back home I would never think like that. For me, I would be happy to marry any Muslim person. He doesn't have to be Bangledeshi. He could come from another country as long as he was Muslim whereas if I were back home I would never be thinking of that. He would definitely be Bangladeshi.

It is clear that this generation of immigrants is moving between two cultures and obviously they find themselves in a difficult position.

However it could be seen as a great opportunity for them to build together with others in their generation something new, a combination of what is good in each culture which would comprise a combination of western modernisation with their pro family/community and religious culture. Will they take advantage of the unique chance they have been given?

Regarding the difficulties that the young immigrants experience it is worthy to reflect with Mondal in his book *Young Muslim British Voices*:

> Being a Muslim in Britain is not a matter of choosing one over the other; instead, it involves a profound negotiation of the different sets of ideas and values that swirl around them in their everyday lives. To put it another way, their journeys into and through Islam, how it shapes and affects their day-to-day existence, and what Islam actually means to them, are all part of an effort to reconcile both 'sameness' and 'difference' (2008:29).

This indicates that the 'pendulum culture' we portray here puts an enormous burden on the young people concerned – and their families - to find the right balance and appropriate methods to combine being Muslim with living in a European environment. The frequent references to young men going to the pub with their friends, but not touching alcohol, indicate one of these critical issues. Some other interviewees, it would appear, did not even find it acceptable to go to a pub with their friends, thus swinging more in the direction of self-conscious adherence to Islamic values. At the end of the day, this indicates that the young people concerned have to do a lot of work for themselves, on themselves, and often by themselves, to find the right path. Seen from this perspective, the challenge of being a Muslim in the West is another form of *ijtihad*, an interpretative process, which can very well be compared to the image of the pendulum.

BIBLIOGRAPHY

Abbas, T. (2005) *British South Asian Muslims: before and after September 11*, ed. T. Abbas, *Muslim Britain, communities under pressure*, Books, London.

Abdelhadi, M. (2006) *What Islam says on religious freedom*, BBC Arab affairs analyst. http://news.bbc.co.uk/1/hi/world/south_asia/4850080.stm.

Abdul-Khalid, A. R. (1997) *Marriage in Islam. The Daar of Islamic Heritage*, Florida.

Ahmed, M. (2008) *Islam, State, and Society in Bangladesh.* eds. J. Esposito, J. Voll, O. Bakar, *Asian Islam in the 21st Century*, Oxford University Press.

Ahmad, F. (2009) *Muslim Women and Higher Education Experiences in the UK*, eds. F. N. Seggie, R.O. Mabokela, *Islam and Higher Education in Transitional Societies*, Sense Publishers, Rotterdam/Taipei.

Ali, A. H. (2007) *Infidel*, Free Press, London.

Alibhai–Brown, Y. (2005) *Revealed: the Brutal truth that hides inside the Burka*, Evening Standard Newspaper, 30.11.2005.

Allam, K.F. (2004) *Koranic Law Does not impose the Headscarf*, La Repubblica, 22.01.2004, http://www.jihadwatch.org/2004/02/the-headscarf-is-just-the-tip-of-the-iceberg.html.

AlSayyad, N. (2002) *Muslim Europe or Euro-Islam: On the Discourses of Identity and Culture*, eds. N. AlSayyad, M. Castells, *Muslim Europe or Europe-Islam. Politics, Culture, and Citizenship in the Age of Globalization*, Lexigton Books, Lanham Boulder, New York, Oxford.

Altorki, S. (1986) *Women in Audi Arabia. Ideology and Behavior among the Elite*, Columbia University Press, New York.

Amara, F. (2007) *Malzenstwa z przymusu. Mity i prawda z terenu*, ed.Ch. Ockrent, *Czarna ksiega kobiet*, Wydawnictwo Boy-Zelenski, Warszawa.

Arab Charter on Human Rights, Council of the League of Arab States, Cairo, adopted on September 15, 1994, http://www.humanrights.harvard.edu/.

The Arab Human Development Report 2005. Towards the Rise of Women in the Arab World, UNDP Regional Bureau for Arab States, New York 2006.

Armstrong, K. (1991) *Muhammad*, Phoenix Press.

Balicki, J., Wells, A. (2006) *Asylum Seekers' Policy v Integration Policy*, Trafford Publishing, Oxford, UK.

Balicki, J. (2010) *Imigranci z krajow muzulmanskich. Wyzwania dla polityki integracyjnej*, Wyd.UKSW, Warszawa.

Bawden, A. (2009) *Interview - Jasvinder Sanghera, director of Karma Nirvana*, The Guardian, http://www.guardian.co.uk/society/2009/jan/14/crime-victims-karma-nirvana 14.01.2009.

BBC (1998) *Female genital mutilation*, http://news.bbc.co.uk/2/hi/health/medical_notes/241221.stm, 23.12.1998.

The Pendulum Culture?

BBC (2003) *Gloucester Voices: Our Untold Stories - Asian Stories*
http://www.bbc.co.uk/gloucestershire/untold_stories/asian/umara.shtml.

BBC (2006a) *The Islamic veil across Europe,*
http://news. bbc.co.uk/1/hi/world/europe/5414098.stm, 17.11.2006.

BBC (2006b) *School sacks woman after veil row,*
http://news. bbc. co. uk/1/hi/england/bradford/6179842.stm, 24.11.2006.

BBC (2006c) *In quotes: Jack Straw on the veil,*
http://news.bbc.co.uk/1/hi/uk_politics/5413470.stm, 06.10.2006.

BBC (2007) *Education Q & A: Muslim Schools,*
http://news.bbc.co.uk/2/hi/uk_news/education/6338219.stm.

BBC (2007b) *Schools allowed to ban face veils,*
http://news. bbc. co. uk/1/hi/education/6466221.stm, 20.03.2007.

BBC(2007c) *BA drops ban on wearing crosses,*
http://news.bbc.co.uk/1/hi/6280311.stm,19.01.2007.

Bennett, C. (2004) *Why should we defend the Veil?* The Guardian, 22.01.2004.

Bowen, J. R. (2007) *Why the French don't like Headscarves Islam, the State and Public Space,*
Princetown University Press, Oxford.

Bowlby, S., Lloyd-Evans, S. (2009) *'You seem very Westernised to me' Place, Identity and Othering of
Muslim workers in the UK labour market,* eds. P. Hopkins, R. Gale, *Muslims in Britain – Race Place
and Identities,* Edinburgh University Press.

Brown, G. (2009) A transcript of a speech on immigration given by the Prime Minister
in Ealing, West London, on 12 November 2009.

Casciani, C. (2009) *Forced marriage plea to schools.* BBC News
http://news.bbc.co.uk/go/pr/fr/-/1/hi/uk/8129466.stm, 02.07.2009.

Cassidy, S. (2010) *Fewer people marrying than any time for a century,* Independent Newspaper,
http://www.independent.co.uk/news/uk/this-britain/fewer-people-marrying-than-any-
time-for-a-century-1896314.html, 11.02.2010.

Cherribi, O. (2003) *The Growing Islamization of Europe,* ed. J. Esposito, F. Burgat,
Modernizing Islam. Religion in the Public Sphere in Europe and the Middle East, Bookcraft Ltd,
Stroud, Gloucestershire.

Crabtree, V. (2007) *Religion in the United Kingdom: Diversity Trends and Decline,*
www.vexen.co.uk/UK/religion.htm, 05.07.2007.

Council of Europe Resolution 1468 (2005): *Forced marriages and child marriages,*
www. unhcr. org/refworld/category, 43f5d5184, 0. html.

Council of Europe (2009) *The urgent need to combat so-called 'honour crimes',* Report
Committee on Equal Opportunities for Women and Men, Council of Europe,
08.06.2009.

Dirie, W. (1998) *Desert Flower* Virago Press, London.

Dirie, W. (2005) *Desert Children,* Virago Press, London.

Electoral Commission (2005) *Black and Minority Ethnic Survey,-Research Study Conducted for
the Electoral Commission,* www.electoralcommission.org.uk.

Bibliography

Entzinger, H., Biezeveld, R. (2003) European Commission Report *Benchmarking in Immigrant Integration*, Rotterdam.

Entzinger, H., Biezeveld R. (2009) UK Government Report *Benchmarking in Immigrant Integration*.

Esposito, J. L. (2010) *The Future of Islam*, Oxford University Press, Oxford.

EUMC (2006) *Muslims in the European Union. Discrimination and Islamophobia*, EUMC, eumc.europa.eu.

FOSIS (2005) *The Voice of Muslim Students* - The Muslim Student Survey, Federation of Islamic Student Studies, http://fosis.org.uk/resources/resource-pool/doc_details/12-fosis-muslim-student-survey-2005.

Forster, H. *African Patterns in the Afro-American family*, Journal of Black Studies (December 1983), http://www.scribd.com/doc/48851/African-Values-and-the-Human-Rights-Debate.

Ghiza, S. (2005) *What does Islam say about relationships?*, http://www.therevival.co.uk/what-does-islam-say-about-relationships-whats-wrong-with-having-boygirlfriends.

Giddens, A. (1991) *Modernity and Self-Identity. Self and Society in the Late Modern Age*, Cambridge.

Gilliat-Ray, S (2010) *Muslim in Britain. An Introduction*, Cambridge University Press, Cambridge.

GIS Project (2009) *Vision of Britain*, University of Portsmouth www.visionofbritain.org.uk/atlas/data-map.

Glasse, C. (2001) *The Concise Encyclopaedia of Islam*, Stacey International, London.

Goodwin, J. (1994) *Price of Honour; Muslim Women Life the Veil of Silence on Islamic World*, Little Brown, London.

Grillo, R. (2010) *British and Others, from 'race' to 'faith'*, eds. S. Vetovec, S. Wessendorf, The *Multiculturalism Backlash. European discourses, policies and practices*, Routledge. London and New York.

Grzymala-Kozlowska, A., (2008) *Integracja – proba rekonstrukcji pojecia*, eds. A. Grzymala-Kozlowska, S. Lodzinski, *Problemy integracji imigrantow. Koncepcje, badania, polityki*, WUW, Warszawa.

Guardian Press Association (2007) *Muslim pupil loses veil challenge*, 21.02.2007 www. guardian.co.uk/education/2007/feb/21/schools. uk.

Gupta, S. *The Concept of Divorce under Muslim Law*, http://www.legalserviceindia.com/article/l393-Divorce-under-Muslim-Law.html

Hai, J. (2008) *The Making of Mr Hai's Daughter*, London, Virago Press.

Hellyer, H. A. (2009) *Muslims of Europe the 'other' Europeans*, Edinburgh University Press.

Hennessy, P. *Burka ban ruled out by minister*, Sunday Telegraph, 18.07.2010.

Heritier, F. (2007) *Kobiety, nauka i rozwoj*, ed. Ch. Ockrent, *Czarna ksiega kobiet*, Wydawnictwo Boy-Zelenski, Warszawa.

Higher Ambitions Report (2009) *The future of universities in the knowledge economy*, Department of Business, Innovation and Skills.

Home Office Press Release (2006) *English Language Tests for those seeking to settle.*

Husain, E. (2007) *'The Islamist'*, Penguin Books, London.

Hussain, J. (2004) *Islam – Its law and society*, The Federation Press, Australia.

Ibrahim, O. H. (2008) *The Myth of the Islamic Headscarf*, Lightening Sources UK Ltd., Milton Keynes.

The Independent (*2008*), *A question of honour: Police say 17,000 women are victims every year*, http://www.independent.co.uk/news/uk/home-news/a-question-of-honour-police-say-17000-women-are-victims-every-year-780522.html. 10.02.2008.

Ipsos MORI (2006) http://www.ipsos-mori.com/researchpublications/researcharchive/poll.aspx?oItemId=315.

Israeli, R. (2009) *Muslim Minorities in Modern States. The challenge of assimilation*, Transaction Publishers, New Brunswick (USA) London (UK).

Jacobson, J. (1998) *Islam in Transition. Religion and identity among British Pakistani youth*, Routledge, London and New York.

Jannah, www.jannah.org/genderequity/equityappendix.html.

Jones, A. (2009) *British warning: Summer is forced marriage season*, Christian Science Monitor, 02.07.2009.

Kadivar, M. (2006) *Freedom of Religion and Belief in Islam*, ed. M. Kamrava, *The New Voices of Islam. Reforming Politics and Modernity – A Reader*, I.B. Tauris, New York.

Kerbaj, R. (2009) *Thousands of girls mutilated in Britain*, The Sunday Times, http://www.timesonline.co.uk/tol/life_and_style/health/article5913979.ece , 16.03.2009

Klausen, J. (2005) *The Islamic Challenge, politics and religion in Western Europe.* Oxford University Press.

Knights, S. (2007) *Freedom of Religion, Minorities, and the Law.* Oxford.

Mail on Sunday, *Burka-ban MP faces court threat from human rights group*, 25.07.2010. http://www.dailymail.co.uk/news/article-1297447/Burka-ban-MP-faces-court-threat-human-rights-group.html.

Maqsood, R.W. (1997) *The Value of the Veil* Q-News, October 1997.

McGolderick, D. (2006) *Human rights and Religion: The Islamic Headscarf Debate in Europe*, Hart Pub., Oxford.

McGhee, D. (2008) *The End of Multiculturalism? Terrorism, Integration and Human Rights.* Open University Press.

McVeigh, T. (2009) *Ending the silence on 'honour killing'* The Observer, http://www.guardian.co.uk/society/2009/oct/25/honour-killings-victims domestic violence, 25.10.2009.

Menski, W. (2008) *Ethnic minority legal studies: managing Cultural Diversity and Legal Pluralism*, London SOAS School of Law.

Bibliography

Gardner, D. (2010) *Now Syria bans the burka and niqab in universities as backlash against Muslim veil grows*, Mail Online, 20.07.2010.

Michalowska, G. (2008) *Problemy ochrony praw czlowieka w Afryce*, Wydawnictwo Naukowe Scholar, Warszawa.

Mondal, A. A. (2008) *Young British Muslim Voices*, Greenwood World Publishing Oxford/Westport, Connecticut.

Monshipouri, M. (2009) *Muslims in Global Politics. Identities, Interests and Human Rights*, Penn, University of Pennsylvania Press, Philadelphia.

Mumford, K. & Power, A. (2003) *East Enders - Family and Community in East London*, Pub. The Policy Press, London.

Muslim Council of Britain (2010) *Muslim Statistics*, http://www.mcb.org.uk/library/statistics.php.

National Curriculum, *Identity and Cultural Diversity*, UK Government http://curriculum.qcda.gov.uk/key-stages-3-and-4/cross-curriculum-dimensions/culturaldiversityidentity/index.aspx.

Nazir-Ali, M. *Times when a ban is right*, Sunday Telegraph, 18.07.2010.

Nazir, S. (2005) *Women's Rights in the Middle East and North Africa – Citizenship and Justice* eds. S. Nazir, L. Tomppert, Pub. Freedom House.

Nesrine, M, (2010) *Why must I cast off the veil?* Sunday Telegraph, 18.07.2010

Newham 2007 Key Statistics, http://www.newham.info/research/downloads/keystats.pdf

Newham College of FE *Ofsted Final Report*, June 2009, http://www.newham.ac.uk/pages/studentshomepage/thecollege.

OECD (2009) *Social Institutions & Gender Index* http://genderindex.org/country/zambia.

Office for National Statistics, *Cohabitation Assumptions*. www.statistics.gov.uk/downloads/theme_population/Marr-proj06/cohabitation.pdf.

Parekh, B. (2006) *Rethinking Multiculturalism*, Palgrave McMillan.

Peach, C. (2005) *Britain's Muslim Population: An Overview*, in *Muslim Britain, communities under Pressure*. ed. T. Abbas, Zed Books, London.

Prince, R. *Burka's can be empowering, says minister*, The Daily Telegraph 19.07.2010

Ramadan, T. (2001) *Islam, the West and the Challenges of Modernity*, Leicester: The Islamic Foundation.

Ramadan, T. (2002) *Europeanization of Islam or Islamization of Europe?* ed S. Hunter, *Islam, Europe's Second Religion. The New Social, Cultural, and Political Landscape*, Praeger, Westport, Con. London.

Ramadan, T. (2004) *Western Muslims and the future of Islam*, Oxford University Press, Oxford USA.

Ramadan, T. (2010) *What I believe*, Oxford University Press.

Reid, S. (2008) *It is one of the great taboos of multi-cultural Britain – and one of the most heart breaking: children born with cruel genetic defects because their parents are cousins*, Daily Mail, 16.02.2008.

Reynolds, J., Mansfield, P. (1999) *The effect of changing attitudes to marriage on its stability, in High Divorce Rates-The state of evidence on reasons and remedies,* volume 1, Papers 1-3- Research series No 2/99, Lord Chancellor's Department.

Roald, A. (2001) *Women in Islam, the Western Experience,* Routledge, London.

Rogers, S. (2010) *Divorce rates data: are married couples more likely to stay together?* http://www.guardian.co.uk/news/datablog/2010/jan/28/divorce-rates-marriage-ons.

Rosser-Owen, D. (1998) *The History of Islam in the British Isles: An Overview,* http://members.tripod.com/~british_muslims_assn/history_of_islam_in_the_bi.html.

Samers, M. (2010) *Migration.* Routledge, London.

Sanhera, J. (2009) *Daughters of Shame,* Hodder and Stoughton, London.

Sarkosy, N. (2009) *Nicolas Sarkozy says Islamic veils are not welcome in France,* www.theguardian,co.uk.

Shah, H. (2009)*The Imam's Daughter,* Ebury Publishing, Random House Group, London.

Shafaat, A. (2006*) Islamic Perspectives: The Punishment of Apostasy in Islam http://www.islamicperspectives.com/Apostasy1.htm.*

Slack, J. (2008) *Muslim husbands with more than one wife to get extra benefits as ministers recognise polygamy,* Mail Online 04.02.2008.

Souad, (2008) *Spalona zywcem,* Swiat Ksiazki, Warszawa.

Stobart, E. (2009) *Forced Marriage Guidelines,* UK HM Government, London.

Syed, S. *Unesco says 6. 5 million children out of school: Illiteracy on rise in Pakistan,* www. dawn. com/ 2006/12/01/top15. htm.

Taheri, A. (2003) *This is not Islam,* New York Post, 15.08.2003.

Tarlo, E. (2010) *Visibly Muslim – Fashion, Politics, Faith,* Berg, Oxford.

Treiner, S. (2007) *Mlode kobiety we Francji wybieraja zycie w stanie wolnym,* ed. Ch. Ockrent, *Czarna ksiega kobiet,* Wydawnictwo Boy-Zelenski, Warszawa.

Tristam, P. (2008) *The Muslim Veil and the Law in Europe, the United States and Canada. Who Allows It, Who Bans It,* www.middleeast. about. com/od/religionsectarianism/a/me080129a_2. htm.

Tucker, J. (2008) *Woman, Family, and Gender in Islamic Law,* Cambridge University Press, Cambridge.

United Nations (1979) *'Convention on the Elimination of All Forms of Discrimination against Women,'* (CEDAW) http://www.un.org/womenwatch/daw/cedaw/.

Universal Declaration of Human Rights (1948) http://www.un.org/en/documents/udhr/.

Ur Rahman, T. (1984) *A Code of Muslim Personal Law,* Vol. 1.

UK Government (2007) *Forced Marriage (Civil Protection) Act 2007.*

UK Government (2009) *Multi-agency practice guidelines: Handling cases of Forced Marriage.*

Bibliography

UK Foreign and Commonwealth Office (2009) *What is a Forced Marriage?* http://www.fco.gov.uk/en/travel-and-living-abroad/when-things-go-wrong/forced-marriage/,Forced Marriage Unit.

UK Home Office (2008) *The Path to Citizenship: next steps in reforming the immigration system,* Border and Immigration Agency.

UK (2009) Multi-agency practice guidelines: Handling cases of Forced Marriage, Forced Marriage Unit, London, June 2009.

Universal Islamic Declaration of Human Rights, 19.09.1981, www.alhewar. com/ISLAMDECL.html.

Vertovec, S. (2002) *Islamophobia and Muslim Recognition in Britain,* ed. Y. Haddad, *Muslims in the West from Sojourners to Citizens,* Oxford University Press.

Wallop, H. *Second marriage falls from favour,* http://www.telegraph.co.uk/relationships/7215219/Second-marriage-falls-from-favour.html. 12.02.2010.

Weiss, A. (2008) *A provincial Islamist Victory in Pakistan: the Social Reform Agenda of the Muttahida Majlis-i-Amal,* eds. J. Esposito, J. Voll, O. Bakar, *Asian Islam in the 21st Century,* Oxford University Press.

Wessels, A. (2006) *Muslims and the West. Can they be integrated?* Peeters, Leuven.

Wilkinson, S (2008) *Muslims in Post-Independence India,* eds. J. Esposito, J. Voll, O. Bakar, *Asian Islam in the 21st Century,* Oxford University Press.

Witkowski, S.(2009) *Wprowadzenie do prawa muzulmanskiego,* Wydawnictwo Naukowe Scholar, Warszawa.

World Health Organisation(2010), *Female Genital Mutilation,* http://www.who.int/mediacentre/factsheets/fs241/en/.

Welchman, L. (2004) *Women's Rights & Islamic Family Law: Perspectives on Reform,* Zed Books, London.

Women's History Resource Site, *Purdah,* Kings College, History Department London, http://departments.kings.edu/womens_history/purdah.html.

World Health Organisation (2010) *Female Genital Mutilation,* http://www.who.int/mediacentre/factsheets/fs241/en/.

Zyzik, M. (2003) *Malzenstwo w prawie muzulmanskim,* Elipsa, Warszawa.

TABLES & FIGURES

Table 2.1 Numbers of Britons of Pakistani and Bangladeshi descent, and
      percentage born in Britain (1951-2001)   25

Table 2.2 Muslims in Britain by age (2008)   25

Table 2.3 Sex of students   29

Table 2.4 Distribution of students according to country   30

Table 2.5 Distribution of students according to passports   31

Table 2.6 Students according to declared religion   32

Table 2.7 Distribution of Muslim and Christian students according to continent   33

Table 2.8 Apportionments of students - religion & continent   33

Table 2.9 Students reflections on parents' attitudes to values of their country
      of origin   35

Table 2.10 Distribution of students according to first language   36

Table 2.11 Ability to speak English and to write English   37

Table 2.12 Family attitudes towards following the customs/ traditions of
      their parents' home country   38

Table 2.13 Family attitudes towards eating national food   39

Table 2.14 Family attitudes towards traditional weddings/ birthday
      celebrations   39

Table 3.1 Aspirations of students to go to university   53

Table 3.2 Students' expectations with reference to further study   54

Table 3.3 Students' attitudes towards young women being permitted to work
      outside the home   56

Table 3.4 Attitudes of students towards a young wife staying at home to care
      for her parents-in-law   58

Table 3.5 Students' hopes for future lifestyle.   59

Table 3.6 Parents' aspirations for their children aged thirty   60

Table 3.7 Students' hopes for future residence   60

Table 3.8 Position taken on having another ethnic group living next door   62

Table 3.9 Christian/ Muslim aspiration to belong to a sports /dance
      or drama club   63

Table 3.10 Muslim male/female aspiration to belong to a sports /dance or drama club — 64

Table 3.11 Christian/Muslim wish to belong to a library — 64

Table 3.12 Muslim male/female wish to belong to a library — 65

Table 3.13 Christian/Muslim desire to give voluntary help or charity — 65

Table 3.14 Muslim male/female desire to give voluntary help or charity — 66

Table 3.15 Muslim & Christian willingness to vote in elections — 66

Table 3.16 Students discriminated against or badly treated because of ethnicity — 67

Table 3.17 Parents discriminated against or badly treated because of ethnicity — 67

Table 4.1 Attitude of students towards co-habiting — 77

Table 4.2 Students' attitude towards woman marrying first boyfriend — 77

Table 4.3 Students' opinions with reference to the allowance of arranged marriage in UK — 81

Table 4.4 Students' opinions on the government stopping brides/ bridegrooms being imported from abroad — 83

Table 4.5 Knowledge of husband/wife being chosen from overseas — 83

Table 4.6 Students' awareness of others in forced marriages — 90

Table 4.7 Students' awareness of help available to those in danger of forced marriage — 91

Table 5.1 Comparison Muslim and Christian attitudes towards UK law allowing polygamy — 96

Table 5.2 Position of students on divorce instigated by wife — 103

Table 6.1 UK society's opinions regarding the Muslim veil being worn in various occupations (%) — 121

Table 6.2 Agreement with the French government's secular law that prevents Muslim women from wearing their *hijab* (headscarf) — 130

Table 6.3 Position of students regarding acceptance of permission to wear religious symbols in school — 131

Table 6.4. Opinions on whether UK schools should allow young women to wear the *burka/niqab* (garment that covers the entire face and body) — 132

Table 7.1 Position of students on their identity — 150

Table 7.2 Identity of the second generation of Muslims in the UK (%) — 150

Table 7.3 Position on feeling British (%) — 151

Tables and Figures

Table 7.4 Comparison between Christians and Muslims regarding how strongly they feel British   151

Table 7.5 Position of students on belonging nowhere.   152

Table 7.6 Religious practices of Christian and Muslim students   153

Table 7.7 Frequency of prayer   155

Table 7.8 Prayer patterns - Muslim males first and second generation (%)   155

Table 7.9 Parents' faith   156

Table 7.10 Showing attendance at church/mosque for mother   156

Table 7.11 Showing attendance at church/mosque for father   157

Table 7.12 Mothers' prayer pattern   158

Table 7.13 Fathers' prayer pattern   158

Table 7.14 Christian and Muslim attitude towards choice of religion and state's non interference   161

Table 7.15 Opinion on whether UK law should allow immigrant communities to punish one of their members if they change their religion.   162

***

Figure 2.1 Ratio of Muslims to Christians in questionnaire group (%)   32

Figure 2.2 Students who watch English channels on television (%)   37

Figure 3.1 Attitude of Muslim students to future education (%)   53

Figure 3.2 Comparison Muslim male and female students' attitudes towards young women being permitted to work outside the home (%)   56

Figure 3.3 Point of view regarding whether a young wife should stay at home, live with and look after her parents-in-law (%)   58

Figure 3.4 Comparison of Muslim & Christian number of close friends within own ethnic group (%)   61

Figure 3.5 Comparison of Muslim & Christian number of close friends within other ethnic groups (%)   61

Figure 3.6 Number of friends from own ethnic group and other ethnic groups (average)   62

Figure 4.1 Comparison between male and female Muslims born in UK and born abroad in relation to the idea of co-habiting. (%)   76

Figure 4.2 Comparison between male and female Muslims born in UK and born abroad, in relation to arranged marriage (%)   81

Figure 5.1 Muslim attitudes towards polygamy (%)   97

The Pendulum Culture?

Figure 5.2 Position of Muslim students on divorce instigated by wife (%)   104

Figure 5.3 Position taken on allowing female circumcision (%)   109

Figure 6.1 UK Society's view on whether veils are a visible statement of separation and difference or whether Muslim women are segregating themselves by wearing a veil (%)   120

Figure 6.2 UK Society's view on Muslim women's right to wear the veil (%)   120

Figure 6.3 Muslim Students' position in relation to the French government's secular law that prevents Muslim women from wearing their *hijab* (headscarf) (%)   130

Figure 6.4 Students' attitude to UK schools allowing young women to wear their *hijab* (headscarf) and young men the turban if the young person also wears his/her school uniform (%)   131

Figure 6.5 Students' attitude on UK schools allowing young women to wear the *burka/ niqab* (garment that covers the entire face and body) (%)   133

Figure 7.1 Sense of not belonging - students born in the UK (%)   152

Figure 7.2 Religious practices of Muslim males born outside and inside the UK (%)   154

Figure 7.3 Muslim (male and female) attitudes towards freedom of choice of religion (%)   162

Figure 7.4 Opinion regarding UK law allowing immigrant communities to punish one of their members if they change their religion? (%)   163

APPENDIX

1. QUESTIONNAIRE

London is a multicultural society. Over 300 languages are spoken by the school children. The purpose of this Questionnaire is to look at young people in Newham and their parents and how they perceive their lives in UK Society with its many cultures and ethnic groups. This project is being conducted by a group of researchers from Poland & the UK.

Your answers are anonymous.

QUESTIONNAIRE   (For 17-24 year olds)   ID...... ....

A)   PERSONAL CHARACTERISTICS

	(please tick)	Mine	My Mum's	My Dad's
A1	Male / female			
A2	Age (completed years)			
A3	Where born (country)?			
A4	What nationality on passport?			
A5	What is first language (mother tongue)?			
A6	Level of education attained (Primary, Secondary, College, University)			

	If you were not born in the UK	(if you were born in the UK please go to Question A9)
A7	When (year) did you arrive in UK?	
A8	With whom did you come to the UK? (please tick no more than 3 answers)	
1	My mother & father	
2	My mother	
3	My father	
4	My brother/ sister	
5	My uncle/ aunt	
6	My grandparent/s	
7	Another person not a relative	
8	No-one, I came on my own	

The Pendulum Culture?

	What is your Religion? (please tick)	I am	My mum is	My dad is
1	Church of England			
2	Roman Catholic			
3	Methodist/ Baptist			
4	Greek/ Russian Orthodox			
5	Muslim			
6	Hindu			
7	Sikh			
8	Jewish			
9	Other (please specify)			
10	atheist (non-believer)			

A10 How often do you attend a church/ masjid (mosque)/ temple/synagogue, etc.? (to pray, for a religious service or for religious education) (please tick)		I attend	My Mum attends	My dad attends
1	Every day			
2	A few times a week			
3	Once a week			
4	Sometimes			
5	Never			

A11 How often do you pray at home/ at work? (please tick)		I pray	My mum prays	My dad prays
1	Several times a day			
2	Once a day			
3	A few times a week			
4	Sometimes			
5	Never			

B) LANGUAGE

	How good are you at: (please tick)	Excellent	Very good	Good	Poor	Fail	N/a
B1	written English?						
B2	spoken English?						
B3	writing mum's language?						
B4	speaking mum's language?						
B5	writing dad's language?						
B6	speaking dad's language?						

Appendix

B 7	Which other languages can you speak?	How well do you know them?				
	I speak:	Excellent	Very good	Good	Poor	Fail
1						
2						
3						

B8	What language do you usually speak at home?	
B9	What other language do you speak at home?	

B10 Have you ever acted as an interpreter in your family? (please tick)		
1	Yes, for a few years, when we first arrived in UK	
2	Yes, still every day	
3	Yes but only a few times	
4	Never	

	How good is your dad at (please tick)	Excellent	Very good	Good	Poor	Fail	N/a
B11	written English?						
B12	spoken English?						

	How good is your mum at (please tick)	Excellent	Very good	Good	Poor	Fail	N/a
B13	written English?						
B14	spoken English?						

B 15	What TV channels do your parent/s watch at home? (please tick)	Yes, always	Some-times	Rarely	No, never
1	English Channels				
2	TV Channels in their mother tongue				
3	Other Foreign Channels				
4	They don't watch TV.				

B 16	What TV channels do you watch at home? (please tick)	Yes, always	Some-times	Rarely	No, never
1	English Channels				
2	TV Channels in your mother tongue				
3	Other Foreign Channels				
4	I don't watch TV.				

		English	Other (please give language)	Both languages	N/a
B17	If you pray, what language do you pray in?				

C) IDENTITY/ CULTURE/ VALUES

C1	How would you describe your National identity?	I am:

C1a	Do you feel you have more than one identity? Have you another identity?	Yes / No If yes, I am also:

	(Please tick)	Yes	Sometimes	No
C2	If you are not a British citizen would you like to be one?			
C3	Do you mind if someone asks you where you come from?			

C4	If someone asks you: 'Which country do you come from?' How would you answer?	My country is:

C5 How strongly do you feel British? (please tick)		
1	Very	
2	Quite	
3	Somewhat	
4	Not very	
5	Not at all	

C6 Do you sometimes feel that you belong nowhere? (please tick)		
1	Yes, often	
2	Sometimes	
3	Rarely	
4	Never	

C7 How many really close friends do you have among… (please tick)		0	1	2	3	4	5	6+
1	Other people of your Ethnic group							
2	Members of other ethnic groups?							

C8 How many really close friends does your mum have among… (please tick)		0	1	2	3	4	5	6+
1	Other people of her Ethnic group							
2	Members of other ethnic groups?							

C9 How many really close friends does your dad have among… (please tick)	0	1	2	3	4	5	6+
1 Other people of his Ethnic group							
2 Members of other ethnic groups?							

C10 Does your family follow the customs and traditions (including: eating habits, holidays, clothing, music, art, etc.) of your or your parents' country /countries of origin? (please tick)	
1	Yes, very much
2	Yes, to some extent
3	Sometimes
4	No, never
5	No, my family is strongly against following traditions

	The customs/ traditions we follow (please tick)	Always	Some-times	Rarely
C11	We eat our national food			
C12	We have traditional weddings/ birthday celebrations			
C13	We celebrate our families national & religious feasts			
C14	I wear traditional clothes			
C15	My mother wears traditional clothes			
C16	We listen to our own culture's music			
C17	Our home is decorated in a traditional way			

C18	Some people fear the arrival of more immigrants. Do you? (Tick all that apply)	I am	My Mum is	My Dad is
1	Afraid they will take our jobs			
2	Afraid they will take our housing			
3	Other (please explain)			
4	Happy to welcome the arrival of more immigrants			

C19 Which are the most important obstacles to different ethnic communities living peacefully together in one community? (Tick all that apply)		
1	Lack of knowledge about other ethnic groups' values	
2	Lack of opportunity to communicate with others	
3	Fear of others with different cultures	
4	Fear of losing one's own ethnic identity therefore mixing only with own ethnic group	
5	We don't all hold the same values	
6	Other (please explain)	

The Pendulum Culture?

C20	Which of the following values give your life meaning? (Please tick no more than 4 answers)	
1	Love	
2	Friends	
3	Education	
4	A job which you like	
5	Deep religious faith	
6	Faith in an ideal	
7	Finding one's own place in society	
8	Family happiness	
9	Money, comfortable life	
10	Having children	
11	Living a quiet life	
12	Action, having a goal in life	
13	Other – (give details)	

C21	Which of the answers for question C20 is the most important for you?	

C22	Do you think it is important to take part/participate in the following:			
	(please tick all that apply)	Yes	Maybe	No
C22a	Belong to a sport's/ dance/ drama group			
C22b	Belong to a library			
C22c	Give voluntary help to others/ charity			
C22d	Vote in elections			

	Views on Marriage/ Family Life (please tick)	Yes, definitely	May be	Definitely not
C23	Do you think UK Law should allow immigrants have more than one wife?			
C23a	Do you think your parent/s have the same opinion as you, regarding question C23?			
C24	Do you think a young wife should stay at home, live with and look after her parents in law?			
C24a	Do you think your parent/s have the same opinion as you, regarding question C24?			
C25	Should a young woman be allowed to have a job outside the home?			
C25a	Do you think your parent/s have the same opinion as you, regarding question C25?			
C26	Do you think a woman should be allowed to divorce her husband?			
C26a	Do you think your parent/s have the same opinion as you, regarding question C26?			
C27	Do you think it is okay for a man and woman to live together without marrying?			
C27a	Do you think your parent/s have the same opinion as you, regarding question C27?			

C28	Do you think 'arranged marriages' should be allowed in the UK?			
C28a	Do you think your parent/s have the same opinion as you, regarding question C28?			
C29	If you accept arranged marriages: Do you think the UK Government should stop the bride/bridegroom being brought to the UK from abroad?			
C29a	Do you think your parent/s have the same opinion as you, regarding question C29?			
C30	Do you think a young woman should marry the first young man she goes out with?			
C30a	Do you think your parent/s have the same you, regarding question C30?			
C31	Should UK law allow forced marriages?			
C31a	Do you think your parent/s have the same you, regarding question C31?			

	Views on Religion / Culture (please tick)	Yes, definitely	May be	Definitely Not
C32	Do you agree that religion is a personal choice and the State should have no say in that choice?			
C32a	Do you think your parent/s have the same opinion as you, regarding question C32?			
C33	Do you think UK Law should allow immigrant communities to punish one of their members if they change their religion?			
C33a	Do you think your parent/s have the same opinion as you regarding question C33?			
C34	Do you agree with the French Government's secular law that prevents Muslim women from wearing their *Hijab* (headscarf)?			
C34a	Do you think your parent/s have the same opinion as you, regarding question C34?			
C35	Most UK schools have a school uniform. Do you think that UK schools should allow young women to wear the *Hijab* (headscarf) and young men the turban if the young person also wears his/her school uniform?			
C35a	Do you think your parent/s have the same opinion as you, regarding question C35?			

C36	Do you think that UK schools should allow young women to wear the *Burka/ Niqab* (garment that covers the entire face and body)?			
C36a	Do you think your parents have the same opinion as you, regarding question C36?			
C37	Male circumcision is allowed in the UK but in many countries female circumcision is also practised. Do you think the UK law should allow female circumcision?			
C37a	Do you think your parent/s have the same opinion as you, regarding question C37?			

	Immigration / Discrimination (Please tick)	Yes, definitely	May be	Definitely Not
C38	Have you ever suffered from discrimination/ or been treated badly because of your ethnic group?			
C38a	Have your parent/s suffered from discrimination or been treated badly because of their ethnic group?			
C39	Would you be happy to have another ethnic group living next door?			
C39a	Do you think your parent/s have the same opinion as you, regarding question C49?			
C40	Some people in the UK worry about the number of immigrants coming into England because they are afraid that there will be a clash of cultures/ values. Do you agree?			
C40a	Do you think your parents have the same opinion as you, regarding question C40?			

C41	What do you think about your parents' attitudes to the values of their country of origin? (please tick only one)	
1	They always keep those values	
2	They sometimes keep those values	
3	They sometimes ignore those values	
4	They forget to keep those values	

Appendix

D) FUTURE

	Further Education (please tick all that apply)	Yes	No
D1	Do you hope to study at university and get a degree?		
D2	Are you thinking of going abroad to study?		
D3	Are you thinking of going abroad for work experience?		
D4	Are you thinking of receiving religious education in your country of origin?		

D5	Do you think you will fulfil the desire to go to University?	
1	Yes, because: (please tick)	
1a	I am hard working & clever	
1b	My parents want me to go to university	
2	No, because: (please tick)	
2a	I have difficulty with English	
2b	My parents want me to marry as soon as I leave college	
2c	My parents want me to start work as soon as I leave college	

D6	What would you like to be doing when you are 30 years old? (please tick only one)	
1	Married with children, working as a	
2	Married, working as a	
3	Single, working as a	
4	Other… (please say what you would like to be doing)	

D7	What do you think your parents would like you to be doing when you are 30 years old? (please tick only one)	
1	Married with children, working as a	
2	Married, working as a	
3	Single, working as a	
4	Other… (please say what you think your parents would like you to be doing)	

D8	Where would you like to be living when you are 30 years old? (please tick only one)	
1	Where I am now	
2	Somewhere else in the UK	
3	Somewhere in Europe outside the UK (please say where)	
4	Somewhere else in the world (please say where)	
5	I do not know	

The Pendulum Culture?

D9	If you would like to get married when you are older would you like to marry someone: (tick all that apply)	
1	Your parents chose for you	
2	From Your mother/father's home country/ ethnic group	
3	Who shares the same religious belief	
4	You have chosen, of any race, colour or religion	

D10	If you think your parents would like you to get married - would they like you to marry someone: (tick all that apply)	
1	They chose for you	
2	From Your mother/father's home country/ ethnic group	
3	Who shares the same religious belief	
4	You have chosen yourself, of any race, colour or religion	

E) SIBLINGS

E1	How many brothers and sisters have you? (please give number)		
1	I have		brothers older than me
2	I have		brothers younger than me
3	I have		sisters older than me
4	I have		sisters young than me

		Yes (how many?)	No (how many?)
E2	Did any of your older brothers go to University?		
E3	Did any of your older sisters go to University?		

E4	How many married brothers have you?	
E5	If you have married brothers (please tick)	
1	Did your parents chose his wife for him?	
2	Did he choose his own wife?	
3	Was his wife to be already living in the UK?	

E6	How many married sisters have you?	
E7	If you have married sisters (please tick)	
1	Did Your parents chose her husband for her?	
2	Did she choose her own husband?	
3	Was her husband to be already living in the UK?	

Appendix

F.   FINALLY

		(Please tick)	Yes	No	Not sure
F1		Do you know anyone who went abroad as a single person and came back with a husband/ wife who was born in another country?			
F2		Do you know anyone who was forced to marry?			
F3		Do you know where you could go for help if your friend was being forced to marry someone against her/his will?			

F4 Is there anything else you would like to tell us?

F5 We would find it very helpful to our study if you would be happy to be interviewed, if so please give:	
YOUR FIRST NAME	
YOUR PHONE NUMBER	

Thank you for completing this questionnaire.

2. QUESTIONS FOR SHORT INTERVIEWS

1   How old are you? (in years)

2   Where were you born?

3   When did you arrive in UK?

4   How would you describe your faith?

5   Which language do you use most of the time?

6   How would you describe your identity?   Why?

7   In an ideal world what would you like from life?

     (family, education, job etc)

8   What do you think your life will really be like?

     (family, education, job etc)

9   What difficulties will you have?

     (language, religion, culture, peer pressure, freedom, discrimination, money etc)

10   Anything else you would like to tell us?

11   Who has an easier life?

     Philosophical question. If you had a choice would you prefer to have been born a girl or a boy.

3. SUPPORT GROUPS

FEMALE CIRCUMCISION

FORWARD – Advice and support for women affected by FGM
Unit 4,
765-767 Harrow Road
London NW10 5NY
0208 960 4000
www.forwarduk.org.uk
forward@ forwarduk.org.uk

BLACK WOMEN'S HEALTH AND FAMILY SUPPORT – support for
African women regarding social issues and especially prevention of FGM
1st Floor
82 Russia Lane
London E2 9LU
0208 980 3503
www.bwhafs.org.uk

FORCED MARRIAGE

THE HONOUR NETWORK HELPLINE 0800 599 9247

KARMA NIRVANA
Unit 6
Roschill Business Centre
Normanton Road
Derby
DE23 6RH
Phone number: 0133 260 4098
Website: www.karmanirvana.org.uk

THE FORCED MARRIAGE UNIT
Phone number: 0207 008 0151
Website: www.fco.gov.uk/en/travel-and-living-abroad/when-things-go-wrong/forced-marriage/

CLEVELAND CHOICE-LINE 0800 599 9365

HENNA FOUNDATION
2 St Martins Row
Albany Road
Cardiff
CF24 2JJ
Phone Number: 029 2049 6920 / 029 2049 8600
Email Address: info@hennafoundation.org+
Website URL: www.hennafoundation.org